PRISON POWER

Marisol, now; the struggle
the struggle is now; the struggle
is towards.

3/28/19

RACE, RHETORIC, AND MEDIA SERIES
Davis W. Houck, General Editor

PRISON POWER

How Prison Influenced the Movement for Black Liberation

Lisa M. Corrigan

University Press of Mississippi / Jackson

www.upress.state.ms.us

The University Press of Mississippi is a member
of the Association of American University Presses.

First printing 2016

∞

Library of Congress Cataloging-in-Publication Data

Names: Corrigan, Lisa M., author.
Title: Prison power : how prison influenced the movement for Black liberation
/ Lisa M. Corrigan.
Description: Jackson : University Press of Mississippi, [2016] | Series:
Race, rhetoric, and media series | Includes bibliographical references and
index.
Identifiers: LCCN 2016008491 (print) | LCCN 2016042417 (ebook) | ISBN
9781496809070 (cloth : alkaline paper) | ISBN 9781496809087 (epub single)
| ISBN 9781496809094 (epub institutional) | ISBN 9781496809100 (pdf
single) | ISBN 9781496809117 (pdf institutional)
Subjects: LCSH: African Americans—Civil rights—History—20th century. |
Civil rights movements—United States—History—20th century. | Black
power—United States—History—20th century. | African American
men—Effect of imprisonment on—History—20th century. |
Imprisonment—Political aspects—United States—History—20th century. |
African Americans—Politics and government—20th century. | United
States—Race relations—History—20th century. | BISAC: SOCIAL SCIENCE /
Ethnic Studies / African American Studies. | POLITICAL SCIENCE / Political
Freedom & Security / Civil Rights. | SOCIAL SCIENCE / Archaeology.
Classification: LCC E185.615 .C675 2016 (print) | LCC E185.615 (ebook) | DDC
323.1196/073—dc23
LC record available at https://lccn.loc.gov/2016008491

British Library Cataloging-in-Publication Data available

To Linda Corrigan
And to The Ralph and Claudia "Mayhem" Schaffner

CONTENTS

ACKNOWLEDGMENTS

This book would not have been possible without many colleagues, collaborators, co-conspirators, and friends who helped along the way. Thanks first to Tom Kane and Ted Windt, who spurred my interest in Cold War politics and the dialectic between presidents and protestors. These men taught me how to think and teach about politics in ways that continue to enrich both my students and me. Along with the brilliant Kellie Robertson, they also steered me toward Shawn J. Parry-Giles, under whose guidance this book began. I'm deeply indebted to her primarily for her patience. Full stop. But I'm also appreciative of her time, feedback, and advice. She taught me how to *work*. And she didn't try to curb my (intellectual) risk-taking, for which I am deeply grateful.

The University of Maryland Communication Department and the McKeldin Library provided me with support while I was writing the initial draft of this project. In the intervening years between this book's inception and its completion, I was quite lucky to learn from a wonderful number of talented professors including Elsa Barkley Brown, Robert N. Gaines, Meyer Kestnbaum, Katie King, Trevor Parry-Giles, Carla Peterson, Mari Boor Tonn, and Mary Helen Washington.

I'm also thankful to Claude Marks, director of the Freedom Archives in San Francisco, for his invitation to work in the archives, and to Noelle Hanrahan, whose audio archives of her interviews with Mumia Abu-Jamal were so helpful in the early draft of this project.

The University of Arkansas provided me with institutional support and funding while I reshaped this project and edited the final draft. Thanks to my colleagues Myria Allen, Lindsey Aloia, Trish Amason, Steve Boss, Bob and Laurie Brady, Rob Brubaker, Sidney Burris, Lynda Coon, Nick Copeland, Lauren DeCarvalho, Pearl Dowe, David Fredrick, Tom Frentz, Jennifer Hoyer, Christine Labuski, Susan Marren, Angie Maxwell, Alexandra Pappas, Mike Pierce, Tom Rosteck, Laurent Sacharoff, Todd Shields, Kathy Sloan, Steve and Lindsley Smith, Trish Starks, Dot Stephens, Brett Sterling, Raja Swamy, Ted Swedenburg, Ron Warren, and Jan and Rob Wicks.

I worked through the ideas in this book at many conferences and workshops including the National Communication Association conferences, the

Roots, Race and Resistance Conference, the Mid-Atlantic Popular/American Culture Association convention, the Cultural Studies Association convention, the Southern States Communication Association conventions, the Rhetoric Society of America conventions, the Organization for the Study of Communication, Language, and Gender conference, and the Rethinking Prisons conference where moderators, fellow panelists, and audience members helped me shape the ideas in this book.

Participating in Northwestern University's Doctoral Conference on Dissent helped me incubate these ideas. In particular, thanks to Angela Ray, for her thoughtful feedback and support, and to Dilip Gaonkar for his incisive critiques and for introducing me to Lauren Berlant, whose work has had a tremendous impact on my research. Additionally, I'm grateful for the continued friendship and collaboration with Wendy K. Z. Anderson, Maegan Parker Brooks, Christian Lundberg, John Lynch, and Elesha Ruminski, whose feedback on earlier portions of this project were invaluable. Finally, a portion of chapter 2 was published as "Claiming Urban Space for the Rebellion: Rap Brown and the Performativity of Black Power," in the *National Journal of Urban Education and Practice* 6, no. 1 (2012): 53–68.

I've also been lucky to call some of my former students friends, and they have certainly worked through some of these ideas with me inside and outside of the classroom. Thanks to Jake Barkman, Bart Belaire, Hashintha Bulumulla, Skye de Saint Felix, Amanda Edgar, Lee Fang, Ryan Gliszinski, Ragan Hensley-Nichols, Emily Ironside, Jamie Kern, Alex Ladd, Alex Marino, Molly McCormack, Molly Rawn, Hillary Scott, and Ginney Wright.

I am especially grateful to join the University Press of Mississippi's extended family of collaborators. First and foremost, I want to thank Vijay Shah for his enthusiastic support for this book. Additionally, series editor Davis Houck has been an incredible mentor, and I am extremely appreciative of his intellectual generosity and friendship. Likewise, I want to extend my deepest thanks to the thoughtful, constructive feedback from both anonymous reviewers.

As I finished editing this project, I am indebted to the friendship, banter, support, and feedback of Adjoa Aiyetoro, Caitlin Bruce, Peter Campbell, Karma Chávez, James Darsey, Marilyn DeLaure, Bonnie Dow, Cara Finnegan, Kris Harrison, Stephen Heidt, Steve Herro, Jim Jasinski, Dick Jensen, Joseph Jones, Bryan McCann, Chuck Morris, John Murphy, Sean O'Rourke, Adolph Reed Jr., Touré Reed, Cindy Richards, Pete Simonsen, Caleb Smith, Jennifer Mellon, Mary Stuckey, Robert Terrill, Davi Johnson Thornton, Anjali Vats, Eric Watts, Kirt Wilson, and Tim Wise.

My online community of support has been vital in helping me work through some of the ideas presented in this book, especially when I can't see these folks because I live in a far-flung place in the American mid-South. Much love to Joseph Boston, Ben Chappell, Tommy Curry, Ravina Daphtary, Marcia Dawkins, Kali Halloway, Rachel Hastings, Andre Johnson, Max Parthas, Gilberto Rosas, Amoja Sumler, and Kimberly Thomas.

I've also been so lucky to be surrounded by a brilliant, thoughtful crew that has sustained me for many years including Phil Elwood, Stephen Stetson, Ebony Utley, Susana O'Daniel, Tony de Velasco, Leslie Dinauer, David Kizzia, Jennifer Lowrey, Jodi and Justin Nimmo, Belinda and Bjørn Stillion-Southard, Leslie Harris, Laura Weiderhaft, Jean Gibson, and Lisa Webb.

My family has been unflinchingly supportive of this project from the beginning. Thanks to my mother, Linda Corrigan, for her unwavering dedication to my pursuit of higher education and to my sister, Emily Corrigan, for the constant witty repartee about popular culture and for her brilliant work helping me to line edit some of the prose of this project, and to Luis Morera, for bringing his own love of higher education into the family.

Of course, this book is dedicated to The Ralph and Claudia "Mayhem" Shaffner. For reasons that should be obvious.

PRISON POWER

INTRODUCTION

Often the path to freedom will carry you through prison.
—Martin Luther King

On February 16, 1960, Martin Luther King spoke to the first sit-in demonstrators in Durham, North Carolina, at the invitation of Durham minister and Southern Christian Leadership Conference (SCLC) board member Douglas Moore. After touring the city, King addressed a large rally of supporters at White Rock Baptist Church where he touted imprisonment as a creative resource for the student movement. He explained that the suffering from imprisonment augments humanity and staves off bitterness in the face of social violence. King argued that imprisonment offered "an opportunity to transfigure ourselves and American society. Let us not fear going to jail. If the officials threaten to arrest us for standing up for our rights, we must answer by saying that we are willing and prepared to fill up the jails of the South. Maybe it will take this willingness to stay in jail to arouse the dozing conscience of our nation."[1] King's speech in Durham points to the transformational potential of imprisonment and its emergence as a central tactic in civil rights agitation. It also connects imprisonment to moral suasion as a strategy to change southern consciousness about white supremacy and segregation. King's arguments in Durham prefigured decades of black liberation struggle that led through America's jails and prisons as activists heatedly debated the role of imprisonment in the organizational structure and strategy of civil rights agitation in the South.

Prison Power traces the influence of imprisonment on the black liberation movement as well as the influence of black liberation on imprisonment to understand how imprisonment served multiple and divergent goals in the civil rights and Black Power movements. Like John Sloop, I am interested in charting a "cultural history of 'prisoners' and 'punishment,'"[2] though in this case, the locus of inquiry is on debates conflating public protest and crime that justified expansion of the prison system in response to the black freedom struggle. It seeks to uncover the multiple influences that imprisonment had first in southern jails and later in northern prisons, particularly as the federal and state governments augmented local police forces in the wake of the urban rebellions of the mid-1960s.

Although Michelle Alexander has recently claimed that the major expansion of the prison-industrial complex took place in response to Reagan's War on Drugs with the introduction of crack cocaine into Los Angeles and the disparate sentencing between crack and powder cocaine, this book demonstrates that the criminalization of black youth activism in the black freedom struggle served as a major justification for the expansion of the prison system.[3] In fact, *Prison Power* demonstrates that federal repression of the civil rights movement and later the Black Power movement gave birth to mass incarceration during the Johnson administration.

Throughout *Prison Power*, I discuss the *strategy* and *experience* of imprisonment in southern jails versus northern penitentiaries as reflected in the rhetorical productions that emerged from black freedom activists. Southern jails and prisons emerged as containment zones for black labor after the failure of Reconstruction, and their connection to the plantation economy and slavery is clear. Northern prisons, while certainly serving to discipline black bodies, occupied different space in the urban political imaginary, especially after the Watts rebellion in 1965 as the Johnson White House urged the criminalization of rioters and then again after the Attica prison revolt in 1971 when Governor Nelson Rockefeller sent in armed state troops to quell the rebellion, ultimately leaving thirty-nine dead.[4]

My purpose in *Prison Power* is to center imprisonment in the history of black liberation as a rhetorical, theoretical, physical, and media resource as activists developed movement tactics and ideology to counter white supremacy. In highlighting imprisonment as a site for both political and personal transformation, I underscore how imprisonment shaped movement leaders by influencing their political analysis and organizational strategies. I suggest that prison became *the* critical space for the transformation from civil rights to Black Power, especially as southern civil rights activists faced setbacks in achieving equality. In centering the prison as a locus of political inquiry, Black Power activists produced autobiographical writings, essays, and letters about and from prison beginning with the early sit-in movement. Rhetorical analysis of the extremely popular, though understudied, autobiographical accounts of the Black Power movement written by incarcerated Black Power icons showcase narrative features explicating four tenets of Black Power including pride in blackness; disavowal of nonviolence; identification with Third World revolutionary movements; and engagement with black masculinity. Sustained incarceration in northern penitentiaries magnified the importance of these rhetorical dimensions of Black Power ideology for imprisoned intellectuals, suggesting that prison was a critical space for theorizing resistance to state repression as the black liberation movement evolved.

Prison Power demonstrates how autobiographical Black Power writings have contributed important articulations of identity politics and critiques of the prison-industrial complex. Although identities are plural and fluid, the Black Power movement was invested in the performance of new, "stable" essentialized black identities to confront similarly mythical notions of "whiteness." Rhetorically, these identity choices helped to craft Black Power identities that worked against the middle-class southern civil rights persona as much as it challenged white supremacy. The performance, for example, of what Rap Brown calls "militant blackness" or the New Afrikan blackness found in Assata Shakur's memoir, are rhetorical attempts to deploy a seemingly stable identity that Black Power activists depicted as "authentic," especially as organizational needs drive such rhetorical processes.

The arguments in *Prison Power* underscore how Black Power rhetoric influenced political actors within the movement and outside of it, particularly as prison became a central facet of their resistance. Most rhetorical scholars have accepted that social movements are composed of symbolic, rhetorical acts as the state clashes with social movement organizations and leaders.[5] This inherently confrontational dialectic produces moral conflict about unmet social needs, which distinguishes social movement rhetoric from other forms of discourse. Thus, social movements are constantly shoring up alliances, recruiting members, defining problems, and proposing solutions as the state pushes back against modifications to the status quo. All of this work is rhetorical, in the sense that it is only through the articulations of difference and similarity that political change happens. Thus, the political *is* the rhetorical.

"Black Power" is a particularly salient space in which to interrogate how political deliberation is articulated rhetorically, since it calls into question the modes by which discourses of state power are produced, circulated, and challenged. While some Black Power statements are directed outward for white listeners and readers, much of the impetus for Black Power is directed toward the creation of rhetorical identification *among* black people. Thus, "[t]he rhetoric of black power is essentially a call for the black man to rediscover himself as a substantial human being. Its primary themes center around black pride, black cohesiveness, and the need for political and economic power."[6]

Still, rhetorical confrontation functioned dialectically for Black Power activists.[7] Activists used the confrontational posture to redefine political terms and relationships, reorder priorities to transcend difference, norm black people to different assumptions about themselves and others, and assign blame to white liberals and ineffectual black politicians. Revolutionary language, often borrowed from Third World liberation movements, helped build the ethos and internationalism of Black Power political programs, though the revolutionary posture of Black Power led to early condemnations of the movement as violent and reactionary.

However, we would be remiss to understand the Black Power as an *act* of violence or as a strategy of political warfare instead of as a strategy of agonism that highlights inequality and brutality to create new patterns of political identification. Instead, scholars should see Black Power as a series of symbols dramatizing oppression and resistance; it is "more consummatory than instrumental" because rhetors build identification through the reshaping of rhetorical forms that expose institutional violence, political alienation, and social inequality.[8] As an agonistic discourse, Black Power "is redressive" and functions as a way of "reaffirming loyalties, testing them or offering new ones to replace old loyalties, always expressed in a kind of muted symbolic display designed to elicit a response which changes attitudes and values without major and unlimited conflict."[9] Thus, the rhetorical style of confrontation has often re-entrenched the binaries that served as such problematic demarcations in public life.

The Black Power Vernacular

In *Prison Power* I introduce the critical optic of the "Black Power vernacular" to describe how Black Power activists deployed rhetorical forms in their writings that invented new forms of black identification and encouraged support for black liberation from prison. In using Black Power vernacular forms, imprisoned activists improved their visibility while simultaneously documenting the racist abuses of the judicial system. This new vernacular emerged to force various publics to acknowledge and end the massive brutality perpetrated against black people in prison and in the streets in the name of law and order thereby helping to shore up support for Black Power organizations and initiatives. Documenting and tracing the rhetorical and political contours of slavery and incarceration built interest in the prison as a locus for both ideological inquiry and political mobilization. Consequently, a new vocabulary emerged from the state to push back against social movement activism by castigating white men as the victims of Black Power "crime." Without the publication of the prison writings of black activists from both the southern civil rights movement and from the Black Power movement, the lives and struggles of these activist women and men would have been completely eclipsed by the dominant discourse eliding "crime" and "protest."

Thus, in publishing accounts written in a vernacular language accessible for many working and middle-class Americans, these discourses crossed out of the walled prison spaces and into the public consciousness, transforming attitudes about imprisonment and criminality. These writings demonstrated the intellectual and rhetorical acumen of black activist prisoners, who were reeducating the non-incarcerated about the relationships between prison, imperialism, national party politics, police power, and activism. Imprisoned activists forcefully articulated the circumstances that produced mass incarceration of poor brown and black citizens and described the racialized origins and legal processes that constrained their trials, imprisonment, and release. Consequently, the Black Power vernacular helped write black incarceration into the history of black repression in America that began with slavery. And, as I have argued elsewhere, the Black Power vernacular has borrowed from other locales, movements, and times to cross-pollinate and reassemble a radical black politics for modern times.[10]

Building on the work of Grant Farred, who defines black vernacularity as a general "repertoire of representation, a politics of being, particular to a racialized, ideologically marginalized constituency," I suggest that the vernacular emerging from the Black Power movement provided a historically specific rhetorical response to increased state violence as the civil rights movement continued to meet tremendous resistance to desegregation in the South.[11] Vernacular rhetoric often takes the form of countercultural discourse, where the rhetoric developed "a chain of rhetorical moves . . . outside of the common cultural storehouse of characterizations and narratives."[12] As the vernacular translates subaltern existence into a series of symbols that build a landscape of political resistance, it creates accessible narratives for the oppressed to use in pushing back against racist, classist, nationalist narratives. And in creating an idiom to oppose structural inequality, the black vernacular historically emerged in nontraditional rhetorical arenas.[13] Vernacular figures operate outside of established avenues of political power, often creating new spaces from which to enter into critical public discussion on the issues of the day. For black leaders, these spaces historically included places like the pulpit, the mutual aid society, and the grassroots organization. Shaped by the formal exclusion from the political sphere as well as the fact that they speak to a broader audience, vernacular speakers must negotiate dual goals: creating exigency for political action among their vernacular public and appealing to formal political agents and publics included in the policymaking process.

This complex negotiation creates constraints for the black vernacular intellectual who is appealing to black audiences while also attempting to engage white audiences or at least address them as they eavesdrop on black rhetorical production. Thus, the vernacular intellectual "articulates an equivocal relationship to hegemony, a complex negotiation with the dominant group that is characterized by a self-conscious difference and defiance."[14] In doing so, vernacular forms emerge from social movements and their creation of popular oppositional symbols. In speaking about popular resistance and popular culture to power, the vernacular intellectual must create and utilize a repertoire that can speak to those excluded from formal political language.[15] The vernacular intellectual, then, utilizes speech patterns, rhetorical figures, arguments, symbols, and forms that appeal to the popular, rather than the official, audience. Conflicts arise, however, when official audiences eavesdrop or misinterpret vernacular forms, either accidentally or intentionally. The result is an inevitable clash over definitions, values, and narrative.

This book charts the ways in which the Black Power vernacular utilized a new *space*, that of the prison, to reframe black oppression and resistance as the black liberation movement evolved. Prison writers functioned as vernacular intellectuals as they introduced and utilized vernacular vocabularies, speaking from and to vernacular communities, and yet were removed from the very spaces and peoples that build the vernacular culture from incarceration and/or exile. The articulations of prison writers emerge via informal networks where the writing of their ideas itself is subversive; they must circumvent formal prison networks that wish to suppress social critique of prison power. Thus, the reading, writing, and thinking of prison writers functions as perpetual resistance from within an incredibly circumscribed physical, mental, and affective space.

As Black Power emerged in 1966 as a term reorienting civil rights activism along a different set of personal and political concerns, it also acquired a rhetorical potency based upon the *ways* in which it was expressed. The Black Power vernacular was characterized by innovation and reinventions of both rhetorical content and style. While the exigencies of the 1960s and early 1970s differed from earlier moments of black protest, many of the rhetorical forms were extensions of earlier vernacular practices. The stylistic repertoire of the Black Power vernacular primarily was based upon the confrontational rhetoric that emerged in the civil rights, feminist, student, antiwar, and anti-imperialist movements in the country, the hemisphere, and around the world.[16]

Confrontational strategies are attractive because there is a "strong sense of success, so strong that it may be a can't-lose strategy," particularly for long-suffering black liberation activists who had nothing left to lose.[17] Black Power activists articulated this "nothing left to lose" posture in several ways: they argued that black people are already socially dead and therefore, can't be killed again; they argued that they could be reborn, perhaps as martyrs;

they argued that they had the tenacity for a revolutionary fight whereas white conservatives did not; and they argued that black people had a global understanding of oppression and how to work together to destroy it.[18] With nothing left to lose, Black Power vernacular intellectuals highlighted the brutality of white supremacy and created new means of unification for black activists through confrontation (particularly over police brutality), though the polarization produced by the vernacular posture demanded that black humanity had to be accepted on black terms.

Thus, confrontational rhetorical strategies reoriented coalitions of power away from white liberals and toward black community actors as black nationalism replaced desegregation. The Black Power vernacular was aggressive, exhibiting a rhetorical pugilism that allowed for no compromise and pursuing direct conflict with statist ideology through a mixture of charisma, wit, hyperbole, and moral outrage, which created a palette for the confidence and play that underscored much of the rhetorical production of the movement. While critics might say that these (mostly) twenty-something Black Power interlocutors were either naïve or foolish to pursue such an aggressive posture toward the US nation-state, activists like Stokely Carmichael, James Forman, George Jackson, Eldridge Cleaver, Huey Newton, and those in this study have been harassed, beaten, tortured, and jailed while very little progress has been made to build healthy, safe black communities free from police brutality and violence. Additionally, the stylistic elements of the vernacular style bolstered the confidence of activists and intellectuals to pursue revolutionary ideals through new language. For example, the choice of "Black Power" rather than "Negro power" suggested a move away from white definitions of black culture and toward a term that "was associated with youth, unity, militancy, and pride."[19] The Black Power vernacular embodied these stylistic attributes in its pursuit of a new vision of blackness in the United States and abroad, as Black Power intellectuals connected the legacy of slavery to global anticolonial struggles. The new Black Power vernacular became a rich "vernacular rhetorical tradition," particularly for black youth, "in spite of the dominant culture's damaging characterization of them and their 'degenerate' surroundings."[20]

Renaming was central to the confrontational posture of the emergent Black Power vernacular, which helped reframe and reconstitute black resistance. Names are useful in expressing "powerful imagery. So naming—proposing, imposing, and accepting names—can be a political exercise," particularly in the case of black America.[21] Activists renamed themselves and their organizations, invented new political tropes, and used invective to rename political enemies as a way of shifting rhetorical power. Renaming served to resituate black activists themselves toward psychological, historical, and cultural resources that propelled activism forward and expressed changing values. Thus, the political strategy of renaming within the Black Power vernacular was aimed not at civil rights for individuals or promoting integration but in developing a powerful new way for black Americans to interact with one another that indexed their own experiences and afforded them a new sense of political agency.

Naming was part of a larger political strategy to exert more control over the rhetorical landscape and redefine black interests through new vocabulary. Black Power intellectuals were notable because they

> participated in public debates not only as barely recognized spokespersons, but in a vocabulary unaccredited and often disparaged by ruling blocs—of both hegemonic and subjugated constituencies. The vernacular intellectual is constituted, as it were, by vernacular articulation. By introducing and strategically deploying vernacular speech patterns, idioms, and metaphors; iconic figures . . . alter, quite literally, the very language of the dominant discourse.[22]

In shifting public rhetorical culture, Black Power intellectuals centered the experience of *imprisonment* by highlighting the history of surveillance, brutality, and terror of living in a culture that prided itself on equality, while it continued to exploit black communities.

In doing so, the Black Power vernacular translated the experience of black people into a discourse that signposted strategies of political resistance in a "state organized according to its ignorance" of black life.[23] It does so in a register that utilizes irony to bridge the gaps separating white and black Americans rhetorically and materially. As Maegan Parker Brooks has suggested, the black vernacular "features a complex ironic appeal that seeks to circumvent physically violent action by redirecting the doomed socio-historical drama between white and black Americans."[24] Thus, Black Power intellectuals actually use "irony's inherent dialogic potential" to circumvent revolutionary violence.[25] In doing so, Black Power vernacular signaled the rejection of accepted modes of rhetorical address and traditional vocabulary in favor of "a new positioning and idiomatic language."[26] They posed new strategies of identification that occupied spaces of white fear about masculinity, revolutionary violence, and retribution, and that interrogated race, gender, and class, since these spaces provided new opportunities to organize and theorize.

Revolutionary idioms were particularly useful in building the Black Power vernacular because it worked to confer Third World legitimacy on Black Power intellectuals, particularly as they made the case for black America as an internal colony. This idea grew out of the "black belt thesis" circulated by the Communist Party of the USA, which argued that the Black Belt states in the South comprised an internal black colony, "an incipient Black nation with the right to self-determination."[27] In arguing that the United States was a colonialist regime, Black Power intellectuals like Harold Cruse, Robert Allen, Stokely Carmichael, and Eldridge Cleaver connected the plight of black America to anticolonial movements worldwide. For example, Harold Cruse used the colonial analogy in his formative 1962 essay, "Revolutionary Nationalism and the Afro-American," which was widely read among black freedom activists and which bears quotation at length:

> From the very beginning, the American Negro has existed as a colonial being. His enslavement coincided with the colonial expansion of European powers and was nothing more or less than a condition of domestic colonialism. Instead of the United States establishing a colonial empire in Africa, it brought the colonial system home and installed it in the Southern states. When the Civil War broke up the slave system and the Negro was emancipated, he gained only partial freedom. Emancipation elevated him only to the position of a semi-dependent man, not that of an equal or independent being . . . The only factor which differentiates the Negro's status from that of a pure colonial status is that his position is maintained in the "home" country in close proximity to the dominant racial group.[28]

The colonial analogy and its attendant idioms helped to express a new relationship between black Americans and the state that rejected integration as a model for identification with whiteness and instead embraced a more oppositional model of relationality, demonstrating the power of vernacular to reframe nationalism around blackness.

At the level of argument, the Black Power vernacular highlighted the history of black incarceration through the use of the internal colony metaphor, which elucidated the relationship between the institution of slavery in the United States and colonialism throughout the rest of the world. For example, Stokely Carmichael and Charles V. Hamilton's pioneering treatise *Black Power: The Politics of Liberation* (1967) includes a chapter on "White Power," where they write that colonialism in the United States "has had social repercussions which date back to slavery but did not by any means end with the Emancipation Proclamation. Perhaps the most vicious result of colonialism—in Africa and in this country—was that it purposely, maliciously and with reckless abandon relegated the black man to a subordinated, inferior status in the society."[29] The colonialism analogy provided a wider lens than "blackness in America" by which to connect them to sympathetic audiences worldwide.

In doing so, imprisoned Black Power intellectuals used colonization as a way into the political strategies and ideologies of Third World intellectuals like Che Guevara, Fidel Castro, Mao, Patrice Lumumba, and other anticolonialist writers. Guevara's *foco theory*, developed in *Guerrilla Warfare* (1961), was especially important to the Black Power vernacular because it promoted guerrilla strategy as a template for revolutionary action. Guevara attributed the success of the Cuban revolution to the guerrillas' investment in vanguardism, where small groups of insurrectionists executed fast, deadly strikes on governmental targets to overthrow the Batista regime.[30]

Black Panther field marshal and prison writer George Jackson elaborated on Guevara's *foco theory* as a model of black resistance in his 1971 prison text, *Blood in My Eye*. There he described the "urban People's War" as one structured upon "the connections, interactions, processes and effects of a people at war under the leadership of a vanguard" within the "Black Colony." Using Guevara's *foco theory*, Jackson argued that the Black Panther Party (BPP) should model themselves as a "tightly knit, totally committed and separate military vanguard" committed to what he calls "the true internationalism."[31]

The Black Power vernacular appropriated internationalist, revolutionary idioms to reorient black publics to new notions of blackness, the white nation state, and activism, by linking black struggle in the United States to a larger history of anticolonialism.[32] For example, Huey Newton describes how the BPP assigned black, anticolonialist literature as part of the ideological education of new members:

> We read the work of Frantz Fanon, particularly the *Wretched of the Earth*, the four volumes of Chairman Mao Tse-Tung, and Che Guevara's *Guerrilla Warfare*. Che and Mao were veterans of people's wars, and they worked out successful strategies for liberating their people. We read these men's works because we saw them as kinsmen; the oppressor who had controlled them was controlling us, both directly and indirectly. We believed it was necessary to know how they gained their freedom in order to go about getting ours.[33]

Reading these central texts helped propel the creation of the Black Power vernacular by exposing Black Power activists to new frameworks for interpreting black struggle in an international context that theorized oppression and resistance from the experiences of black people rather than from the preferences and dictates of white liberal governmental officials.

Revolutionary idioms referencing guerrilla warfare, armed struggle, imperialism, anticolonization organizing, self-determination, and Third World solidarity helped to created what Thomas Kent has termed a thick "discourse community," where layers of language help to solidify organizational identification.[34] The revolutionary idiom became an intrinsic rhetorical feature of the Black Power vernacular, helping to connect the movement in the United States to anti- and postcolonial movements abroad and reframing civil rights as anti-imperialist agitation.

As Black Power leaders emulated Third World heroes, the intensification of state repression began. Thus did the production of Black Power's prison autobiographies help connect American imperialism abroad to state-sanctioned violence against poor black and brown people in the United States as well as to the burgeoning prison-industrial complex. By connecting American imperialism abroad to the expansion of the prison-police state from slavery to the present, Black Power prison writers connected it to liberation movements across the globe. Certainly some of Black Power's objections to white supremacist violence, police brutality, economic exploitation, and cultural domination had their genesis in earlier moments of black resistance to white supremacy in the civil rights movement (and chapter 1 will trace them), but the prison discourse of the Black Power movement crystallized radical black intellectualism around Third World solidarity to create salient rhetorical resources and a new audience for critiques of the prison-industrial complex from celebrities within prison walls. Unfortunately, this crystallization also made the Black Power movement an enemy of the US government between the Johnson and Reagan administrations.

Prison Power highlights how prison texts provide authorizing discourses that cement imprisoned Black Power leaders as "living martyrs" through their vernacular narratives about the conditions that produced urban activism against segregation, cultural domination, police brutality, and economic exploitation. The writings of H. Rap Brown, Mumia Abu-Jamal, and Assata Shakur (all convicted for killing police officers) are powerful expressions of the cultural and political tension surrounding movement politics, police repression, and imprisonment at the end of the 1960s and the beginning of the 1970s. These discourses demonstrate how the Black Power movement regenerated Black Power through vernacular prison texts even after the FBI sought to disrupt, discredit, and destroy the movement through its Counter Intelligence Programs (COINTELPRO) and the expansion of "law and order" policies that built mass incarceration beginning in the Johnson administration.

A Note on Method

In assessing the rhetorical and historical successes and failures of the Black Power movement to generate political identification by mobilizing imprisonment and narratives about imprisonment, I understand the role of the critic in the way that Culpepper Clark and Raymie McKerrow suggest, seeing the critical rhetorical historian as a "raconteur" who uses social science to craft her stories about the rhetorical nature of history.[35] As a raconteur, I am interested in the ways that activists narrate their own history as it relates to the history of black imprisonment in America, and I seek to explain how narrativizing this history of imprisonment functioned in the black liberation movement. Specifically, *Prison Power* traces the history of prison culture in the Black Power movement alongside the arguments that situated prison as a strategy in the liberation of black Americans while simultaneously justifying prison expansion to crush the black liberation movement. I see both rhetorical criticism and rhetorical history as the overlapping space from which to understand how various political actors understand political transformation. I contend that in this decade where social movements defined public culture, political officials and social movement leaders shaped the lives of ordinary Americans as they theorized and implemented new civic strategies. Thus, the rhetorical and political relationships among the White House, Congress, and black liberation activists helped to define the pace and nature of social change as it pertained to black life in America.

Because of my commitment to the critical work that charts the history of ideas, *Prison Power* uses rhetorical history and criticism to tell the story of an actively changing tapestry of ideas around civil rights, civil disobedience, political transformation, and law and order. I agree with Jennifer Mercieca, who explains, "rhetorical discourse must be—in fact, can only be—understood by placing it within the complex web of dominant ideas and events in its immediate historical context."[36] I suggest that the ideas and arguments articulated by the political actors invested in or against Black Power can only be understood within the complicated history from which they emerged. Context is important for two reasons: "first, ignoring context prevents modern scholars from understanding how, why, and to what effect historical discourses were composed and circulated; second, ignoring context robs those who came before us of their own history and attempts to remake the world in our own image—it is the epitome of academic hubris."[37] Thus, the relationship between texts and context form the narrative of this book to help understand how the role of prison shifted and changed throughout the modern struggle for black liberation.

Although the prison activism of the Black Power movement is acknowledged in monographs that focus on one movement organization or on one Black Power figure, none deal systematically with the role that prison played in the evolution of Black Power ideology or rhetoric in a way that showcases how prison intellectuals contributed to ideological shifts in the movement for black liberation. And while Black Power historiography is enjoying a remarkable renaissance as an object of scholarly inquiry across disciplines following the 2005 publication of Charles Jones's *The Black Panther Party Reconsidered*, which reintroduced the politics and literature of the Black Power movement to a new generation, more critical work remains to be done. This is particularly true since no volume to date has looked at the relationship between prison and the rhetorical formulation of Black Power ideology from the writings of the movement leaders.[38] Though the field of rhetoric has started to produce more prison studies, very little contemporary rhetorical scholarship focuses on the Black Power movement except in passing, despite a rash of early studies on the Black Power phenomenon in the 1960s and early 1970s.[39] *Prison Power* seeks to fill this gap between the rising tides of Black Power historiography and prison studies by discussing the rhetorical forms and strategies of the Black Power ideology as they emerged from prison politics.

Prison Power uses an intersectional perspective that looks at how race, gender, and class interact to build rhetorical identification in the prison manifestos of H. Rap Brown, Mumia Abu-Jamal, and Assata Shakur in the next stage of the Black Power movement. In the case of Black Power, I argue that the regeneration of the movement began due to the assassinations of major civil rights leaders like Malcolm X (1965), Martin Luther King (1968), Fred Hampton (1969) and the incarceration of others like Huey Newton (1967), Rap Brown (1970), and Angela Davis (1970). From 1967 on, the Black Power movement was compelled to (re)calibrate itself through the writings of prison leaders who formed the intellectual vanguard of this next phase. As such, this book augments most sixties historiography, which primarily has "focused on developments prior to 1969 and 1970 and, when considering the late sixties, has done so from a white male leadership perspective. Black and white women's and black men's voices from late in the decade are not heard in sixties stories already told."[40] As Wini Breines has argued persuasively, "The leadership and culture of black people in the sixties have been erased precisely from the moment when their power was pervasive and persuasive."[41] I suggest that this erasure was due, at least in part, to the *imprisonment* of these Black Power icons, thereby structuring their erasure from the rhetorical and critical canon. Thus, I concur with Bryan McCann's argument that the "victim" frame or ideograph in prison discourse (particularly that focused on the death penalty) has rhetorical utility despite its limitations.[42]

Black Identity: Representing Race, Gender, and Class

I undertake this task of situating Black Power texts within their contexts, aware of the humility necessary to address what rhetoricians Gesa E. Kirsch and Jacqueline Jones Royster have outlined as key foci of this kind of rhetorical work, including an attention to the intersecting relationship between gender, race, and ethnicity; status and its relationship to class position; geographical sites of rhetorical production; and rhetorical domains, genres, and modes of expression. In doing so, I also understand that this approach must be "dialogic [balancing multiple interpretations], dialectical [seeking multiple viewpoints], reflective [on intersections of internal and external effect], reflexive [about unsettling one's conclusions about and deferring argumentative closure], embodied, and anchored in an ethos of care, respect and humility" toward the historical participants and the rhetorical and political constraints within which they were operating at the time.[43]

Race, gender, and class function together to create the conditions for oppression and privilege, and the negotiation of these identity markers is the terrain over which activists struggle for autonomy, identity, and power. In the process, the activists' discourse reifies as well as destabilizes traditional notions of race, gender, and class as central components of Black Power identity. *Prison Power* examines the way that gender, race, and class circulate through Black Power in this new phase of agitation. Consequently, I understand that the historical actors debating and implementing Black Power in the culture were operating in the midst of a culture war that magnified rhetorical strategies and responses as they emerged in the public domain.

While I have endeavored to treat each figure in this history fairly and with care, I confess that my biases—where they are obvious—tend toward vigorous public argument and self-determination, even when the actors disrupt the stability of the established order. At the same time, despite the fact that Lyndon Johnson fell out of favor with civil rights and Black Power leaders and they with him, I have a deep sympathy for him. Johnson's presidency seems to be grossly constrained (particularly by Kennedy's assassination) in ways that made it impossible for him to achieve his own personal and political goals, including major civil rights and domestic progress with the Great Society. As such, I try to the best of my ability to demonstrate where such constraints emerged and propelled Johnson, in particular, to react to Black Power as he did. Still, one major tension in this book surrounds issues of rhetorical authority and the right to speak, particularly in the case of dissenting speech. Andrew Lakritz suggests that appeals to the author's own subject positioning can be problematic because, while it might

> generate rhetorical authority, it cannot in itself address another important issue: that the very structure of authority that allows us to identify and empathize inserts us back into the structure of inequality the identification would dismantle. In other words, because I am an elite I have the luxury of feeling empathy for the oppressed. The very authority I have permits such identification, which undoubtedly threatens and maintains that authority at the same time.[44]

In this book, my intent is to dialogue with the ideas presented by these Black Power writers, rather than speak for them. Aware of my elite subject positioning, I occasionally provide longer context for the comments made by the writers taken up in this study to help them explain in their own words what they are arguing for. In doing so, I acknowledge the dynamics involved in my silence in the text as well as the silencing of others. I note these dynamics here to underscore my own authority and the role that it plays in structuring my approach to these texts and their writers.

Accordingly, I take up Dale Bauer's poignant question on rhetorical authority: "What authority can 'I' claim in a world where the very concept of authority . . . has been rendered problematic and undermined?"[45] I am particularly interested in how these prison writers frame their authority and rhetorical identifications in such a tumultuous period of racial repression as well as what the rhetorical identifications of these writers ask their auditors to *do*. These texts document the emergence of a new racial consciousness that enables the writers to critique the politics of race, class, and gender that inscribe their bodies and that circumscribe their relationships with the state. Their narratives privilege resistance over capitulation and document the betrayals involved in building movements.

Précis of Chapters

Prison Power offers a close textual reading of H. Rap Brown's (now Jamil al-Amin's) *Die Nigger Die!* (1969); Mumia Abu-Jamal's *Live From Death Row* (1996), *Death Blossoms* (1997), and *All Things Censored* (1999); and Assata Shakur's *Assata: An Autobiography of Assata Shakur* (1987). Each of these vernacular writers seeks to regenerate activism by articulating Black Power ideologies while indicting the prison-industrial complex. In doing so, they connect their own images to martyred legacies of proto-Black Power leaders, situating themselves in the historical progression of black martyrdom from slavery to the present and supporting ideologies of self-defense and/or armed struggle. In addition, they position the police and the (white) government as enemies and see police brutality and covert repression as exigencies that must mobilize new activists around police brutality, political prisoners, and prison reform. These activists also employ strategies that highlight the importance of self-reliance and black pride, which underscore that the cultural nationalism of their projects become part of the collective identity necessary for oppositional consciousness. In the case of Assata Shakur, the emphasis on black pride is also connected to expressions of hope for the future, which has the potential to inspire new groups of activists. Although explicit similarities exist across the manifestos, clear differences also exist within their strategies of regeneration.

More specifically, chapter one examines black resistance, imprisonment, and "law and order culture" that began with the sit-ins. It marks the evolution of the jail-ins as a political strategy while tracing the kinds of prison manifestos that shaped the rhetoric of the movement for black freedom to showcase how prison writings served as pragmatic discourses for interrogation of black subjectivity in the emergent "law and order" culture. From Albany to Soledad, black intellectuals employed the Black Power vernacular to help describe and analyze the relationship between incarceration and segregation.

Chapter two centers on former SNCC chairman and former honorary member of the Black Panther Party, H. Rap Brown/Jamil Al-Amin, and his autobiography, *Die Nigger Die!*[46] This chapter examines the intersection of blackness, masculinity, and class to elucidate the politics of representation, especially at the end of the Johnson administration. It highlights Brown's emergence as a black badman through his performance in the dozens, his defiance of authority, and his critiques of political liberals, but it also underscores the extent to which texts travel through time, since the book was rereleased in 2002. Since Brown's actions formed the basis of massive FBI repression of black liberation and since his book was published *before* the era of mass incarceration (and it was written under house arrest rather than from death row or exile), his observations primarily focus on the relationships between white supremacy, white liberalism, and state repression.

In chapter three I examine three anthologies of essays penned by former Black Panther and current John Africa Society member Mumia Abu-Jamal from Pennsylvania's Huntington Prison. Abu-Jamal's writings center police brutality and the abuses of the prison-industrial complex in his analysis of white supremacy by documenting police and judicial corruption in Phila-delphia. They also feature prophetic constructions of black masculinity as Abu-Jamal extends ideological formations of Black Power through narratives about the men on death row and through the nostalgia of black leaders like Malcolm X, Huey Newton, and Martin Luther King Jr.

Chapter four focuses on former Black Panther and Black Liberation Army member Assata Shakur and her autobiography, *Assata: An Autobiography of Assata*. I examine Shakur's autobiography to understand how she reconstitutes a black female identity within this new phase of the Black Power movement while critiquing the prison-industrial complex through both poetry and prose that is complicated with her simultaneous reification of black masculinity.

The final chapter examines the intellectual legacy of these Black Power activists and after the war on terror marked them in order to speculate about how their discourses travel in new ways through the lens of "terrorism," rather than "crime." In this context, Brown, Abu-Jamal, and Shakur continue to recirculate for a new generation of Black Power activists. To such ends, the notion of the leader and their heroic image is a key force in the perpetual regeneration of Black Power that also functions to mobilize conservatives against black liberation through the lens of the war on terror. This final chap-ter poses questions about the continued utility of the Black Power vernacu-lar, particularly about the relationship between imprisonment and American empire-building.

Rooted in the traditions of textual criticism and cultural studies, this book carefully analyzes the various textual dimensions of these autobiographical manifestos to understand how Black Power leaders have been able to regener-ate their ideology from spaces of prison and exile. I explain how these narra-tives help to build and rebuild the momentum for black liberation even as the movement's leaders are imprisoned and prohibited from agitating for social change in public. I explore how various dimensions of the manifestos both enlarge the scope of Black Power ideology and constrain the movement's ability to really transform the racial landscape in America by examining the successes and the limitations of their political and textual strategies. In the process, I reflect upon how these manifestos utilize identity politics, which demonstrates that the intersections of class, race, and gender are complex and polyvalent, enhancing the appeal to audiences who see these activists as celebrities and living martyrs, sacrificing themselves to continue regenerating the ideology of Black Power. Ultimately, I acknowledge the importance of these autobiographies as discourses that construct Black Power in ways that undermine the credibility of the prison-industrial complex and make Black Power relevant today.

CHAPTER ONE

Prison Power
Speaking and Writing Black Resistance

A n FBI memorandum dated June 20, 1966, describes Student Non-violent Coordinating Committee (SNCC) chairman Stokely Carmichael's interview on the CBS program *Face the Nation* as he clarified his position on "Black Power" after the March Against Fear. The memo describes questions directed toward Carmichael about the relationship between Black Power and violence:

> When pressed as to how the Negroes should obtain control, Carmichael at first stated it should be by organizing politically and registering to vote. However, in response to an inquiry as to whether he would use violence in obtaining this power, he indicated that if the Negroes were prevented from obtaining this control legally, they would have to obtain it in other ways. When pressed further, he stated that if all legal means were exhausted, then violence would be justified.[1]

Carmichael's description of Black Power here and elsewhere harnessed Martin Luther King Jr.'s proclamations of civil disobedience justifying the "jail, no bail" strategy earlier in the decade alongside Malcolm X's maxim "by any means necessary," forming a bridge between these two articulations of black resistance. But it was clear from the questions in this interview that the white media was interested in framing Carmichael's cry for "Black Power" as the start of a race war initiated by blacks against whites.

As his Black Power stance garnered more attention, the FBI initiated a comprehensive review of his arrest record to demonstrate that Carmichael was dangerous. An FBI memo dated July 13, 1966, lists Carmichael's arrests in Jackson, Mississippi; Baltimore, Maryland; New York City, New York; Cambridge, Maryland; Bolivar County, Mississippi; Fort Deposit, Alabama; and Greenwood, Mississippi, for offenses ranging from being a participant in the

1961 Freedom Rides to desegregate public transportation, to "being loud and boisterous" in New York, to "distributing handbills without a permit" in Alabama. The memo condemns Carmichael for his public criticism of the FBI and for making "derogatory references to the Bureau over a CBS News Special report on 7/1/64, stating that the FBI never did 'a damn thing,' and that the FBI had been most derelict in the field of civil rights."[2]

The FBI objected to Carmichael's characterization of its civil rights record and condemned Carmichael as a racial troublemaker. FBI director J. Edgar Hoover warned of a "black messiah" emerging from civil rights organizations to fully challenge white supremacy, writing in a March 4, 1968, memorandum to his field offices that, "Martin Luther King, Stokely Carmichael and Elijah Muhammad all aspire to this position."[3] Consequently, the arrest records of activists like Carmichael led to the use of the "rabble-rouser" trope by federal officials to demonize Black Power leaders as "outside agitators" stirring up otherwise docile black communities. In popularizing new forms of civil disobedience, black activists promoted disrespect for unjust laws and for legal authority, making it possible for conservatives to paint them as perennial dangers to law and order, leading to mass incarceration as the Black Power movement rose and fell.

This chapter traces rhetorical and political history of imprisonment before and after the birth of Black Power, focusing on major moments of activist imprisonment as well as movement discourses written from prison. In charting the role of prison in the movement, the chapter also discusses the emergence and legitimacy of Black Power as a slogan, as a theoretical device, and as a series of rhetorical strategies designed to be a particularly historical intervention into the stagnating discourses of "civil rights" and "law and order." I contend that incarceration became a major strategy used by *both* black activists and white conservatives during the Black Power era; consequently, the period following 1966 marked a new phase of Jim Crow as Black Power became a rallying cry against state repression.

I also argue that the legitimacy of Black Power—as a term of art, as a series of vernacular signs, and as an organizing principle in a new phase of the black liberation movement—hinged upon whether the state or the activists controlled the frame and how closely it became associated with violence. Because the Black Power slogan and ideology were articulated by activists with extensive rap sheets as the state circumscribed their activism, Black Power ideology took up the relationship between state repression and incarceration as a place to excavate new arenas for the black liberation struggle, particularly in the memoirs of movement activists. The repression of political dissent is the violence that spawns resistance; certainly Black Power activists understood this dynamic in a visceral way, since thousands had been imprisoned for working against segregation and for political representation. Particularly within the leadership of SNCC, the conversation changed from voter registration to more radical tactics, as activists grew frustrated with the constant harassment and violence initiated by state agencies.

In detailing the coterminous relationship between black liberation activists and white politicians, it is clear that white proclamations about black deviance have had the effect of forcing black rhetors to dramatize black experience through strategies that necessarily reference such proclamations. Hortense Spillars suggests that black culture "carries both its *statement* and *counterstatement*" in its articulation, meaning that black intellectuals are constrained by white political assessments that overdetermine their standpoint through opposition rather than understanding.[4] Consequently, I see the writings of imprisoned Black Power activists as a natural extension of earlier "jail, no bail" strategies and as part of a continuous strategy of interrogating white supremacy through prison. But by the time that Black Power emerged as a movement of its own, it served to justify the imprisonment of movement leaders and the eradication of movement organizations, thereby changing the relationship between black freedom and black imprisonment.

Black Power as a Turning Point

Stokely Carmichael's assertion of "Black Power" in 1966 marked a moment when activists were able to reframe black liberation especially considering the Johnson White House's loss of political capital due to Vietnam and major legislation stalling after the passages of the Civil Rights Act of 1964 and the Voting Rights Act of 1965. SNCC activists, and later, the Black Panther Party, turned to new rhetorical and political strategies to articulate how state repression and the emergent "law and order culture" were making the nonviolent pursuit of civil rights impossible. Black activists made the case for expanded political participation in an increasingly hostile white America.

The backlash intensified as 1966 ushered new conservatism with California governor Ronald Reagan and as 1968 welcomed President Richard Nixon. The shifting political landscape was marked by the elevation of more explicitly white supremacist politics at the federal and state level under the rubric of "law and order" as well as the repression of black protest. Writing about the prevailing opinions about white northerners marching with black southerners to protest police brutality, imprisonment, and disenfranchisement, Mary Stanton explains that the majority of white Americans by 1965 deemed demonstrators "professional agitators" trying to "gain influence for themselves."[5] So as black liberation activists struggled for new ways to intervene in a political system that formally excluded their participation, whites further marginalized their efforts.

As a symbol and slogan, Black Power was an intentionally confrontational, yet rhetorically ambiguous provocation.[6] Young black activists embodied the confrontational posture of the term, alienating some whites and blacks and splintering SNCC as it became increasingly separatist. Still, rhetorician Donald McCormack has suggested that in Black Power's formative years, "the ambiguity of the slogan was very much a source of vitality," since new textual antecedents for Black Power expanded the ideological direction of the black liberation movement.[7] The strength of Black Power "was based on some essential truths about racism in America, and so it eventually proved to be a powerful tool of persuasion."[8] These truths pointed to the legacies of slavery in modern political life, highlighted violence in black communities by white agents of the state, and protested the lack of basic services in black communities. Through contemporary prison writings and their historical antecedents, the Black Power movement expressed a new vernacular in this phase of black liberation struggle.

The Black Rhetorical Tradition and the Genre of Prison Writing

While the rhetorical shift from civil rights to Black Power found its voice with Stokely Carmichael in 1966, black texts have cited imprisonment as a constant feature of life in America since slavery. H. Bruce Franklin's landmark text *Prison Literature in America: The Victim as Criminal and Artist* (1979), inspired by Black Power literary activism from the late 1950s through the 1970s, marked the first extensive scholarly treatment of the genre of prison literature and dozens of studies soon followed. Franklin's studies were particularly incisive about the early slave narratives, which helped to drive the development of methods that traced prison literature as an "identifiable genre" by defining slavery as a form of institutionalized imprisonment.[9] Franklin asserted that "America is itself a prison, and the main lines of American literature can be traced from the plantation to the penitentiary" as black Americans experienced "being legally kidnapped, plundered, raped, beaten, chained, and caged."[10] His study lent academic credibility to statements made by Black Power activists about the unique way that Jim Crow emerged against civil rights activism in the mid-twentieth century.

Black Power intellectuals articulated the relationship between nation-building, slavery, and forced labor as they used the rhetorical strategies of the global Third World Left to reframe their analysis of black oppression in the United States. As Franklin points out, the "descendants of these Africans are in many senses the truest Americans, for the Afro-American people were created in the United States, their unpaid labor provided the capital base for the political economy of modern America, and their culture has, for more than a century, been central to American culture in general."[11] Franklin catalogued writings that bolstered Black Power critiques of white supremacy and spoke to the constant surveillance and confinement of black Americans under slavery and in the emergent prison system. His studies also catalogued the way in which black orators have utilized vernacular speech, idioms, and storytelling to build the case for emancipation. Within this context, Black Power's rhetorical posture is more comprehensible as a logical extension of earlier iterations of imprisonment and resistance. And, as Black Power activists used black history to craft their vernacular messages about the continuity of black oppression in the United States, they pointed to the features of black life that arose from reformation ideas about the value of incarcerated laborers. Black Power activists looked to the entire history of the prison as a rhetorical resource for investigating the power of white supremacy over black America.[12]

While slavery was not institutionalized as punishment for crime prior to the Civil War, the Thirteenth Amendment legally provided just such a rationale for the perpetuation of this cheap labor. It reads, "Neither slavery nor involuntary servitude, except as a punishment for crime whereof the party shall have been duly convicted, shall exist within the United States, or any place subject to their jurisdiction." Thus, the amendment actually wrote slavery into the Constitution for those convicted of crimes. This rhetorical and legal change had drastic repercussions for former slaves as southern states, led by Mississippi in 1865, drafted legislation that defined nearly all former slaves as criminals for vague offenses ranging from "mischief" to "insulting gestures" but also for not being in a labor contract, all while the freedmen were not yet extended voting rights. The Black Codes inspired the creation of southern penitentiaries to hold these new black "criminals." After Reconstruction, the discipline of the southern prison regime extended to every aspect of black life, constraining black bodies and black voices through tremendous bodily violence and torture. "Actual imprisonment, the threat of imprisonment, and day-to-day imprisonment on the tenant farms or in the ghettos," writes Franklin, "were central to the life of Black people."[13]

While the Black Codes did not survive Reconstruction, they created the conditions for the birth of the southern penitentiary, as the Thirteenth Amendment became the rhetorical mechanism to harness black labor in southern prisons. This system of exploitation of former slaves was intrinsically linked to the development of industrial capitalism, but it was also driven by the fee system emerging in the South where sheriffs were only compensated based on the number of prisoners arrested. Thus, "the law" and "lawlessness" converged in the southern disciplinary official who could transgress "the law" at will and with no repercussion, particularly when these indiscretions involved black Americans. This fact was not lost on black freedom activists, who understood the collapse of law into lawlessness as an intrinsic condition of white supremacy.

Prison writings testified to the conditions of the new plantation economy as it emerged in prisons and prevented black people from holding property, moving freely, and economically competing as new prisons structured post-bellum white supremacy. Franklin elucidates how whites "devised a pervasive, intricate apparatus of law, custom, and brute force to keep the Blacks in perpetual bondage. Central to this historical redefinition of the role of Black people was an ideological redefinition of them. No longer were they just a sub-human race; now they were to be thought of as a race of criminals."[14] Franklin concludes that this "definition was to become increasingly important throughout American culture, right up through the white code words of the 1960s and 1970s, such as 'black militants,' 'welfare cadillacs,' 'violent-prone,' 'crime in the streets' (as opposed to 'safe streets'), and 'racial disorders' (as opposed to 'law and order')."[15]

Certainly, the state's response to civil disobedience from the 1950s to the 1970s hinged on the rhetorical redefinition of black people as "pathological criminals" and of "protest" as "crime." These rhetorical moves were honed as Reconstruction failed and the black intelligentsia questioned the retreat from guarantees of black citizenship found in the Reconstruction amendments to the Constitution.

The prison writings of the 1960s highlighted the continuity of imprisonment as a feature of black life in America and created new rhetorical modes of expressing the psychological and physical impairments that slavery and imprisonment created in black communities. The vernacular rhetorical strategies within black prison memoirs from slavery on demonstrate how these texts offered deep meditations on life and death and on the relationship between prison and slavery. Grant Farred explains, "Overburdened by structural lack (historic absence of material resources and access to capital), vernacular speech is politicized as much by its content, though much of that may be superimposed, as by the absences of formal political channels of redress or representation."[16] Consequently, vernacular rhetorical strategies in emergent prison writings were tied *intrinsically* to issues of sovereignty, citizenship, and group identity. Thus, black Americans, marginalized by public culture and denied access to the political sphere, looked for spaces from which to forge individual and group identities.

By the 1970s, writings by imprisoned intellectuals like Martin Luther King Jr., Malcolm X, Stokely Carmichael, Angela Davis, George Jackson, and Eldridge Cleaver circulated widely and were found on bestseller lists across the country. Black newspapers, magazines, and journals included the writings of black prisoners and those formerly incarcerated not only to expose inhuman prison conditions but also "to make clear the continuities in the circumstances for African Americans inside and outside prison walls."[17] Former political prisoner Angela Davis explains that these writings were vital in creating political and intellectual space for prisoners because "[t]here is always the tendency to push prisons to the fringes of our awareness so that we don't have to deal with what happens inside of those horrifying institutions. And there is the tendency also to look at the prisoners as having deserved what they have met with there."[18] Given the tremendous number of activists that had seen the inside of America's jails and prisons as a result of the black freedom movement, a reimagination of "the black prisoner" seemed necessary for the movement.

As activists forged new ways of thinking and talking about civil rights and black liberation, they had to contend with how civil disobedience should be used, particularly after it failed to fundamentally end segregation. Violence became a large part of the conversation as (mostly) white media outlets pushed back against a more radical civil rights agenda. Prison writers often took the most radical stance in the rhetorical posturing of the Black Power movement, since these intellectuals had, in a very real sense, less to lose. Joy James explains that imprisoned writing often centers on violence: "violence by the state to squash dissent and destroy dissenters; violence deployed to 'disappear' the incarcerated or detained; violence carried out by dissenters and prisoners in self-defence or to wield power."[19] Importantly, James also contends that prison writings are suspect rhetorical vehicles for sustained critiques of the state because "Americans are more familiar with (inured to?) state violence, particularly when it is directed against disenfranchised or racially or politically suspect minorities."[20] Because violence is at the center of the struggle for citizenship, Black Power activists centered slavery, imperialism, and colonialism in their analyses, demonstrating how racism and classism functioned together to create systemic inequality, enforced by state-sanctioned violence, under the pretense of democracy.

These topics were part of a series of recognizable black-speaking positionalities (outlaw, criminal, outcast, martyr) that helped amplify the topoi of warfare. Invocations of the history of slavery demonstrated the ways in which the arbitrary state power in the 1960s and 1970s (via unjust laws, a corrupt legal system, state-sanctioned violence, and a passive federal government) functioned in similar ways to Jim Crow. The Black Power writings of the 1960s and early 1970s employed a vernacular that highlighted structural racism while also resisting the constructions of pathological blackness iterated by white politicians, demonstrating that Black Power writers could participate in the major literary and political discourses shaping contemporary culture.

Beginning with the Montgomery Bus Boycott in 1955, sit-ins and jail-ins used by activists in Alabama, Mississippi, and North Carolina walked the line between making demands about equality and trying not to offend white liberals. By August 1961, sit-ins included over 70,000 participants and produced over 3,000 arrests, creating the participants and audiences for the emergent prison discourse of the movement.[21]

Jail became a site of social transformation for activists where, in the words of Martin Luther King Jr., the "poverty of conscience of the white majority" was exposed.[22] Because of this process of moral actualization, many black citizens followed King's lead to jail. From the early days of the struggle, black preachers in Alabama realized that the only way to unify their efforts was to follow King "wherever the struggle led him, including jail," according to Houston A. Baker, who adds that this ironically created "a new space of black freedom: the entire criminal justice system of the American South. As discussed previously, with the sit-ins, the most thunderous cry of black public resistance was 'jail, no bail.' This cry indisputably defined a new southern black public consciousness that instituted a body-on-the-line revolution."[23] In defining a new sense of black consciousness that involved the embodied knowledge of imprisonment, jail-ins created a new community of civil rights practitioners that saw imprisonment as rhetorical action. While jail was often boring and occasionally violent, it did engender a certain feeling of invincibility among activists, particularly those that were jailed repeatedly. Activists saw that the jails couldn't hold all of their numbers, and they were regularly praised for their courage through letters and op-eds in the papers. As a result of the mass imprisonment of civil rights activists, "the entire apparatus of white policing and surveillance, which had evolved from the 'patter-rollers' in the armed camp of slavery, was converted, mostly by young black students, into a vocational site for liberation. The white-controlled space of criminality and incarceration was transformed into a public arena for black justice and freedom."[24]

As the movement transformed southern jails and prisons into spaces for freedom and justice, several moments defined the southern movement's pairing of rhetorical manifestos and embodied resistance: Albany (1961–1962),

Birmingham (1963), Mississippi Freedom Summer (1964), and the march from Selma to Montgomery (1965). While civil rights historians have often recounted the events that transpired in these cases, the following accounts highlight the emergence of prison writing to understand how jail transformed the black liberation activists, the black freedom movement, and the state's resistance to desegregation. Beyond these southern campaigns, the Black Power movement used vernacular prison writings, especially autobiographies, to challenge the jail-in strategy by highlighting the role of prison in maintaining white supremacy in urban spaces.

The Albany Movement (1961–1962)

As the sit-in movement captured the imagination of students in North Carolina, direct-action protests using the "jail, no bail" strategy spread across the Deep South led by SNCC activists Charles Jones, Charles Sherrod, and Cordell Reagon. Their Albany movement in Georgia eventually included the Southern Christian Leadership Conference (SCLC) led by King, who visited Albany for the first time in December 1961. While King had intended to appear only briefly to support the movement, he was swept into nonviolent protests, leading to his arrest. When King returned to Georgia in July of 1962 for his arraignment, he was sentenced to forty-five days in jail or a $178 fine for parading without a permit and disorderly conduct; King chose to be jailed alongside hundreds of other protestors.

March leader and Albany native Dr. William Anderson recalled, "going to jail was about the worst thing that could happen to a Negro in Albany, Georgia, prior to the civil rights movement . . . They thought that for you to go to jail and risk losing your job was as bad a thing as you could do."[25] Anderson recalled that the SNCC activists changed people's minds about the role of prison in the struggle for equality because "they came down and went to jail like they were going to a Sunday school picnic. That was a dramatic difference from anything these people had been taught to do."[26] King concurred with this assessment, suggesting in his autobiography that Albany was important to the struggle because, in his words, "Negroes, wielding nonviolent protest in its most creative utilization to date, challenged discrimination in public spaces, denial of voting rights, school segregation, and the deprivation of free speech and assembly."[27]

Although Albany activists exercised a wide array of tactics, the jail-in was the strategy that leaders remember most vividly. Charles Sherrod explains what activists had hoped would come of their imprisonment in Albany: "We were going to break the system down from within. Our ability to suffer was somehow going to overcome their ability to hurt us."[28] Sherrod suggests that Albany was significant because of the sheer numbers of those going into Georgia jails. Around seven hundred people had already been jailed when they decided to call in King and the SCLC.[29] Sherrod remembers, "We didn't know what we were doing. We'd never done it before. Nobody had never got that many people to go to jail. And I'm not talking about just the hoi polloi, I'm talking about the upper crust . . . Even some white folk went to jail with us, from Albany."[30] Sherrod suggests that the unity that imprisonment brought demystified the prison experience and helped to transform many members of the community into coalitional activists.[31]

However, SNCC's William Hansen noted that King's imprisonment raised the visibility of the Albany movement. He explains, "As much as we may disagree with MLK about the way he and SCLC do things, one has to admit that he can cause more hell to be raised by being in jail one night than anyone else could if they bombed city hall."[32] In acknowledging the national press coverage that King brought, Hansen suggests that King's imprisonment had symbolic value for the protestors and for the nation, due to his stature and his rhetorical abilities. The contribution of jailing well-recognized leaders created opportunities for those leaders to comment on segregation from jail.

But chief of police Laurie Pritchett studied King's nonviolent methods, and he retrained his police officers to adapt to King's strategies and trained the Albany police force in nonviolence to combat the bad optics of police brutality that became particularly infamous after Birmingham.[33] Albany is remarkable particularly *because* social movement participants and state agents used the jails as the major point of contention as the insistence for desegregation mounted. Jail, then, was the defining feature of the Albany movement for activists and officers alike.

Albany was a strategic location for the "jail, no bail" strategy, given its position in the Deep South as well as the endurance of the movement there. But it was also rhetorically significant because King wrote his first manifesto and his first prison letter in Albany and thus began a genre of prison writings from the movement that continued throughout the decade. Rarely mentioned by scholars, King composed the "The Albany Manifesto," on July 15, 1962, and charged Pritchett and city administrators for "a long history of double-talk, unkept promises, subtle intimidation and lack of integrity" in dealing with segregation in Albany. King also cited the mass imprisonment of activists as a reason for continued marches in Albany, saying: "we insist that it is our right under the Constitution and the Bill of Rights to peacefully protest our grievances; and whereas it is a true saying that no Negro can exercise that right without provoking arrest and conviction; be it therefore resolved that we shall never again bargain away our First Amendment privilege to so peacefully protest. . . ."[34] Though a mere two pages long, the "Albany Manifesto" demonstrated the relationship between imprisonment and moral suasion as King attempted to persuade a reluctant black population to demonstrate under the threat of arrest.

Southern activists and imprisoned intellectuals used manifestoes and open letters, as King did, to communicate with a larger (often white and northern) audience about the gross violations of civil rights by those sworn to uphold civil rights and about the conditions of American prisons. King's first prison letter, written in Albany, titled "A Message From Jail," dated July 21, 1962, and published in the black New York newspaper *The Amsterdam News*, explained the reason for his imprisonment and the justification for remaining there. King explains that Albany has "been the site of the largest mass demonstrations and jail-ins in the nonviolent movement in the South."[35] Responding to white critics of the Albany movement who charged that civil disobedience "fosters disobedience for the law and encourages lawlessness," King said these critics missed the crucial distinction between racists who flouted the law and refused to pay any penalty whatsoever and the activists, like King, whose "decision to break the law and willingly pay the penalty for it evidences the highest respect for the law."[36] King used this open letter to circulate the idea that law enforcers themselves were lawless and that black activist citizens felt a social obligation to protest the abrogation of law by those entrusted to uphold it. King's point, of course, was to simultaneously highlight the daily inequalities that made black citizenship nearly impossible because of structural racism, violence, and imprisonment and to also showcase the black devotion to citizenship, suggesting that in their civil disobedience, activists were showcasing a more sophisticated and ethical adherence to the spirit and intent of desegregation laws. While King's letter was not as rhetorically sophisticated as his letter from Birmingham and it did not describe his prison experience in Albany, it did serve as a brief description of the situation for those on the outside and helped to rally northern support for nonviolent civil disobedience. As a rhetorical witness, King's authority on state violence only grew after Albany, giving him a nearly unimpeachable credibility through the mid-decade.

King's autobiography describes how imprisonment influenced the Albany movement, describing the crowd's "spirit of enthusiasm" at the release of movement participants just before Christmas 1961 "when seven hundred Negro citizens were finally released from prison. Out of the jails came men and women—doctors, ministers, and housewives—all of whom had joined the ranks with a gallant student leadership in an exemplary demonstration of nonviolent resistance to segregation."[37] King's description carefully highlights the men and women radicalized by the Albany movement and their imprisonment, suggesting such a possibility for other middle-class black Americans across the South. Tactically, King's strategy paid off because Laurie Pritchett had to choose between keeping King in jail for a month or more, risking the possibility of every civil rights leader in the country descending on Albany, or arranging for King's bail to be posted to end the public relations tumult in the city.[38]

Albany provided the opportunity for King to fine tune the vernacular that he would continue to employ in defending civil disobedience as a strategy of inclusive citizenship. Rhetorician Gerard Hauser explains that prisoners of conscience who are imprisoned by virtue of their political "disagreement with a hegemonic power" resort to rhetorical strategies that highlight their unique position as a witness to state violence.[39] Hauser writes that political prisoners inhabit "a unique rhetorical space. Unlike convicted felons who break the law for personal gain or through criminal recklessness, blind passion, or folly, [prisoners of conscience] are incarcerated for the threat of their ideas. . . . When their legal violations do involve acts of violence, they stem from embracing ideas at odds with the existing order."[40] By providing a competitive rhetorical perspective, the writings of political prisoners create an ethical and political exigency to prompt innovative political conflict. As a result, "[t]heir ability to display an alternative political vision can be so compelling . . . that repressive regimes are willing to liquidate leading dissidents" to silence their voices, says Hauser.[41] King certainly harnessed this power to create exigency through the embodied resistance of his imprisonment alongside the SCLC and local community organizers.

Birmingham (1963)

By the time that King was arrested in Birmingham during the confrontation with public safety commissioner Eugene "Bull" Connor and wrote his famous 1963 prison manifesto, "Letter From Birmingham Jail," thousands of protestors in America's most segregated cities had already been jailed. Like Albany, the Birmingham jail became the centerpiece of embodied resistance in the movement's triumphalist narrative of Birmingham. In *Why We Can't Wait* (1964), King explains why jail was so central to southern civil rights, particularly in Birmingham. He writes,

Jailing the Negro was once as much of a threat as the loss of a job. To any Negro who displayed a spark of manhood, a southern law-enforcement officer could say: "Nigger watch your step, or I'll put you in jail." The Negro knew what going to jail meant. It means not only confinement and isolation from his loved ones. It meant that at the jailhouse he could probably expect a severe beating. And it meant that his day in court, if he had it, would be a mockery of justice.[42]

Because jail loomed as such an enormous social threat, southern activists including King tried to fill the jails to demystify and de-stigmatize imprisonment, particularly for middle-class black Americans. King hoped to induce more middle-class blacks (and whites) to financially support the movement. King explains that as a result of jail-ins, "to the Negro, going to jail was no longer a disgrace but a badge of honor. The Revolution of the Negro not only attacked the external cause of his misery, but revealed him to himself. He was somebody. . . . He was impatient to be free."[43] As King explains, imprisonment was an inevitable path to freedom that transformed the consciousness of passive black citizens.

This was especially true as movement leaders argued for the use of schoolchildren in Birmingham. King's chief of staff, Wyatt Tee Walker, justified this movement tactic, saying, "[w]e knew we were right to use the children. One of the basic tenets of the nonviolent philosophy is that it is the kind of struggle in which everyone can participate—young, old children, adults, blind, crippled, lame, whatever—because it is a moral struggle."[44] He adds, "I think someone quotes me as saying six days in Jefferson County Jail would be more educational to these children than six months in the segregated Birmingham schools that they were attending."[45] Walker's comments suggest that imprisonment provided an embodied political literacy about race relations in America, and he compares it to the underfunded black schools in the city to underscore how transformative the direct action in Birmingham was in politicizing the children.

Because of the media coverage of the brutality of Birmingham, King's imprisonment was even more compelling than in Albany. Thus did King's "Letter From Birmingham Jail" prove to be the most enduring manifesto of the southern civil rights movement because of King's "authority to direct thought and action against the existing order."[46] In his indictment of federal inaction protecting civil rights workers one hundred and one years after emancipation, King articulated several interrelated dimensions of the southern civil rights movement that circulated in the Black Power movement several years later. First, he highlighted the willingness and courage of civil rights activists to confront racial inequality. Second, he described the rampant police brutality in the South, suggesting that the Justice Department's unwillingness to break with the racist police structure in the South imperiled civil rights activists, making substantive change impossible. Without federal support, King argued that black citizens have an impossible task in seeking equality: "A ruling state apparatus, accustomed for generations to act with impunity against him, is able to employ every element of unchecked power. A slow-moving federal suit, or sporadic and frequently ineffectual federal mediation, is scarcely more adequate to support the Negro in such a one-sided engagement than would be a pat on the back."[47] Finally, King impugned the federal reluctance to use marshals to enforce desegregation orders and their refusal to use the Interstate Commerce Commission to desegregate public transportation, clearly blaming the Kennedy administration for inaction on civil rights while simultaneously suggesting that the passage of major civil rights legislation would be a defining moment of success.

King's appeal ends with a note toward audience, suggesting that many southerners welcomed federal leadership on civil rights to help remake communities marred by segregation and violence. King suggested that these new southerners "would welcome the curbing of the up-dated, iron-booted Klansmen. . . . The dignity of the federal government would be radiantly enhanced if it arrayed a trained, self-confident force of federal marshals against these armed usurpers who have stomach for battle only with the unarmed and nonviolent."[48] King's Birmingham manifesto indicted southern law enforcement officers for their brutality, suggesting that the incivility of white culture prompted the demonstration.

His letter asserts King's visibility *from prison*, a move that the imprisoned can't often perform. Hauser explains that state imprisonment "rests on a calculation that once they are off the public stage they will be forgotten, and if their treatment is horrendous enough, quite possibly they will recant" and, barring such a confession, "the regime calculates that removal from public view will toll the dissident's political death knell and possibly deliver a mortal blow to the ideas for which he or she stands."[49] Without these oppositional political visions, the hope is that leaders will be driven underground.[50] But King's own visibility as a political and spiritual leader meant that he couldn't be disappeared.

Certainly, Birmingham shocked the nation, and King's letter framed the protest for readers outside of Alabama. Afterward, there was optimism that the sheer scale of Birmingham would prompt major legislation despite the fact that King's relationship with the White House was quite strained by 1963. Still, Lyndon Johnson's speechwriter Harry McPherson boldly suggests that

King's imprisonment was a primary reason that Johnson was able to get the Civil Rights Act of 1964 and the Voting Rights Act of 1965 passed after Kennedy's assassination. McPherson explains, "King's suffering was the catalyst. His being beaten, his being hosed, his being put in jail, all of the suffering that he endured, in every case brought a legislative response."[51] Because of Birmingham, McPherson argues, "the legislators, the Wilkinses and the Lyndon Johnsons, used that national anger and outcry against the treatment that King and his people had suffered at Selma and Birmingham and elsewhere, used that as the momentum builder to get the legislation through."[52] King's imprisonment, his letter from the Birmingham jail, and the images of dogs and fire hoses being used on schoolchildren created a political pressure that, at least in McPherson's mind, helped compel federal civil rights legislation.

However, it was King's vernacular that helped these visual historical images to resonate with audiences that existed outside of the black southern experience. Ecclesiastical training shaped King's vernacular profoundly, determining the kinds of narratives and metaphors he used to mobilize new activists. King relied heavily on the jeremiad as a vernacular rhetorical form and the Exodus narrative to postulate deliverance (religious and political) from segregation. He employed this vernacular strategy to position black Americans as Israelites who were delivered from Egyptian tyranny by God. Gary Selby contends, "This history of self-identification provided a source of social knowledge that King could exploit to evoke the kind of collective identity that theorists have insisted is essential for a social movement to exist, as well as a basis for his appeals to unity in the black community."[53] According to Selby, this rhetorical choice allowed King to couch black experience in the religious myths that gave King "a theological justification for engaging in collective action."[54]

Writing in *The Nation* in 1964, King argued that Birmingham focused the nation's attention on the brutality and imprisonment of nonviolent activists, especially the children. King wrote that in just a few months,

> more than 1,000 American cities and towns were shaken by street demonstrations, and more than 20,000 nonviolent resistors went to jail. Nothing in the Negro's history, save the era of Reconstruction, equals in intensity, breadth and power this matchless upheaval. For weeks it held spellbound, not only this country, but the entire world. . . . Negro power had matured and was dynamically asserting itself.[55]

Using the vernacular term *Negro power*, certainly a precursor to the term *Black Power*, King described *imprisonment* as the source of maturation fueling the movement's dynamism. He concluded this essay with a statement supporting activists and calling for federal action, declaring: "as Negroes have marshaled extraordinary courage to employ nonviolent direct action, they have been left—by the most powerful federal government in the world—almost solely to their own resources to face a massively equipped army."[56] King capitalized on what McPherson described as important political pressure to argue for the passage of what became the Civil Rights Act of 1964, suggesting that executive attention would compel the use of federal marshals to enforce the law after its passage.

Mississippi (1961–1965)

Imprisonment served as a radicalizing force for movement activists in Albany and Birmingham, but it also served SNCC activists working in Mississippi. There, the terrorism of the white police drove many activists (particularly during the Freedom Rides) into Parchman Prison, the state penitentiary. Formerly a massive antebellum cotton plantation, Parchman was still a working farm, turning a profit with the aid of black convict labor. This irony was not lost on SNCC activists imprisoned there as Stokely Carmichael points out in his autobiography: "It was designed, organized and run along the lines of an antebellum slave plantation for *humanitarian* reasons in the 1890s."[57] Carmichael discusses the continuity of black slavery at the site of Parchman, demonstrating the long role of imprisonment in black life since black lives continue to be seen as expendable, particularly by the prison guards who carried cattle prods to assault prisoners. Describing it as one of the two most brutal penitentiaries in the South and calling it a "concentration camp" and "hellhole," Carmichael details the "serious torture" the SNCC activists withstood there.[58] Assaulted with fire hoses for singing hymns and padlocked to wrist breakers, SNCC activists were eventually bailed out of Parchman, half-starved and exhausted, but the brutality of the experience connected them forever.

As the movement slouched toward Black Power, prison became an increasingly politicized space as SNCC activists went back to Mississippi in 1963–1965 to lay the groundwork for what eventually became the Mississippi Freedom Democratic Party (MFDP) through massive voter registration drives. As media outlets showered attention on white summer volunteers in Mississippi, black members of SNCC were increasingly discouraged by the attitudes of white volunteers. Historian Cheryl Greenberg describes how SNCC members worried that white members might always compromise a truly black vision of activism in the South, particularly after "the intensive FBI search for (white) civil rights workers Andrew Goodman, James Schwerner and (black) James Chaney during Freedom Summer, agents dredging the river discovered the black bodies of lynchings they had never bothered to investigate."[59] Given the daily violence in Mississippi and the slow pace of change, it seems that a radicalization of the movement was in some ways inevitable. And, with the early resistance of the Kennedy administration to the black freedom movement along with the Johnson administration's preoccupation with the war in Vietnam, Black Power was a likely shift as activists lost hope in the ability of whites to fundamentally shift their attitudes about black people and segregation. Additionally, King's overwhelming command of the movement alienated many younger activists who saw the SCLC as too conservative.

Still, voter registration in Mississippi was a laudable goal, though extremely difficult due to pervasive violence and imprisonment, which propelled radicalism among SNCC members. Harassment and intimidation were extremely pervasive as black residents saw the retaliation of whites. Those black residents that attempted to register to vote suffered from economic retaliation in the form of boycotts, political and physical persecution, fire bombings, and police harassment. The violence during the summer was staggering. Three volunteers were murdered, four shot and wounded, fifty-two beaten, and 250 arrested. Thirteen black churches were razed to the ground with seventeen other churches and community buildings damaged by fire bombings.[60] Conspicuously absent from the summer's voter registration activities was the protection of federal officials. While 136 FBI agents were dispatched to Mississippi, they were there with strict orders to observe rather than protect as the Justice Department protested a lack of precedent for interference.[61] With the lack of federal protection, violence escalated. Still, activists were able to convince about 17,000 black residents to fill out voter registration forms, though only 1,600 were allowed to register. In addition, 80,000 black residents registered as members of the newly formed Mississippi Freedom Democratic Party.[62]

By the time that the MFDP had its showdown with the Democratic Party at the 1964 Democratic convention, civil rights workers had seen an incredible amount of violence inside and outside of prison. Fannie Lou Hamer, vice chair of the MFDP delegation at the national convention, recalled the brutal prison beatings she endured along with other women in Mississippi working to register black voters. In her heartbreaking account of state repression of the voter registration work in Mississippi, she described a state highway patrolman explaining to another, "I want you to make that bitch wish she was dead."[63] Hamer told the nation, "Five mens in this room while I was one Negro woman, being beaten, and at no time did I attempt to do anything but scream and call on God. I don't know how long this lasted, but after a while I must have passed out. And when I did raise my head up, the state highway patrolman said, 'Get up from there, fatso.' But I couldn't get up."[64] The white police officers ordered five black prisoners to beat Hamer with brass knuckles; she was sexually assaulted in jail and the physical abuse was so severe she nearly lost an eye.[65] At the hearing for the civil rights workers, Hamer recounts that the policemen who beat her were on the jury and they charged her and her colleagues with disorderly conduct and resisting arrest. Hamer glosses Abraham Lincoln's 1858 speech accepting the Republican nomination as a US senator. In the most rousing portion of the speech, which bears quotation at length, Hamer explains:

> A house divided against itself cannot stand; America is divided against itself and without their considering us human beings, one day America will crumble. Because God is not pleased. God is not pleased at all the murdering, and all of the brutality, and all the killings for no reason at all. God is not pleased at the Negro children in the state of Mississippi suffering from malnutrition. God is not pleased because we have to go raggedy each day. God is not pleased because we have to go to the field and work from ten to eleven hours for three lousy dollars.[66]

Her speech is remarkable because, as rhetorical scholar Maegan Parker Brooks suggests, Hamer's vernacular "appeared paradoxical as she sought authority by claiming powerlessness."[67] Brooks suggests that Hamer's vernacular "used this paradox as a trope of invention" enabling her vernacular persona "to establish the authority to speak, encourage oppressed audiences to recognize the potential for change, and challenge the nation's self-conception in such a manner that prompted both black and white audiences to work toward social transformation."[68] Hamer's vernacular persona, grounded in her experience as a women and victim of extremely brutal violence, as a sharecropper, and as a daughter of slaves drove her indictment of southern white supremacy. Centered within her account of white supremacist violence was her experience in the southern jail, where an auditor or reader of her rhetorical text cannot easily dismiss the brutality she encountered. Hamer's self-conscious reference to her lack of education and her limited rhetorical repertoire allows her vernacular to evidence the veracity of her claims.

Although Johnson worried that seating the MFDP delegates at the convention would cost him southern votes and encourage a convention walk-out, he allowed vice-presidential hopeful Senator Hubert Humphrey, along with several other Democratic leaders, the opportunity to craft a compromise. The final result of that compromise was an offer of two seats to the MFDP, filled by delegates chosen by the Democratic Party without input from the MFDP leadership. Hamer and the other leaders of the MFDP soundly rejected the compromise and started the work to document the massive evidence of racial discrimination at the voting booth. When it was completed, the MFDP documented black exclusion from voting by compiling "over 15,000 pages of sworn testimony documenting the harassment, reign of terror, and violence aimed at potential black voters."[69]

Given the sheer volume of data collected by the MFDP about violence, intimidation, harassment, and imprisonment, it seems reasonable that workers were both frustrated with the Johnson administration and feeling betrayed as well as concerned about their own personal safety. SNCC activist Cleveland Sellers recalled this moment in the organization's history in his memoir, writing, "The national Democratic party's rejection of the MFDP at the 1964 convention was to the civil rights movement what the Civil War was to American history; afterwards, things could never be the same."[70] If Black Power was an unavoidable destiny, this rift between the Johnson administration and the civil rights organizers in the Deep South propelled the movement to the Left.

Selma to Montgomery March (1965)

The march from Selma to Montgomery proved to be another turning point in the southern movement as activists marched to protest the murder of twenty-six-year-old Jimmie Lee Jackson, whose grandfather was whipped bloody by a state trooper during a peaceful march earlier in February 1965. Rushing to his grandfather's aid, Jackson carried the bloody man into a café where state troopers beat Jackson and shot him in the stomach. He died several days later and civil rights organizations descended on Selma to protest the killing. Jackson's death was more evidence of systematic police brutality in the South and it "provided a martyr for the cause of black voting rights," according to historian Lloyd Earl Rohler.[71] Jackson's death also suggested that the sheer magnitude of violence against civil rights workers had to be addressed rhetorically and politically in a more comprehensive way. As activists wondered about the limits of nonviolence direct action, the murder of Jimmy Lee Jackson settled the issue for many SNCC workers who were ready to change the conversation away from nonviolence to Black Power.

New York Times journalist Roy Reed described the 3,200 protestors marching to the Alabama state capitol to petition Governor George Wallace to guarantee civil rights for black Americans. Reed remarked on the gravity of the march, saying it "appears destined for a niche in the annals of the great protest demonstrations."[72] Reed noted that the march was organized as "the culmination of a turbulent nine-week campaign that began as an effort to abolish restrictions on Negro voting in the Alabama Black Belt and widened finally to encompass a general protest against racial injustice in the state."[73] He added that violence and imprisonment marred the protest, however, with "two men dead and scores injured. Some 3,800 persons have been arrested in Selma and neighboring communities."[74]

The sheer numbers of those imprisoned in the march from Selma to Montgomery suggest that as the decade wore on, violence against demonstrators increased, exposing more activists to the experience of imprisonment as well as more imprisoned violence. But activists utilized this tension more frequently. For example, in anticipation of Martin Luther King's arrest in Selma, the SCLC drafted a fundraising advertisement for the New York Times. And King wrote another open letter, this time from the Selma jail after his arrest on February 1, hoping to build momentum for the passage of a federal voting rights bill. King's letter begins with an acknowledgment of his acceptance of the Nobel Peace Prize in 1964, and he suggests that the Nobel committee probably did not anticipate that he would be back in prison less than sixty days after receiving the award. Harnessing an international audience, King asserts that "[b]y jailing hundreds of Negroes, the city of Selma, Alabama, has revealed the persisting ugliness of segregation to the nation and the world. When the Civil Rights Act of 1964 was passed many decent Americans were lulled into complacency because they thought the day of difficult struggle was over."[75] King's letter describes the poll taxes and literacy tests that SCLC activists were protesting at the time of their arrest, saying: "THIS IS SELMA, ALABAMA. THERE ARE MORE NEGROES IN JAIL WITH ME THAN THERE ARE ON THE VOTING ROLLS."[76] King added, "This is the U.S.A. in 1965. We are in jail simply because we cannot tolerate these conditions for ourselves or our nation."[77]

Rhetorically, King used this letter to quantify the paltry numbers of black Americans that could vote in Alabama and to compel northern financial support for the movement as it continued to make its case in the streets and jails of the American South. King concluded the appeal, asserting, "Our people are eager to work, to sacrifice, to be jailed—but their income, normally meager, is cut off in these crises. Your help can make the difference. Your help can be a message of unity which the thickest jail walls cannot muffle."[78] Financial support is articulated here as a vernacular rhetorical message of unity that can overcome the trauma of imprisonment for the activists fighting for the right to exercise the franchise. As Hauser explains, vernacular interlocutors "rely on a rhetoric that addresses its immediate audience or an audience of readers and viewers in a way that interrupts what we were doing and demands a response."[79] Certainly that is the case in the Selma letter where the full-page letter interrupts the reader's attention to demand that they support the movement.

The march from Selma to Montgomery also marked a rhetorical turning point because King spent much time during the march with SNCC's Stokely Carmichael debating the role of nonviolence in the movement. Watching the state troopers beat and kill nonviolent protestors was too much for SNCC activists like Carmichael, who felt that the nonviolence had outlived its utility. The violence at the Edmund Pettus Bridge combined with the death of Jimmie Lee Jackson radicalized SNCC activists even further, creating rifts in SNCC that exposed competing visions about the movement's future.

The new Black Power vernacular augmented this rift and expressed a more militant stance against the brutality of segregation. King's vernacular genius "had been his unique ability to combine militance with moderation. He had consistently been radical enough to push American toward major change while staying near enough to middle-class opinion and institutions to affect and direct them."[80] However, after 1965, King faced an uphill battle because his characteristic charisma was unable to overcome the rhetorical posture of the Black Power movement or the new distance of white liberals. And by mid-decade, King was trapped "between young black militants who called him a compromising Uncle Tom and established black leaders who echoed white charges that he was radical and unpatriotic."[81]

King's vernacular could not overcome these competing rhetorical conditions, and it became increasingly difficult for King's message to mobilize new action for civil rights with a rhetorical strategy relying primarily on biblical language. For example, it was problematic to suggest direct-action events while employing a narrative of redemption that did not spring from the civil disobedience itself, but instead, relied upon the idea that God would deliver them. Particularly as younger activists began to use Marxism, the Cuban Revolution, and Third World anticolonialism to inform their analyses of structural racism, the persuasive power of the religious myths lost cultural cache. As King's popularity declined, Black Power leaders like Carmichael energized the movement with new vocabulary, ideas, and strategies as activists were no longer content to witness racial atrocity but instead sought to radically disrupt public space through more radical confrontations. Historian Francesca Polletta explains, "[a]fter years of brutal repression and a practically non-existent federal response, SNCC workers after 1964 were more intent on gaining power than appealing to a liberal establishment now perceived as corrupt."[82]

For example, SNCC activists invited Malcolm X to speak at meetings in both 1964 and 1965 as leaders explored more radical perspectives on black consciousness and power.

As his influenced waned after being alienated by the Johnson White House over his dissent on the Vietnam War and on the War on Poverty, King lost ground among white liberals across the country who lumped him in with Black Power leaders because he refused to denounce them and because he was slowly adopting some of their vernacular inventions in his own discourses. Historian David Howard-Pitney adds, "[w]hereas King had once appeared to many whites as a patriotic dissenter in whom they could take pride, after 1965 they considered him mainly a radical rabble-rouser or, worse, a traitor."[83] This was particularly ironic, since white elites had done much to create the King phenomenon from sending financial support, to encouraging news coverage, to agitating on behalf of the SCLC. But, by the time of his death, "America's elite regarded King as a dangerous threat" that "they themselves had done much to create."[84]

Class became a major component of King's changing rhetoric as Black Power helped to radicalize his perspective on segregation, particularly in the North, but which presented him with rhetorical and political problems. Accordingly, "When black jeremiads expanded their agendas to include structural economic changes that would reconstruct the North, too, a reform consensus among blacks and white Northerners failed to materialize. Most whites, including many who had lent crucial support to the struggle against slavery and for blacks' legal rights, balked at subsequent proposals for economic change."[85]

As the Black Power movement began to utilize a vernacular that highlighted *class* and used Marxism as a major component of their theoretical paradigm about oppression in the United States, the state made a concerted effort to eradiate them through infiltration and assassination. Still, the arguments being made by Black Power proponents influenced King, who began incorporating it into his own vernacular.

Black Power and the Black Panther Party

Within the Black Panther Party for Self-Defense, a black revolution seemed inevitable given the limited success of the southern civil rights movement and the increasing brutality of state officials. In 1966, young, optimistic college students and disenfranchised ex-convicts in Oakland saw California as a fertile ground for revolutionary black action. Seizing on California's place in the American imaginary, the Black Panthers became the new cowboys of the late 1960s and early 1970s, ushering in a new era where power would be displaced and challenged by outlaws who elucidated the corruption of the political regime. Amy Ongiri cogently describes this culture of the mid-1960s as new conservatism emerged in the American consciousness:

> The rhetoric of law and order positioned African Americans firmly within a discourse of lawlessness and disorder that they had traditionally been assigned by the dominant culture. The Black Panther Party would radically refigure this discourse, restructuring the relationship between the African American outlaw figure and a romanticized notion of revolution to provoke identificatory possibilities across a broad spectrum of potential supporters. The Black Panther notion of vanguardism successfully created allies out of the formerly uninitiated and apolitical through the wide-ranging appeal of an ideology scripted through an easily decipherable iconic language of images: the raised fist, the black jacket and beret, the gun.[86]

The aesthetics of the Black Panthers catapulted the group into popular culture and media attention on the organization turned Panther leaders into celebrities as Hollywood elites like Marlon Brando and Jane Fonda and East Coast liberals like Tom Wolfe sought to be associated with Panther fundraising.

But the organization was also gaining coverage from their organizing about the constant police harassment that characterized life on the West Coast. The prominence of Black Power in California became obvious on May 2, 1967, when Panthers arrived armed at the state capitol in Sacramento. Loading their weapons on the statehouse lawn, Panthers assembled to protest the racial profiling of black motorists. Then-governor Ronald Reagan was so unnerved by the presence of the Panthers, that he ended a speech early to flee the scene.[87] While Bobby Seale read a prepared statement to reporters that refuted the Mulford Act, a bill specifically targeting the Panther Party and designed to stop black residents from carrying loaded weapons, armed Panthers flanked him and media scrambled to cover the emerging story.[88] Speaking against the Panthers, Speaker Pro Tem Carlos Bee suggested that the stunt on the capitol lawn would speed passage of the Mulford bill while assemblyman Don Mulford himself said he would make the bill even tougher, subsequently adding a provision to prohibit firearms in the state capitol.[89] Less than three months later, the Mulford Act would become California law, providing one of the strictest gun control measures of the 1960s. The Mulford Act "succeeded in ending the Black Panthers' armed police patrols" though some Panthers continued to illegally carry, leading to confrontations with the police.[90] These confrontations provided the rationale for the FBI's Counter Intelligence Programs of disruption and surveillance against radical groups like the Panthers. By 1968, Hoover had placed the BPP at the top of his list for targeted demolition.[91]

Black Power's presence in California clarified on February 17, 1968, at the Oakland Auditorium, when the BPP, along with the Peace and Freedom Party, held a rally for Black Panther chairman Huey Newton, who had been imprisoned for allegedly killing a police officer. This coalition sought to "Free Huey," and in the speeches that punctuated the rally, prominent members of the Student Nonviolent Coordinating Committee including Stokely Carmichael, Rap Brown, and James Forman spoke along with Panthers Kathleen and Eldridge Cleaver, about the necessity of freeing Huey Newton from prison because his imprisonment signified the way in which black men were being persecuted around the country. Claiming that Newton was only "guilty of being black," the Panthers framed blackness as a sign of permanent social incarceration, inside and outside of prison.[92] At this rally, the Panthers announced a merger with SNCC and appointed SNCC leaders to posts within the BPP. Stokely Carmichael was appointed field marshal, Rap Brown (the new chairman of SNCC) became minister of justice, and James Forman was given the title minister of foreign affairs.[93] Seven thousand people attended the rally, raising over $10,000 for Newton's defense and a follow-up event the next day at the Los Angeles Sports Arena was well attended, demonstrating the sheer mass of people committed to securing Newton's release from prison as well as the importance of mobilizing against imprisonment.[94]

At the rally, speakers exhorted the necessity of revolutionary action, demonstrating that the movement's relationship to imprisonment had changed. In her own prison memoir, the *Autobiography of Angela Davis* (1971), Angela Davis recalled the rally, praising Rap Brown's electrifying speech.[95] Brown's speech was popular with the audience, who didn't want him to yield the podium to Carmichael. They were excited by Brown's vernacular and urged him to continue speaking as he characterized the Johnson administration's use of "law and order rhetoric." In his rally speech, Brown exclaimed:

> OK, we going to talk about law and order versus justice in America, then. You see, Lyndon Johnson can always sit up and talk . . . he can always raise an argument about law and order, because he never talks about justice. But black people fall for that same argument, and they go around talking about law breakers. We did not make the laws in this country. We are neither morally nor legally confined to those laws.[96]

Using King's famous arguments in the "Letter From Birmingham Jail," Brown makes the distinction between just and unjust laws while adding context about the erasure of black voices in the promulgation of law, particularly those precedents established under the banner of "law and order." But unlike King, Brown's vernacular uses an entirely secular context and accessible language to suggest that black activists needed to hone a more critical appraisal of political power.

Following Brown, Stokely Carmichael spoke at length about the need for black Americans to struggle alongside other people of color working against American imperialism and colonization abroad. He also repudiated the prison strategy of the southern civil rights movement, of which he had been so central, explaining: "It is no need for us to go to jail today for what we say. They did that to brother Malcolm X: they just offed him for what he was saying. We have to progress as a race."[97] Knowing that the penalty for organizing continued to be death for black leaders, Carmichael sought a broader vision for black liberation that problematized the role of prison in the movement.

The move away from jail-ins marked the changing tide of movement strategy. Where southern activists were rarely in jail long, given the sentencing guidelines for their relatively minor infractions for civil disobedience, in northern cities, black activists were being arrested and imprisoned for long sentences. Also different was the fact that northern groups like the BPP were recruiting *from* prison and they were including long-term prisoners in their organizational identity and ideological platform, significantly changing the relationship between imprisonment and the black liberation struggle. Imprisonment and police brutality formed the basis for the short-lived collaboration between southern SNCC activists and northern BPP activists at the Free Huey rally and other collaborations in 1969. But the alliance between SNCC and the BPP was short lived due to the disagreements about the necessity of coalitions with white organizations. Still, this moment in 1968 demonstrated the way in which the black vernacular became a common rhetorical strategy utilized by both popular organizations as well as the importance of prison in helping to shape Black Power coalitions as they mobilized around Huey Newton's case and as they expanded their urban influence.[98] Undoubtedly, the BPP shifted the conversation around civil rights, partly out of necessity.

With the birth of COINTELPRO in 1967, the Panthers became a prime target for FBI harassment. A letter to select field officers in 1968 demanded "imaginative and hard-hitting counterintelligence measures aimed at crippling the BPP" by destroying coalition-building, eroding relationships between party leadership (particularly between Newton and Eldridge Cleaver), and exacerbating tensions between the BPP and other California black national-ists, particularly Ron Kargena's US organization. This plan turned deadly in January 1969 when Los Angeles Panther leaders Alprentice "Bunchy" Carter and John Huggins were shot in a UCLA classroom by US members George and John Stiner and Claude Hubert.[100] In his autobiography, early Us member and black arts legend Amiri Baraka describes the death of Carter and Hug-gins and how it marked the point where the FBI "escalated their 'intervention' into the conflict. They'd shoot at one organization, knowing that the other would get blamed, and that the organization shot at would retaliate in kind."[101] The FBI's constant provocation, documented in countless internal memos, stoked warfare between the US and the BPP, providing political cover for FBI and local police intervention, but also spurring tremendous fundraising and agitation from the BPP and their allies.

And although Huey Newton's case was a prominent example of how the Panthers used prison to agitate outside of the penitentiary walls during the reactionary Nixon administration, it was only one of many high-profile cases that forced a public conversation about this new phase of black activism and the role of the police and the FBI in working to undermine black liberation organizing. The 1969 Chicago 8 trial (including Black Panther Bobby Seale, whose case was severed to be tried separately), the 1969 trials over the murder of Panthers Bunchy Carter and John Huggins the New Haven Panther trials in 1969, the misconduct case in the assassination of Chicago Panthers Fred Hampton and Mark Clark, the massive global organizing to free former UCLA professor Angela Davis in 1970, and the 1971 Panther 21 trial in New York were all high-profile cases involving police and FBI malfeasance against Panthers.[102] As a result of the dramatically high number of assassinations, the huge num-ber of FBI informants, and the police harassment of Panthers across the coun-try, activists were now exposed to the inside of northern penitentiaries, not southern county jails. This repression spurred more global activism as Panthers used global examples of American repression to theorize about incarceration, police power, new conservatism, and urban white supremacy. Building a new coalition with SNCC leaders, the BPP sought to make connections and scaffold experience about imprisonment and activism in the late 1960s.

Mississippi Freedom Democratic Party: Imprisonment and Political Organizing

Although SNCC had transformed southern organizing with student inno-vation and bodily resistance, the organization also propelled the Mississippi Freedom Democratic Party. In 1968, taking a page from SNCC's playbook, the

BPP in concert with the Peace and Freedom Party approved Huey Newton, Bobby Seale, and Kathleen Cleaver as candidates on their platform in the 1968 elections. Additionally, Eldridge Cleaver was chosen as the party's presidential candidate in 1968 running on a platform dedicated to black liberation and opposing the war in Vietnam.[103] The nomination of these Panthers to run for political office gave the BPP a global visibility that helped to publicize their cause and also gave them the space to build coalitions with other progressive causes from environmentalists to workers' justice organizations. It also demonstrated that they could work with those white liberals and white radicals that were the majority in the Peace and Freedom Party.[104]

But the Black Panther Party differed from SNCC in their membership and recruitment. Under Newton's leadership the BPP recruited heavily from the California prison systems because of the visibility of the prisoners' rights movement and the successful organizing of the black Muslims who made the penitentiary a hotbed of civil disobedience. Major prison riots in California's four major penal facilities—Soledad, Alcatraz, San Quentin, and Folsom—in the 1950s paved the way for political agitation around prisoners' rights pertaining to reading, writing, and First Amendment protections and shifted the landscape around prison culture in California that continued through the 1970s. The publication of San Quentin death row inmate Caryl Chessman's books *Cell 2455, Death Row* (1954), *Trial by Ordeal* (1955), *The Face of Justice* (1957), and *The Kid Was a Killer* (1960) demonstrated that memoirs could bring attention to individual cases and to the brutality of the prison system. In fact, as Donald Tibbs explains, "many convicts followed [Chessman's] lead. Inmate after inmate argued that their writing, too, was the best evidence that they were fully and successfully rehabilitated and different now compared to when they were sentenced."[105]

While Chessman made substantial strides in paving the way for prison intellectuals to use literature as a critical intervention into discourses of law and order, Malcolm X's memoir *The Autobiography of Malcolm X* (1965) also made a substantial impact on the genre of prison writing. Malcolm's autobiography and speeches shaped black liberation language but it also shaped socialism and communism as discourses throughout the global Third World Left.[106] Malcolm's use of street language, his jazz cadence, his pan-Africanism, his syncretic religious parables, and his aphorisms all created a rich, innovative tapestry of black vernacular that provided countless resources for Black Power intellectuals after his assassination in 1965.

As Huey Newton recounts, Malcolm's speeches and writings were part of the Panther education program and were indispensible to Panther ideology, particularly about prison. Malcolm was, in Donald Tibbs's estimation, Black

Power's "muse" as they adopted his literacy models to develop study plans and reading lists to inform their ideology and their political discourses.[107] Newton goes so far as to claim "Malcolm's spirit is in us."[108] Certainly, prison was a central location for theorizing black political resistance to incarceration, police brutality, economic injustice, and political underrepresentation in memoirs in addition to serving as a rhetorical exigency in and of itself as in the case with rallies for BPP members on the inside. Elsewhere, Newton elaborates on the influence of Malcolm and remarks that the BPP arose from the recognition that nonviolence was a failing strategy in California. Newton explains, "We had seen how the police attacked the Watts community after causing the trouble in the first place. We had seen Martin Luther King come to Watts in an effort to calm the people, and we had seen his philosophy of nonviolence rejected. Black people had been taught nonviolence; it was deep in us. What good, however, was nonviolence when the police were determined to rule by force?"[109] Newton was impressed by Malcolm's logical mind, his street savvy combined with his academic perspective, his lectures, and his practicality; the iconic minister became a role model for Newton.[110] In his memoir *Revolutionary Suicide* (1973), Newton, harnessing Malcolm's disdain, denounces nonviolence as a tactical dead end for black organizing against the militarization of urban centers. Malcolm's autobiography eventually inspired similar best-selling prison books from Black Power intellectuals like George Jackson, Angela Davis, and Eldridge Cleaver and certainly provided a template for the Black Panther Party's manifesto, the "ten-point program." All of these writings indicted segregation, the racial inequality in the judicial system, and police brutality.

If Newton's writings elevated Malcolm's ideologies, Minister of Information Eldridge Cleaver extended Malcolm's ideas about blackness itself as a site of imprisonment, writing: "It is only a matter of time until the question of prisoner's debt to society versus society's debt to the prisoner is injected forcefully into national and state politics, into the civil and human rights struggle, and into the very consciousness of the body politic. It is an explosive issue which goes to the very root of America's system of justice, the structure of criminal law, the prevailing beliefs and attitudes toward the convicted felon."[111]

This militarization of America's cities prompted the Panthers to promulgate their self-defense policy. Panthers would openly carry shotguns and follow police officers harassing black motorists. As Bridgette Baldwin has persuasively argued, "the Panthers' conscious posture and performance of armed self-defense garnered both positive outcomes (street credibility with urban black youth and, later, Third World revolutionaries) and negative consequences (a distorted image of the BPP as a revolutionary 'gang' obsessed with irrational violence)."[112]

The popularity of the BPP's ideologies about self-defense made the organization extremely popular in American cities, and the very real disruption by local police and the FBI only confirmed the kinds of critiques they were offering black urban residents. Aesthetically and rhetorically, the BPP enhanced the Black Power vernacular by masculinizing it through rhetorical forms that created a powerful cultural resonance. The raised fists, rifles, berets, leather jackets, afros, and sunglasses all functioned to build a visual vocabulary of resistance. In their heroic resistance to police brutality and imprisonment, Black Panthers articulated freedom through sustained righteousness that works as an "antidote to invisibility or conditional visibility within American culture more broadly."[113] Particularly as they connected the plight of inner-city black communities to the international struggle against colonialism, the Panthers augmented the Black Power vernacular with sustained and thoughtful critique of white supremacy and militarism. Reading from Executive Mandate Number One in front of the California statehouse in Sacramento, surrounded by armed Panthers, Bobby Seale explained: "As the aggression of the racist American government escalation in Vietnam, the police agencies in America escalate the repression of black people throughout the ghettos of America. Vicious police dogs, cattle prods, and increased patrols have become familiar sights in black communities."[114] Seale suggested that armed self-defense was the only option available.

However, reading the COINTELPRO memos suggests that these statements were not the rantings of a paranoid personality but the reaction to sustained targeting that painted the BPP as a threat poised to annihilate American society. Still, this confrontational posture was a large part of the identificatory politics of the BPP, and certainly it provided visibility for multiple publics in the late 1960s, as it both responded to and fed the punitive measures of the FBI's COINTELPRO schemes and local repression. But this consequence was not limited to black activists. Rather, as Ward Churchill documents in declassified FBI documents, COINTELRPO may have started with Black Power, but it soon engulfed the students of the New Left active in the free speech and antiwar movements. For example, citing their "nonconformism in dress and speech," a COINTELPRO FBI memo to Albany on October 10, 1968, demonizes hippies for their clothing and bead necklaces, shaggy hair, lack of personal hygiene, "publicized sexual promiscuity, experimenting with and the use of drugs," among other traits found undesirable. The memo explains, "These individuals are getting strength and more brazen in their attempts to destroy American society, as noted in the takeover of Columbia University." The memo concludes with a definitive statement about how the New Left movement should be "handled," in rhetoric that mirrors COINTELPRO directives on the BPP: "It is believed therefore, that they must be destroyed or neutralized from the inside."[115] The finality of this statement and the brutality that it contains is striking given the list of offenses that New Lefters are accused of perpetrating, but the use of drugs is part of the cycle of demonization that fed into the War on Drugs, which began a little over a decade later.

This connection between the COINTELPRO mission to destroy the BPP (with other progressive movements), changed as COINTELRPO was forced to end when a small group called the Citizens Commission to Investigate the FBI broke into an FBI field office in Media, Pennsylvania, on March 8, 1971, and stole hundreds of classified documents that detailed the surveillance and repression of US citizens. In April, Senator Edward King called for Hoover's resignation over the revelations, and the FBI was forced to shut down COINTELPRO.

Despite this nominal curbing of domestic intelligence powers in 1971, some scholars point to the War on Drugs as the successor to COINTELPRO. Ward Churchill, certainly the most prominent expert on COINTELPRO's war against the BPP, explains that the "still evolving U.S. political/intelligence/military complex does not appear to be devoted to direct political repression. Rather, its purpose seems primarily to have been to intensify the condition of pacification to which COINTELPRO had reduced oppressed communities, especially communities of color, by the early 1970s." Churchill explains that the War on Drugs is a direct consequence of COINTELPRO: "Leaving aside the fact that U.S. intelligence agencies have been heavily involved in the importation of heroin and cocaine since at least the early 1960s—and that if the government were really averse to narcotics distribution in the inner cities, the FBI would have assisted rather than destroyed the BPP's anti-drug programs" and would have supported rather than crushed the BPP's initiatives to politicize street gangs rather than criminalizing them.[116] The War on Drugs is certainly one contemporary example of how the repression and imprisonment of the Black Power movement lasted beyond the organizations that made up this shift in the black freedom struggle. But, as we will see in the conclusion, the legacy of repression, imprisonment, and law and order culture along with black resistance have also become bulwarks in the rhetoric surrounding the war on terror as the rhetorical strategies utilized by the state has remained salient.

Wielding Black Power from Within and Without

A superficial account of the demise of the Black Power movement and its major organization, the Black Panther Party, would perhaps point to the youth of the movement's leaders and suggest that inciting a black revolution was naïve and foolish. Such an account might also fault Black Power rhetors for bringing the FBI crackdown upon themselves, without accounting for the massive repression of the nonviolent movement for civil rights in the South that preceded it. But blaming the victims for centuries of political disenfranchisement would not reveal the complexities of the struggle for black freedom, particularly as states' rights politicians and the FBI worked to hamper civil rights activism before, during, and after the height of Black Power. This reading would also obscure how the Black Power movement was reacting to (rather than driving) the alienation of white liberals as the Johnson White House cut ties to civil rights activists following their opposition to the war in Vietnam. Particularly after the (literal) death of nonviolence following King's murder, the judicial and legislative paths to social change were foreclosed as new conservatism characterized black activism as black-on-white crime. With the COINTELPRO assassinations of Black Power leaders, it became clear that the black freedom struggle would not be permitted to continue.

Thus, I suggest that Black Power was a *reaction* to circumstances beyond the control of either rural or urban black citizens. In a dialogue with anthropologist Margaret Mead, writer James Baldwin described black America's shift in tactics due the hostile climate characterized by the ascendancy of Nixon and Reagan and the assassination of King. He argued that the movement for Black Power was

an *absolute* reaction, a reaction of real fury, because a whole generation is now growing up—is grown up—which is unlike my generation. This generation knows. It has seen it with its own eyes and has heard it with its own ears: the nature of the lies the white people told black people for generations. . . . What they are doing is repudiating the entire theology, as I call it, which has afflicted and destroyed—really, literally destroyed–black people in this country for so long. And what this generation is reacting to, what it is saying, is they realize that you, the white people, white Americans, have always attempted to murder them. Not merely by burning them but murdering them in the mind, in the heart.[117]

Baldwin's assessment speaks to the necessity of confrontation in these years as the possibility for compromise ended with Nixon's election. And in managing their devastation at the assassination of King, Black Power activists saw no path forward with the SCLC's conciliatory rhetorical posture. Thus did SNCC's more militant posture evolve and inspire groups like the Black Panthers.

Nonetheless, Black Power's demise was at least partly predictable, though not entirely because of the failures of Black Power activists. In the words of the historian Peniel E. Joseph, "Black Power accelerated America's reckoning with its own uncomfortable, often ugly, racial past, and in the process spurred a debate over racial progress, citizenship, and democracy that would scandalize as much as it would change a nation."[118] Although the harsh criticisms of the US government penned and uttered by nonviolent southern civil rights leaders like those highlighted in King's publication of *Why We Can't Wait* in 1964 pointed to the outrageous lack of progress on civil rights one hundred years after the Emancipation Proclamation and after almost ten years in the streets, very few material changes had improved black life.

The following chapters examine how imprisoned and formerly imprisoned black liberation activists articulated Black Power ideology in their memoirs to understand the multiple ways that the Black Power vernacular appeared in this new period of agitation as sentences became longer for more serious infractions in the struggle for black liberation. As COINTELPRO was used to destroy the black liberation movement and was explicitly utilized by the FBI to imprison Black Power leaders indefinitely, the importance of imprisonment in the black freedom struggle became intrinsic to Black Power rhetoric and organizing. What emerges from these chapters is an account that showcases how the success and failures of Black Power as this rhetorical frame pivoted upon who controlled and crafted the meaning of the term, the portraits of the activists, and the assessment of Black Power goals. Because the Black Power slogan and ideology were articulated by imprisoned and formerly imprisoned activists, particularly as the FBI and local police targeted their activism, Black Power ideology took up the relationship between state repression and incarceration as a place to excavate new arenas for the black liberation struggle, particularly in the memoirs of movement activists.

In charting the complicated and shifting relationship between black liberation activists and white politicians, it is clear that white proclamations about black deviance forced black rhetors to dramatize their experience through strategies that necessarily referenced the bogeymen that white fears conjured. But Black Power activists also used political critique, historical evidence, anecdote, personalization, hyperbole, and invective (among other strategies) to problematize the very limited commitment of state and federal officials to civil rights as the 1960s neared a close. Certainly the Nixon administration magnified the "law and order" frame and neither Ford nor Carter pushed back. Thus, the lenses that characterized black activism as black crime were stable by the time Reagan was inaugurated, making the demonization of the black freedom struggle part of his racial history of America. Still, the prison writings of these Black Power activists showcase the new conversations about repression and liberation that emerged in the Black Power period as well as the strategies that prison memoirists utilized to bridge new audiences and activists even now.

CHAPTER TWO

Producing the Black Badman

The Politics of SNCC in the Era of Rap Brown

S NCC was well-known for the southern sit-ins and jail-ins during the 1960s. However, by the beginning of 1966 ideological battles raged in SNCC between the old guard, led by executive secretary James Forman and chairman John Lewis, and the new guard, led by Stokely Carmichael and later H(ubert) "Rap" Brown. Because of the growing dissatisfaction with SNCC's position on nonviolence, the disappointment with traditional modes of political power, the increasing influence of Malcolm X's separatism, and differing positions on the Vietnam War, SNCC split into two factions. The first, led by Forman and Lewis, was still committed to an interracial struggle for civil rights. The second followed Carmichael, elected chairman in 1966, and embraced Malcolm X's separatism.

Carmichael's articulation of the Black Power slogan popularized black separatism signaled a rhetorical shift in the southern movement, but its emphasis on power and race consciousness also undermined SNCC's multiracial coalitions, which changed SNCC's organizational strategies. As SNCC embraced Black Power, "[s]ome of SNCC's workers even spoke of guerrilla warfare against the white power structure."[1] Because of their often-adversarial relationship with the federal government as well as the ubiquity of violence against civil rights workers, both SNCC and the Congress on Racial Equality (CORE) "had little to lose by associating themselves with often working-class advocates of armed self-defense. National leaders in SNCC and CORE recognized that in dangerous battlefields like Cambridge, Maryland, Danville, Virginia, and rural Louisiana and Mississippi, their nonviolence organizers' survival depended on indigenous armed militants."[2] But the increasing black militancy created intense strain with the whites that had survived the violence of SNCC's campaigns in the Deep South. SNCC veterans John Lewis and Julian Bond resigned, and their absence undermined SNCC's projects in the South, while also hampering the organization's ability to secure northern funding, especially as memories of the March on Washington and the brutality in Birmingham faded.[3]

SNCC's break with moderate civil rights leaders came in August 1966, first, when Carmichael and others protested the Vietnam War at the August 6 wedding of President Johnson's daughter and, later that month, when they protested the 1966 Civil Rights Act. As a result of the protests, the House of Representatives amended the Civil Rights Act to prohibit crossing state lines to incite a riot and blamed Carmichael and other militants for urban rebellion in the North.[4] As brilliant and tenacious as Carmichael was as an activist and theorist of Black Power, his reign as chairman came to a conclusion in 1967 because of the break with white activists and veteran organizers, the alienation of SNCC from the mainstream civil rights groups, and the ire of the Johnson White House.

Carmichael's promotion of Black Power made the organization more visible while complicating SNCC's relationship with the movement and the federal government, but the rhetorical change made a substantial impact on the political landscape. In a 1969 editorial for *The Black Scholar*, CORE leader Floyd McKissick cogently explained that the shift to Black Power's significance rested in its rejection of white approval in the face of the "short-lived idealism" of white liberals, whose hostility at demands for Black Power unmasked their real disdain for true equality.[5] This rejection of white liberals in favor of black self-determination characterized the confrontational nature of the Black Power vernacular, which became clear as SNCC leadership transitioned yet again.

In May 1967, twenty-three-year-old H. "Rap" Brown was elected chairman of SNCC after Carmichael's resignation. SNCC colleagues praised Brown's rhetorical and physical style. James Forman wrote that Brown's "way of speaking, his whole style, has a grass-roots quality that gave him mass appeal."[6] They thought Brown "would be less abrasive and less vulnerable to charges of irresponsibility and extremism" than Carmichael.[7] Influenced by his SNCC fieldwork in Alabama and Mississippi, Brown suggested organizing "sharecroppers in the South and the ghetto dwellers in the North," demonstrating his commitment to building Black Power across the country.[8] Brown's vernacular appeal combined with his broad vision for black organizing made him a popular Black Power speaker and writer while marking him as a target for the federal government.

Brown's election provided an opportunity to redirect the momentum of SNCC into new action because he and Carmichael were part of what Nancy Whittier has termed a "micro-cohort," or a "cluster of participants who enter a social movement within a year or two of each other and are shaped by distinct transformative experiences that differ because of subtle shifts in the political context."[9] Micro-cohorts, while short lived, share an ideological perspective that dominates their collective identity.[10] This collective identity dominates the culture until the "movement shifts into abeyance on one set of issues" when "its personnel and organization may switch the grounds of the challenge to another set of issues."[11] The declining popularity of nonviolence, the birth of the Black Panther Party, the assassinations of both Malcolm X (1965) and Martin Luther King, Jr. (1968), and the mobilization of urban blacks shaped Carmichael and Brown's micro-cohort. However, Brown's framing of the black liberation struggle as "Black Power" went further than Carmichael's as he "encouraged alienated young blacks to rebel against white authority" and, consequently, "became a symbol for millions of white people who wanted to strike out against the visible symbols of black militancy."[12]

This chapter begins with an examination of the political context and rhetorical politics of urban rebellion as Rap Brown augmented the Black Power vernacular after the Cambridge riots and the subsequent passage of the 1968 Civil Rights Act. To understand Brown's interventions into the Black Power vernacular, I examine the mobile, embodied performativity of black masculinity in Brown's autobiographical manifesto *Die Nigger Die!* (1969), authored while Brown was under house arrest. *Die Nigger Die!* was phenomenally successful (due, in part, to its unsettling title), going through seven printings before being rereleased after Brown's murder conviction in 2002 by publishers at Lawrence Hill in Chicago. But because Brown's vernacular style actually spurred the mass incarceration of black liberation activists, his memoir isn't as concerned with prison conditions or resistance (like Mumia Abu-Jamal's essays or Assata Shakur's memoir, which will be discussed in later chapters). His experiences with incarceration and repression focus more macroscopically on the ways in which white power creates the conditions for black repression and imprisonment.

In charting Brown's resistance to black repression, I highlight Brown's style, his performance as a black badman in games like the dozens, his understanding of the fragility of black boyhood and the politics of black masculinity, and his interest in both self-defense and violence in the text to understand the production of Black Power vernacular. Finally, this chapter considers Brown's descriptions of the problems with both white culture and "Negro culture," which causes the self-hate that makes black communities willingly submit to the nation. Because of his high-profile arrests, his incarcerations, his house arrest, and his time in exile, *Die Nigger Die!* documents Brown's leadership style, his ideologies concerning Black Power, and the political and legal exigencies that necessitated continued Black Power agitation after 1969.

Summer of Rage: Urban Rebellion and the Rise of Rap

The summer of 1967 found Brown in the national spotlight for the urban rebellions sweeping across northern American cities, marking him as a dangerous militant and prompting a shift in the federal criminalization of black activism, especially after the passage of the 1968 Civil Rights Act. In talking about black urban rebellion, Brown "went further than Carmichael in urging his listeners to take up arms against white society" using hyperbole, invective, and revolutionary language to dramatize the consequences of segregation, poverty, and racial violence that circumscribed black lives.[13] That summer, Newark, New Jersey, the location of the worst crime rates in the nation, erupted July 12–17 after police officers rushed crowds protesting police brutality. The Newark riot lasted for five days and nights, killing 26 people, injuring 1,004, and ending with 1,397 arrests.[14] Just days later, Black Power leaders, including Stokely Carmichael and Rap Brown, were assembled in Newark for a conference when the Detroit riots broke out on July 23, leaving 42 people dead, 386 injured, and 5,557 arrested.[15] Newark and Detroit were two of the over 150 cities that experienced riots, rebellions, or acts of civil disorder that summer, and they were sites of intense confrontation about the role of Black Power agitation in the North.[16]

In the wake of Cambridge and Detroit, President Johnson appointed the (Otto) Kerner Commission on Civil Disorders to assess the causes of the violence.[17] The Kerner Commission's final report argued that although black Americans explained riots as the response to housing and employment segregation and discrimination, whites blamed black-on-white violence as the cause of riots. The commission also noted that "while few" blacks perceived "the riots as caused by 'leaders'... nearly a quarter of the white sample cite[d] radical leaders as a major cause."[18] The commission concluded that the root cause of the rebellions was clearly "white racism."[19] This data reveals the extent to which white public officials blamed black leaders for urban discontent. It also provides the rationale for the intense political repression that the FBI launched against the leaders of the civil rights and Black Power movements. Finally, the commission noted that the media exaggerated the rebellions and "failed to report adequately on the causes and consequences of civil disorders and the underlying problems of race relations."[20] Rap Brown echoed this conclusion on the same day that the Kerner Commission was appointed, declaring that violence was "as American as cherry pie," a comment that would haunt him throughout his life because it situated structural violence as an intrinsic part of American culture and because it highlighted the role of Brown's vernacular in marking him as an agitator.[21] Because the white media sensationalized urban rebellions and focused on leaders as the agitators (rather than focusing on structural discrimination), it is easy to see how someone like Rap Brown was targeted by the FBI, particularly after giving such critical, hyperbolic speeches in cities that later rebelled.[22]

For example, the Newark and Detroit rebellions prompted Brown to accept an invitation to speak on July 25 in Cambridge, Maryland.[23] Prior to the speech, Brown had been quoted almost daily in the national press talking about northern racial disparity.[24] With a population of 14,000 residents (one-fifth of which were black), Cambridge was rife with racial disparities, which Brown commented upon in his fiery address. Brown told city residents, "If America don't come around, we going burn it down, brother."[25] He also "warned that black people were faced with genocide as a result of poor living conditions and the drafting of young blacks to fight in Vietnam," telling black listeners to "take over white-owned stores" and "advised blacks to prevent whites from coming into their community."[26] Brown's vernacular intensity in Cambridge was noted, especially by the white press.[27] While no violence occurred during Brown's speech, shots were fired between city police and black residents after the speech. Although he left Cambridge after the speech, Brown's "mere presence evoked images in the minds of white leadership that there was an organized conspiracy afoot to lead Cambridge's Negroes in a rampaging pillage of the town's white business district," precipitating the conflict.[28]

Whites in Cambridge saw Brown as an agitator and scapegoated him for the eruption of black rage, in precisely the ways that the Kerner Commission suggested.[29] The Cambridge police chief even identified Brown as the "sole reason" for the Cambridge rebellion.[30] Brown left Cambridge the following morning just before Maryland governor Spiro T. Agnew sent in the National Guard. At a Washington, DC, press conference after his arrest for inciting the riot, Brown peppered his remarks with rhetorical jabs characteristic of his Black Power vernacular, "calling President Johnson a 'white honky cracker, an outlaw from Texas' and charging that his arrest was the result of a conspiracy involving Johnson and state authorities."[31] These attacks helped undermine black dependency on presidential support for civil rights by characterizing Johnson as a bully and a crook. "He also said that FBI director J. Edgar Hoover was conspiring with them to discredit SNCC and shift the blame for all the rioting from L.B.J." to him.[32] In light of the FBI's counterintelligence surveillance of Brown during these years, Brown was not far off the mark, but his invective against Johnson alienated him from the White House.

Brown used his arrest to rhetorically intervene in the discourses of law and order that were characterizing white responses to urban rebellion. He defended his role in Cambridge by highlighting the exclusion of black participation in the construction of the law.[33] To dramatize this exclusion, Brown commented on how black Americans are subjected to imprisonment inside and outside of the penitentiary: "Neither imprisonment nor threats of death will sway me from the path that I have taken, nor will they sway others like me. . . . More powerful than my fear of the dreadful conditions to which I might be subjected in prison is my hatred for the dread conditions to which my people are subjected outside prisons throughout this country."[34] In these comments, Brown compares the racial repression in American ghettos to imprisonment, while acknowledging the centrality of imprisonment to his Black Power agitation.

Additionally, Brown's statement utilizes a strategy of redefinition in his defense, explaining that black civil disobedience is a direct response to massive white-on-black violence:

> Each time a black church is bombed or burned, it is an act of violence in our streets. Each time a black body is found in the swamps of Mississippi or Alabama, that is violence in our land. Each time black human rights workers are refused protection by the government, that is anarchy. Each time a police officer shoots and kills a black teenager, that is urban crime.[35]

In highlighting the kinds of crimes perpetrated against black youth, Brown redefines violence, anarchy, and urban crime as transgressions instigated *by the state*. This rhetorical shift frames state violence as urban crime to create space for Black Power activists to demonstrate that black activism is a response to a very real need to protect and augment black freedom.

Brown's use of the Black Power vernacular after Cambridge prompted condemnation from white liberals inside and outside of the Johnson administration. These critics couldn't or wouldn't understand the younger generation of activists, and their distaste for (black) youth activism paved the way for the laws criminalizing Black Power speech. White editorials, like this one from the *Chicago Tribune*, called for the administration to "drop the permissive doctrines which condone the acts of rioters and seek to shift their guilt to the law-abiding majority which has not reaped rewards upon them."[36] For example, because the white news framed Rap Brown himself as the "cause" of urban rebellions, Congress passed Senator Strom Thurmond's (R-SC) 1968 Anti-Riot Act, paving the way for intense political repression of Black Power intellectuals as a result of their vernacular choices, linking their rhetoric to their political incarceration.[37] The Anti-Riot Act became explicitly linked to criminalizing Black Power rhetoric when it became known colloquially as the H Rap Brown Act. The act was used to demonize black leaders and functioned as "a legal and spatial tool to control the public spaces of urban America . . . [T]he law, both in design and practice, was used to control dissent by New Left groups precisely by regulating the spatial field in which they moved . . . The hope of such a policy was that protest itself would wither away."[38] J. Edgar Hoover recommended the passage of the act because it gave the FBI expanded jurisdiction over political protests in the cities and landed them major appropriations for new weapons, recruitment, and training for urban repression, specifically targeting black liberation organizations.

Although Brown articulated a provocative perspective on urban resistance, federal officials concluded that his persecution was extreme. Former attorney general Ramsay Clark explained that Brown was charged and tried under an obscure statue and that "although there was a clear violation" the sentence "was unjust" because "five years is pretty extreme."[39] Still, the passage of the H Rap Brown Act severely hampered his ability to recruit and fundraise for SNCC, and these "legal actions taken against Rap Brown . . . established a pattern for the subsequent suppression of highly-publicized radical leaders," particularly in the Black Power movement.[40] Consequently, Brown found his way to the top of FBI director J. Edgar Hoover's Rabble Rouser Index.[41] Hoover saw Brown as the epitome of a new kind of mobile troublemaker, who would travel cross-country inspiring urban rebellion.[42] Hoover unwittingly acknowledged a major rhetorical success of the Black Power vernacular as Brown utilized it: namely, its flexibility. Farred explains, "The vernacular is ideologically mobile, responsive to crises, adaptable to its situation, able to translate and situate itself in nonnative locales"; "[t]he vernacular is situated but not physically—which is to say, geographically—restricted."[43] It is precisely this mobility of the Black Power vernacular that made it popular, especially in northern urban centers, but that also encouraged its eradication by highlighting the tremendous differences between hegemonic and subordinate national groups.

The surveillance and harassment of Brown led to a long rap sheet for Brown. For example, on the night of March 9, 1970, a bomb exploded in a car killing SNCC activists Ralph Featherstone and Che Payne outside of a Maryland courthouse where Rap Brown was to appear the following day on the "inciting to riot" charges. However, instead of appearing, Brown went underground to Canada and was placed on the FBI's "most wanted" list. A year later, he was arrested for the robbery of a Harlem "dope bar" and was given a sentence of five to ten years.[44] Brown completed his sentence, converted to Islam in jail, and took his new name, Jamil Abdullah Al-Amin.

Finally, Rap Brown, now Jamil Abdullah Al-Amin, made headlines again in 2001 when he was captured and arrested in Lowndes County, Alabama, after fleeing the scene of a shoot-out with two sheriff's deputies who were serving him a warrant for failing to appear in court on an outstanding theft charge. He was given life imprisonment instead of the death penalty. At the time of his arrest he had spent over twenty years as a Muslim imam at an Atlanta mosque. *Die Nigger Die!* (1969), Brown's manifesto, catalogues how his confrontational vernacular style influenced and was influenced by law and order culture as the state moved to crush Black Power, and it stands as a testament to the tremendous interest in him as a social movement leader, as a fiery orator, and as a vernacular spokesperson for Black Power ideology at the end of the 1960s.

Brown's Black Power Vernacular in *Die Nigger Die!*

While speeches precipitated confrontation with the state and guaranteed immediate legislative and political backlash, vernacular Black Power treatises like Brown's memoir *Die Nigger Die!* performed the long-term ideological and definitional work of the movement's micro-cohort to identify problems with the state, articulate new goals, recruit and purge membership, inspire political action, and craft ideology.[45] In the case of *Die Nigger Die!* this ideological work is performed with a confidence and arrogance that made the book so incredibly successful after its release.

Brown's articulation of the Black Power vernacular begins on the very first page of *Die Nigger Die!*, where he symbolically links black births to the birth of Jesus. He emphatically asserts that all black births are revolutionary:

> With each new birth comes a potential challenge to the existing order. Each new generation brings forth untested militancy. America's ruling class now experiences what Herod must have at the birth of "Christ": "Go and search . . . and when ye have found him, bring me word again, that I may come and worship him also." America doesn't know which Black birth is going to be the birth that will overthrow the country.[46]

Brown's rhetoric surrounding the black liberation struggle in 1969 relies upon the metaphor of birth as central to the regeneration of Black Power that he sees as critical in sustaining black activism. However, Brown masculinizes this understanding of birth because as Hazel Carby writes, "in the general political and social imagination the birth of future generations is most frequently feminized, while revolution is often represented as a homosocial act of reproduction: a social and political upheaval in which men confront each other to give birth to a new nation, a struggle frequently conceived of in terms of sex and sexuality."[47] This replication of Black Power in 1969 is masculinized and also racialized since Brown sees black people as the harbingers of revolution. In Brown's future, there is no hope for multiracial, cross-class mobilization for social change: there is only black revolution.[48] In using this masculinized form of the birth metaphor, Brown attempts to convert and inspire Black Power advocates by emphasizing the coming black revolution led by a black Christ figure, sent to rectify the racial inequality of America. This explicitly positions him as a leader of the black masses, as a likely black Christ. But, he also promotes Black Power by reconstructing the black masculine hero, the messiah, and the badman. In this way, his strategies of regeneration are premised upon birth metaphors (which are also featured in the writings of Assata Shakur and Mumia Abu-Jamal. Like Abu-Jamal's they rest on masculinized tropes of reproduction predicated upon a history of black male leadership and rebellion). Nonetheless, Brown's performance of the badman persona is his major contribution to the Black Power vernacular, particularly since it succeeded in catalyzing criminalization of Black Power, rhetorically and politically.

Black Heroes, Bad Badmen, and the Dozens: Resisting White Authority

In black history and folklore, the "bad nigger" has historically been an audacious figure with a heightened sense of injustice, and Rap Brown's manifesto is a meditation on the identity politics and strategy of the "nigger" in popular and political culture. In the "Introduction" to *Die Nigger Die!*, Don L. Lee (now Haki Madhubuti), the famous poet of the Black Arts Movement, writes at length about the role of the "bad nigger" in the black liberation struggle and argues that black men must embrace both blackness and masculinity as strategies for resistance. Henry Louis Gates Jr. has suggested that signifyin(g) is a central rhetorical principle at work in black vernacular and that certainly is the case with the Black Power vernacular, particularly in the construction of "bad niggers." Gates writes that signifyin' is "a trope, in which are subsumed several other rhetorical tropes, including metaphor, metonymy, synecdoche, and irony (the master tropes, and also hyperbole, litotes, and metalepsis. To this list we could easily add aporia, chiasmus, and catachresis, all of which are used in the ritual of Signifyin(g)."[49] Thus, rhetors employ constitutive rhetoric as they signify for their auditors; as James Jasinski explains, "an advocate's message awakens (or energizes) certain possibilities or a specific identity (or subject position) for that audience."[50]

Reflecting on the importance of signifying, Lee's prefatory comments suggest that signifying is a distinctly black rhetorical strategy that has "greatly contributed to the survival of blacks."[51] Lee asks black men to embrace black masculinity as an act of resistance toward both middle-class black life and values, or when he calls "Negro culture," and white life and values, a distinction that is also made in the text by Brown. Lee continues, "Any action or behavior which is not endorsed by whites, negroes consider 'acting like a nigger'. . . . The conversation in negro America has always been, 'What are we going to do about them niggers?' never, 'What are we going to do about them white folks?'"[52] Lee suggests that a new cultural conversation about white supremacy and black performativity is necessary in the black community. Until that conversation happens, Lee sees "acting like a nigger" as an important identity move to differentiate between black men who are fighting against cultural imperialism and those "negroes" who are passively accepting the white agenda for "civil rights." Lee says, "To be Black in this country is to be a nigger. To be a nigger is to resist both white and negro death. It is to be free in spirit, if not body. It is the spirit of resistance which has prepared Blacks for the ultimate struggle."[53] Lee sees being a "nigger" as an act of resistance to white social values that prepares men for black liberation struggle. Likewise, his distinctions between "negroes" and "niggers" underscore the class politics that emerged from the space of Black Power as students in SNCC rebelled against the bourgeois, Christian values of King's SCLC.

Serving as a clear constitutive force for black male resistance in an age of intensifying police control, the badman or "bad nigger" is an archetype useful in transforming the Black Power vernacular by connecting the new age of agitation in SNCC to slave revolts. For example, Robert G. O'Meally writes, "if we count Gabriel Prosser, Nat Turner, and Jack Johnson as magnificent badmen in Afro-American history, and Stagolee, Casey Jones, and John Henry as badmen in Afro-American folklore, the difference in white and black perspectives is clear. For blacks, black badmen represent not so much fearful as exemplary figures."[54] He adds, "These badmen . . . were so bad . . . that they threatened to live forever in the eternal arch of myth: to kick ass (as the vernacular would have it) for one lifetime and to take names for the next."[55] The badman makes such an impact on the popular imaginary because he "violates social conventions and spaces, virtually at will and thereby represents not just black disdain for American oppression . . . but the ability to face hardship and to win. The improvising trickster fakes and shifts to freedom; the rawhide-skinned badman blasts and socks to freedom."[56] When the badman does not win, he "nonetheless goes down swinging or shooting, not sorry for his deeds, requesting no mercy at all."[57] Black badmen act out in audacious ways, catalyzed by structural violence against black people, to dramatize the injustices of white supremacy and the ironies of blackness in a white supremacist America.

Although the black badmen archetype abounds in black folklore, fiction, and history, two distinct kinds of black badmen emerge: "the *bad badman* and the *moral badman*."[58] No law governs the bad badman, and he is quick to use violence to settle a dispute, often against other blacks. The bad badman is also stylish and verbally adroit, which illustrate his primacy and role as a leader within a community of male peers. Moral badmen believe in working within the system of American institutions to meet their goals. They "achieve their victories by annihilating stereotyped conceptions about black strength and aggression under pressure; by coolly beating the white man at his own game."[59] Ultimately, the badman lore preserves the black hero, provides hope for a new beginning, and encourages black Americans to fight their enemies more directly. These badman tales speak to the "unsinkability of the human spirit."[60] Modern examples of badmen can be found in America's prisons, where they have been locked away from the public's view. Charles P. Henry urges scholars to see Nat Turner's confessions, convict work songs, "and the prison autobiographies of Malcolm X, George Jackson, Angela Davis and Eldridge Cleaver" as the discourses of badmen (and women).[61] Prisoners and prison autobiographies, then, are common spaces for the badman persona to appear.

As Lee's "Introduction" reveals, Rap Brown can also been added to this category of bad badmen, certainly in terms of his style and his attitude toward self-defense. Black Power historian Hugh Pearson notes that when Brown became the chairman of SNCC, he transformed himself to appear more confrontational: "His natural was larger than Carmichael's, and he constantly wore sunglasses. He no longer sported fratboy-like clothing, choosing instead casual street clothes" or a beret and boots, similar to the uniform of the Black Panthers, which helped to build this style of the freedom fighter and legitimize his masculinity.[62] Cornel West reminds us that most young black men attain power, "by stylizing their bodies" to "reflect their uniqueness and provoke fear in others."[63] By stylizing their bodies and speech to provoke awe, respect, and even fear, badmen seek to both emulate and resist the structure of white patriarchy that constrains their existence as Rap Brown does in *Die Nigger Die!* As Hazel Carby observes: the black male body in "subversive and revolutionary texts connect with the politics of the black male body enacted in the practice of lynching. As an erotic and phallic form of masculinity was assumed and subsumed in representations of the black male rebel, so the eroticism and phallic nature of the ritual dismemberment of black male bodies was an essential part of the attempt to deny to black men the power to resist, rebel, or revolt."[64] Thus, vernacular *texts* create space for embodied challenges to white authority and white violence that complement vernacular rhetorical strategies.

By understanding a figure like Rap Brown as a "bad nigger" whose style is just as important as his texts, the reader is asked to participate in a strategy of Black Power regeneration that links Brown to this entire bodily history of black male resistance including the leaders and martyrs of slave revolts, the prison revolutionaries, and to Black Power's martyr, Malcolm X. This elevation of "bad nigger" leaders lets both Lee and Brown position the Black Power movement against middle-class black preachers like Martin Luther King Jr. or Fred Shuttlesworth who supported integration alongside the piecemeal legislative reforms that constituted "civil rights" while simultaneously pushing back against the white "liberals" who pledged to help black America find jobs, homes, and education but did not address the psychological legacies of the centuries-old brutality that continued to constrain black self-determination.

Of course, one of the results of this move is the exclusion of bad black women and the erasure of the history of black female resistance. This is not totally surprising since Farred reminds us, the "vernacular provides only a partial accounting of resistance, a construction of the intellectual that is at once deeply oppositional and radical and yet is bound by the patriarchal constraints of its historical modality."[65] Still, the move to embrace the black badman helps to propagate the notion that black resistance has always been masculine and that any move to assert black leadership must be done by replicating this brand of black masculinity through boys and through men. Nonetheless, masculinity becomes an important register for the Black Power vernacular.

Black Heroes: Boyhood and Manhood

In the replication of black masculinity as part of a vernacular strategy of resistance to white supremacy, adolescence looms as a critical period of identification and signification, especially in Black Power memoirs. Black boyhood has always been a vulnerable time for young men, as the lives of Emmett Till and many others have demonstrated. Because black boyhood has been haunted with the promise of lynching and torture, young black men have created their own avenues to both emulate and challenge white men. For Black Power memoirists like Rap Brown, an extended examination of childhood was a strategy of explaining the intellectual and rhetorical development of activist leaders.

In *Die Nigger Die!*, Rap Brown's discussion of his adolescence highlights his emergence as a black badman, a "bad nigger," and a community hero, demonstrating how Brown's vernacular "self-representation drew extensively on the experiences and resources of his primary community."[66] At the Blundon Orphanage Home, where his formal education began, Brown learned how to perform for white folks from the missionaries. Of the orphanage, Brown says, "[i]t was operated by white missionaries whose role was similar to that of whites in Africa. Civilize the savage through Christianity. Savages in this case being Black kids from families too poor to support them."[67] There, "[y]ou had to excel in either fighting, running or tomming"; Rap writes that he perfected all three.[68] He adds, "We didn't even have time for a childhood. If you acted like a child, you didn't survive and that's all there was to it."[69] Without a childhood, young boys became men quickly under the watchful eyes of benevolent whites, and they emulated the stronger, tougher boys in their neighborhoods. Here, hypermasculinity and self-protection were socialized within white organizations, though these were also coping strategies necessary for survival in poor urban neighborhoods.

Brown remembers the childhood heroes who earned respect on the streets of the neighborhood as he meditates on the development of leadership in his community. He writes, "In this world, the heroes were bloods who will never be remembered outside our Black community. Cats like Pie-man, Ig, Yank, Smokey, Hawk, Lil Nel—all bad muthafuckas. Young bloods wanted to be like these brothers. They were the men in our community. They had all the women and had made their way to the top through sports and knowing the streets."[70] Brown sees these male heroes as an important part of his youth and as crucial in his understanding of how to prove his manhood: through women, sports, and street smarts. Here, the replication of generations of young black male leaders again takes place through other men, rather than through women who are merely commodities that indicate status, rather than sisters in struggle.

Brown also voices approval of the badmen who are the templates for his Black Power leadership style. Brown tells the reader that he established his reputation the same way as these heroes, boasting, "Once I'd established my reputation, cats respected it."[71] But he sees this space of black boyhood as a place where young black boys were "perpetually at war" because of the tribes and gangs that parceled out neighborhoods in Baton Rouge, Louisiana.[72] For black boys, mobility was limited by gang activity unless you were recognized to be a badman, and then you could move more easily through neighborhoods without having to fight.[73] Although he seems to be acutely aware of the ways in which the competitiveness of the streets spills over into other facets of life in the form of "black-on-black" violence, he still heroizes the badmen of his neighborhood who could move unobstructed through town. This rhetorical strategy of regeneration highlights the ways that Black Power becomes palatable to urban black men because it acknowledges their frustrations and their propensity for both resisting and conforming to white patriarchy through violence. As Michael Kimmel has amply demonstrated, "Violence has long been understood as the best way to ensure that others publicly recognize one's manhood."[74]

Manhood and violence, or at least rhetorical violence, were certainly essential parts of Black Power ideology and performance, and Brown's memoir underscores the centrality of the threat of violence to black boys and men. Brown's discussion of structural violence highlights the importance of community mobility for black men and connects Brown's analysis of youth culture in Baton Rouge to the kinds of restrictions that developed in federal legislation like the H Rap Brown Act, which specifically targeted black male mobility across state lines. Thus, from Brown's memoir we can understand how mobility became a political strategy for black identity and organizing while simultaneously a site of contesting white supremacy.

In acknowledging the complexity of this transition from black boyhood to manhood, Brown attributes the permanence of this warring tribalism among black youth in urban communities to the brainwashing of white culture that pervaded the orphanage but also to the poverty that characterizes black life, particularly in the South. In his critique of this intersection between class and race, Brown argues that black boys and men hardly find themselves living the "American Dream." Brown writes of the fatalism of young black men, saying, "You grow up in Black america and it's like living in a pressure cooker. Babies become men without going through childhood. And when you become a man, you got nothing to look forward to and nothing to look back on."[75] This crisis leads young black men to take up drinking, drugs, or religion to cope with the poverty of their present and the lack of a future.

Brown describes how the politics of class creates hopelessness in black adolescence. "America is the country that makes you want things, but doesn't give you the means to get those things," he explains.[76] This intersectional critique underscores the sense of worthlessness that pervades many impoverished communities and gives the reader insight into the origins of Brown's cultural nationalism as he examines how self-worth in America is directly related to property. If you don't have property, you don't exist. Brown says, "When a race of people is oppressed within a system that fosters the idea of competitive individualism, the political polarization around individual interests prevents group interests. . . . So individuals join tribes or groups to further their own personal ambitions. It's one of the things that keeps us fighting ourselves instead of the enemy."[77] The alternative to this paradigm of competitive individualism is to become a badman, to struggle with a tribe that understands collective oppression and resistance. Brown's rhetorical strategy here is explicitly constitutive as he attempts to recruit among the hopeless by giving them a vocabulary and framework for their anger so that they may direct their energy at the state, rather than at each other. This also allows us to see why Brown views "race war" as an inevitable consequence of race relations: he sees no hope, only the cycles of despair and poverty that have characterized many black communities for centuries. Here, we see how Black Power regeneration has the capacity to tap into the black men who have lived within the conditions of racial inequality in America's cities. Additionally, the political and practical strategy of self-defense is prefigured by poverty and white violence, which create the exigencies that propel black boys and young men to embrace the badman vernacular and posture.

In the absence of a real future, Brown spent his youth in Baton Rouge perfecting his skills at the dozens (the most obvious example of signifyin'), a verbal duel that ruins the reputation of an opponent by making fun of him through repetitive rhyming taunts.[78] By perfecting black vernacular street traditions of the badman, Brown taught himself the rhetorical skills necessary to express his emotions, undermine the credibility of an opponent, humiliate an enemy, rally a crowd in support, tell jokes, and harness his ethos to build his notoriety as a verbal tactician. Brown writes, "There'd be sometimes 40 or 50 dudes standing around and the winner was determined by the way they responded to what was said. If you fell over each other laughing, then you knew you'd scored. It was a bad scene for the dude that was getting humiliated. I seldom was. That's why they call me Rap, 'cause I could rap.'"[79] Hubert Brown was reborn as "Rap" by playing the dozens and in doing so, he built the signifyin' skills that made him popular in SNCC.

Brown's recollection of his prowess at the dozens underscores his appreciation for black cultural forms, forming the basis of his fidelity to Black Power's emphasis on cultural nationalism. He continues, "Hell, we exercised our minds by playing the dozens. . . . And the teacher expected me to sit up in class and study poetry after I could run down shit like that. If anybody needed to study poetry, she needed to study mine. We played the Dozens for recreation, like white folks play Scrabble."[80] Brown's alienation from and rejection of traditional white literary forms like poetry and white pastimes like table games propelled his disengagement from school, but in recounting this moment he is performing as the bad badman, shunning white culture. In anecdotes like this one, Brown documents his commitment to black vernacular styles even as a young black boy, anchoring his persona to a childhood built upon the same values that Brown espouses as a SNCC leader.

Brown's narrative also underscores the importance of self-reliance and security in the regeneration of Black Power, since physical, social, and economic *insecurity* is the foundation of black boyhood. In this way, Brown's memoir pushes back against claims that Black Power was simply antisocial nihilism because it provides warrants and rhetorical context for the development of a black masculine vernacular during the Black Power movement in the face of continued structural racial inequalities that began with the plantation system. It points to the confrontational style as a rhetorical form rather than an instrumental political strategy. As Paul Gilroy explains, "From this perspective, 'nihilism' ceases to be antisocial and becomes social in the obvious sense of the term: it generates community and specifies the fortified boundaries of racial particularity."[81] Thus, Brown's vernacular interventions as a youth and as a Black Power leader were survival strategies, responses to social conditions, and ways of marshaling constitutive rhetorical practices to shore up black communities and individuals constantly under siege.

Insecurity and Authority in *Die Nigger Die!*

In the anecdotes about his childhood, Brown also highlights the illegitimate "authority" exercised by the state, especially against young black boys, providing a personalized account to the Black Power analysis of power and urban space. Consequently, the illegitimacy of state authority provides the warrant for the emergence of bad badman and "bad nigger" behavior. In Brown's characterization, white authority simultaneously creates both white supremacy and black accommodationism. In charting the emergence of these phenomena, Brown's Black Power vernacular "articulates an equivocal relationship to hegemony, a complex negotiation with the dominant group that is characterized by a self-conscious difference and defiance."[82] Brown argues that white authority makes it impossible for black people to narrate their own lives or resist oppressive conditions, especially as "negro america" regurgitates white supremacy within black communities.[83] By internalizing Christian religion rather than confronting slave owners, Brown argues that black Americans began to internalize their own oppression and perpetuate their submission to white power structures through accommodationism, which ultimately made it impossible for them to agitate for freedom since they did not confront the racist assumptions of white religious life. Tracing the consequences of this internalization of white supremacy, Brown's memoir documents the warrants for a new cultural nationalism that centers black life in an effort to create new models for ethics, the law, and public policy.

The indictments of civilizationism in *Die Nigger Die!* are, in some ways, predictable given the history of slavery in America. Gilroy explains, "Because it was so reliant on the institutionalization of their unfree labor, the slaves viewed the civilizing process with skepticism and its ethical claims with extreme suspicion. Their hermeneutic insights grounded a vernacular culture premised on the possibility that freedom could be pursued outside of the rules, codes, and expectations of this conspicuously color-coded civilization."[84] Brown's strategy of regeneration allows for no compromise with the civilizationist impulses of white America, be it Scrabble, verse poetry, or Christian religious sentiment. Brown's disavowal of these forms of white organization, leisure, and literature prompt a positionality demanding a total loyalty to Black Power, black history, and black heroes. While this move clearly helps delineate Black Power enemies in service to the regeneration of the movement, it also helps spur the change in consciousness that Black Power demands and upon which it is premised. Gilroy suggests that this kind of rhetorical expression highlights how Black Power writers presented opportunities to rhetorically or politically transgress the social boundaries of race as a "negation of unjust, oppressive, and therefore illegitimate authority."[85]

Brown's elaboration on the difference between respect and authority invokes race to unmask the whiteness of presidential power through his trademark vernacular in addition to images that illustrate the production of race. Two collaged pictures frame his remarks about respect and authority in the memoir. One image features a round slogan from Johnson's administration, which says "LBJ for the USA" as Johnson looks sternly at the reader. Below Johnson is a picture of President Kennedy, who seems to be signing legislation in the presence of Hubert Humphrey and eight other self-congratulatory white men. In both images, LBJ is at the forefront, positioned to directly address the reader with his stern, Texas scowl. Brown's dialogue on respect and authority is framed by the LBJ picture, but the conversation continues on the following pages replete with images, this time of Hubert Humphrey, whose head is pasted onto Tarzan's body, with Fay Wray at his feet. Next to the image is the slogan, "America's Number One Hero."

On the facing page, Brown's rhetorical pugilism exposes the illegitimate authority of white liberals to dictate the terms of equality. He says, "In this country, authority is a cover for wrong. I don't respect wrong and I don't respect authority that represents wrong. And old cracker ass Lightning Bug Johnson knows that's true, because I told him myself."[86] These pictures indict the ethics of Johnson and Humphrey and serve to highlight the politics of whiteness that frame his interactions with them and articulate Brown's dominance of them. Thus, Brown's vernacular, punctuated by hilarious images, highlights how rhetorical authority is *both* produced and undermined. Grant Farred has argued, "vernacular speech belongs to the colonized or the ghettoized communities of the metropolis. The vernacular is counterposed to (and is less valued than) the formal—or 'proper'—speech of the colonizers or the metropolitanized discourse of the dominant society."[87] Brown's colloquialisms, his verbal confrontation with Johnson's policies, and his badman persona contrast his version of legitimate political authority with Johnson, depicted as a white poseur propped up by illegitimate authority.

Brown continues by recollecting his altercation with Johnson when he visited the White House as the chairman for the Non-Violent Action Group (NAG) during the Selma March. He recalls Johnson as "arrogant as hell and mad 'cause we were there. His whole attitude was, 'What you niggers doin' here takin' up my time.'"[88] According to Brown, the group was polite despite Johnson's disdain, but Brown was insulted by the accommodationist tone that the NAG folks were using with Johnson. He reports that he told the president, "I'm not happy to be here and I think it is unnecessary that we have to be here protesting the brutality that Black people are subjected to. And furthermore, I think that the majority of Black people that voted for you wish that they had gone fishing."[89] This confrontation provides prime rhetorical space for Brown to demonstrate his verbal prowess as a badman as Brown castigates the Johnson White House for its civil rights failures and uses a language of dominance that destroys Johnson's credibility as a man and as a leader through a vernacular that would appeal to urban black readers. He says "Johnson was a big-eared, ugly, red-necked cracker. . . . And when I was tearing into Johnson's ass, Humphrey, who is supposed to be a 'liberal,' was getting madder than a pimp with dogshit on his shoe. So I looked at him and knew where he was at. The little red punk."[90] This penetrating invective helps to undermine the "authority" (and masculinity) of Johnson and Humphrey on civil rights issues, positioning Brown as a legitimate movement leader while also undermining the credibility of the nation's most prominent white liberals on issues of black equality.

In this commentary on white supremacy, Brown's narrative highlights what bell hooks calls "whiteness in the black imagination," demonstrating this vernacular use of alternative history and memory to undermine white authority.[91] Thus, Brown's recollection of Johnson's attitude on civil rights is at odds with popular memory surrounding the Johnson administration's handling of civil rights after Kennedy's assassination and demonstrates the personal and political complexity of the moment. As a result, scholars can read Brown's race analysis and his performance as an urban badman as an intervention into historical whitewashing of the civil rights movement and the Johnson administration's relationship to its leaders. Brown then moves into a discussion of the inevitable black revolution to explain how the illegitimate authority of white supremacy informs black resistance in urban centers.

Forging the Black Revolution

At the center of this discussion of political resistance is the figure of the badman as a social movement leader. Brown moves from personal anecdotes to theoretical analysis to discuss how the vernacular aesthetics of urban black masculinity and the performance of rebellion needs to be understood as an embodied leadership style premised upon bodily and rhetorical confrontation with white people in power and encompassed in the black badman persona. Literary scholar C. P. Henry stresses that both the myth and the reality of the black badman constitute a continuing historical source of revolutionary vision that should be understood as a distinct leadership style, rather than castigated as pathological, dysfunctional, or nihilistic, if not linked to white benevolence.[92] Brown's autobiography is a prime example of this intersection between urban black masculinity and rebellion that forms the template for Black Power leadership at the end of the 1960s. As a leader, Brown articulated his argument for revolution by indicting racial binaries and justifying the need for urban rebellion. Brown writes:

> All of white america is a structure of institutions that says to Black people, "Nigger, you ain't shit!" All standards of excellence, beauty, efficiency, and civilization are such that any comparison between Black and white is designed to favor white and put down Black. And it's ground into a Black person every minute of every day, whether you're at work or whether you're out trying to have fun, it's Nigger you ain't shit. "Die Nigger Die!"[93]

Herein lies the source for the title of the manifesto and the phrase repeated throughout the text as a synecdoche for white attitudes about black Americans. Brown argues that the entire American culture is premised upon these white values, which are replicated by the black institutions that form the backbone of the black middle class. Paired with his critique of institutionalized racism, this statement forms the basis of Brown's own oppositional consciousness and the underlying reason that he cannot perform accommodationism: at its core, accommodationism privileges whiteness by asking nonwhites to accept and conform to existing white norms and behaviors.

Brown delineates between the three Americas coexisting and competing within the nation-state: white america, negro america, and "Black" america.

For Brown, the contradictions within these communities of practice produce the conditions that demand revolution, which he deems as inevitable. As a black badman, Brown seeks strength in black communities through black self-determination that rejects the politics of colorism. He continues:

> Negroes have always been treated like wild, caged animals by the white man, and have always felt the passions of caged animals (because they were living in cages), but they would always act civilized with whites, that is, what white people told them was civilized. But inside, the–civilized negro was an undying hate. This hate, however could only be released in negro america. If it was ever released in white america, it would prove to whites that negroes were savages. That hate became self-hate.[94]

Next, Brown moves from a description of himself as a badman into the theoretical underpinnings of violence and the coming black revolution. Here, Brown sets himself up as a hero opposed to Johnson's white paternalism guised as "civil rights," and he also begins to delineate the theories about black nationalism that inform articulation of Black Power activism, including his philosophy of self-defense and the utility of violence in forging an independent collective identity for black America. His conflict with Johnson at the White House confirms that he saw himself as a badman and refused to capitulate to Johnson's demand for deference from the civil rights leaders. In this move to become the bad badman, Brown also implicitly contrasts himself with the "Uncle Toms" of the mainstream civil rights organizations and uses the anecdote to elevate himself and his ideology above what he perceives is the same egregious accommodationist practices that "negro Americans" had perfected since slavery. Because Brown's interactions with Johnson and Humphrey were so imbued with the same contempt and racial politics that legitimized segregation, he saw the loyalty to them as undermining black self-determination. As the bad badman, however, Brown usurps the power from Johnson and Humphrey and triumphs over them as a badman because he is able to expose them for their own racism in the face of their so-called support for civil rights. Since Johnson can't and won't lead on civil rights, Brown will through a regeneration of Black Power agitation for a black revolution.

Framing the Black Revolution: The Exigencies of Black Power

The aesthetics of urban black masculine rebellion in *Die Nigger Die!* need to be understood as a leadership style premised upon embodied and rhetorical confrontation with whites in power and encompassed in the black badman persona. Like Don Lee in the introduction of the memoir, Brown delineates between three Americas coexisting in the nation-state: white america, negro america, and Black america. Brown sees revolution as inevitable, and he positions himself as a revolutionary messiah squarely in the camp of "Black America" as he reminds Americans about the politics of color that dominate their daily existence. The characteristics of "negro America" seem to be a replication of the color caste that privileges lightness over darkness, straight hair over kinky hair, Anglo features over African features, white middle-class values over black community issues. Centering his analysis on black body image, Brown talks about the long-term consequences of internalizing white power. Like Assata Shakur, this brainwashing and cultural prejudice is internalized at a young age for black people through education and "for Black people, the american educational system is a propaganda machine we don't need. It propagandizes against us. It makes us hate ourselves."[96] Here, the cultural nationalism of Black Power *is* political, just as the direct-action agenda is political. Consequently, cultural aspects of blackness are central to the creation of oppositional consciousness and black solidarity.

Brown's arguments about colorism describe how whiteness becomes the benchmark as a standard of beauty, morality, respectability, intelligence, and historical successes. Because white America has controlled the language of the culture, "They have always known that if they could justify and make their actions legal, either through their religion, their courts or their history (educational system), then it would be unnecessary to actually rectify them because the negro would accept their interpretation."[97] "Negro america" becomes the translator of white racism by placing it under the banner of American patriotism; white institutional racism then permeates "negro" institutions in the same manner that it does in the larger structure of the nation. For Brown, this translation work uses nationalism as the language that codes racism. He adds, "White nationalism divides history into two parts, B.C. and A.D.—before the white man's religion and after it. And 'progress,' of course, is considered to have taken place only after the white man's religion came into being. The implication is evident: God is on the white man's side, for white Jesus was the 'son' of God."[98] As Brown points out, the blending of religious myth with history renders counterhistories and myths of progress moot as whitewashed cultural icons like Jesus stand in for all that is good and right. A black Christ-figure like Brown is then necessary in delivering black America to salvation through separatist philosophy and political strategy. This kind of philosophy certainly makes his transition to Islam in the 1970s much easier as Brown argues that Christianity has also been an obstacle for black self-determination and has been a strategy of co-optation by the state of moderate civil rights leaders like Martin Luther King.

In describing the psychological and physical oppression of black ideas, black life, and black freedom, Brown exposes black frustration, saying, "inside the 'civilized' negro was an undying hate. This hate, however could only be released in negro america. If it was ever released in white america, it would prove to whites that negroes were savages. That hate became self-hate."[99] Brown explains that the internalization of self-hate was a coping strategy, a survival mechanism to deal with the impetus to embrace the promises of the United States and yet deal with the reality of its institutionalized racism. The social and psychological fragmentation of black people and culture was an obvious consequence of capitulating to white norms. Brown sees accommodationism and integration as coping mechanisms that have long outlived their usefulness. In these indictments of white nationalism, Brown elevates a black rebellion predicated upon black culture and black pride.

It is at this point that Brown begins to describe the promises of black America for he sees this as the place where revolution will begin. He argues that "Black america" is important as a distinction because it is the space where folks self-impose their exile from both whites and "negroes." It is a place that offers a "humanism uncommon to white and negro america" because it accepts those that are dually rejected from black and white America for being too black or too poor.[100] For Brown, blackness is not a color but a way of thinking.[101] Blackness is the only site of unity and freedom from the racist history and institutions that fuel self-hate. This becomes the basis for the collective identity that Brown uses to regenerate Black Power.

For Brown, self-exile and rebellion are the foundations of black culture in America, and he links his ideology to that of the leadership of slave revolts. This strategy unmasks the continuity of resistance while simultaneously acknowledging that leaders of slave revolts are widely held as badman heroes renowned for their use of violence to break free from bondage. Brown remarks, that "there has been one continuous rebellion in Black america since the first slave got here."[102] This is an important argument to forge, first, because it asserts a continuous (masculine) legacy and counterhistory of black America, which declares resistance and revolution as intrinsic to the culture.

Second, Brown's argument about the continuity of rebellion underscores his appreciation for the interplay between dominant ideology, subaltern cultures, and self-hate since his depiction makes it quite simple to see how "Black America" and "negro America" come to be positioned against each other. Each large community seeks to preserve its boundaries by maintaining the differences that make it distinct. "Blackness," then, constitutes the kind of racial and gendered identity that Brown offers for those who seek to oppose the arbitrary authority exercised in their communities and the systems of power that guarantee racial inequality. This strategy of regeneration makes positive connotations of blackness a prerequisite to Black Power leadership.

Brown's understanding of the way that race works as a trope of difference for white culture and the way that color and class work for black America is a useful tool in explicating the relationships between these substrata of US culture. Brown makes it possible to see how (white) nationalism fuels the growth of negro america while needing to simultaneously suppress the revolution burning inside of urban black america. This simultaneity constitutes the power of white America. Brown adds, "if you're Black, then you do everything you can to fight the white folks. If you're negro, you do everything you can to appease them. If you're Black, you're constantly in and out of trouble because you're always messing with the man."[103] Blackness constitutes an oppositional identity that opposes the arbitrary authority exercised by white patriarchy. This rhetorical strategy makes positive connotations of blackness a prerequisite for rebellion since Brown sees "Negroes" as just barely removed from the slave system. Brown's close proximity with whites and middle-class blacks as a youth convinced him that he needed an identity that wasn't predicated upon subservience to whites; he says, "I knew I didn't want to be a slave."[104]

It is here that Brown also condemns integration as a strategy of the movement for black liberation. To Brown, integration is an instantiation of white nationalism. Brown argues, "the civil rights movement was concerned with—controlling the animalistic behavior of white people.... We were letting white folks know that they could no longer legislate where we went or what we did."[105] Brown explains that the civil rights movement was never concerned with being able to get close to white people; instead, it was about trying to rein in the violent, uncivilized behavior of whites against blacks in public places. However, Brown's analysis of the dialectic between white nationalism and black resistance doesn't see white culture substantively changing as a result of the civil rights movement and instead argues that black separatism is really the only option for ending white violence and forging a group consciousness that empowers black people to reclaim their movement and their space.

Brown's use of the Black Power vernacular is riveting precisely because it disrupts physical and rhetorical space. It creates tension, exposes hypocrisy, and invites confrontation. In Farred's words, it "inspires hegemonic imitation and yet is despised—feared, even—because it is the incarnation and the articulation of that which is deemed culturally and economically lesser, the speech of the working class or ethnic minority, the discourse of the racial subject."[106] While imitation is certainly one mode of rhetorical transmission of the Black Power vernacular and Rap Brown is intending to inspire it here, "the vernacular can still, in some if not all instances, stand as the enunciation of a threatening, angry resistance, a determination to speak within and against the dominant group with the hint of Fanonian violence." This rhetorical anger demonstrates a committed determination to both address and respond to political violence.[107]

The vernacular idiom is the *lingua franca* of the oppressed. It is the situated knowledge that informs political expression. "Vernacularity has a contradictory function in that it is at once the marker of disjuncture, the form of speech that separates rich from poor, dominant from dominated, the speech that distinguishes black self-representation from its white counterpart, and an ironic conjoining."[108] In other words, the black vernacular marks itself as distinctly subaltern in ways that challenge dominant white rhetorical modes without overcoming those modes. Thus, while the black vernacular can momentarily displace white rhetorical repertoires in renaming or reframing rhetorical moments or political ideas, they never serve to replace them entirely. Consequently, the black vernacular "reassures the hegemonic group of their difference, their discursive, locational separation (that place where they stand, almost literally), and their linguistic superiority to—the command of, historic attachment and association with 'proper' discourse, the formal expression of a particular language—that of the variously raced, gendered, and ethnicized underclass."[109] Logically, then, the black vernacular is what Farred calls a "dependent gesture announcing a dialectical relationship between the vernacular and the formal."[110] Inherent in the vernacular, then is the concept of confrontation. The major question is whether confrontational rhetoric utilized by the underclasses and aimed at police, prison officials, and the state can augment movement organizations in positive ways, despite the blowback from state agents.

Brown's strategies for regenerating Black Power are highly dependent on the confrontational street vernacular that demonizes white authority generally, but he also creates a rhetorical exigency surrounding specific cultural figures: John Kennedy, Bobby Kennedy, Hubert Humphrey, the FBI, and the local police. Brown's understanding of the broken promises of liberalism beginning with the Kennedy White House underscores the extent to which the civil rights movement was on its own. This sense of betrayal fuels Brown's disenchantment with the agenda of mainstream black organizations and forms part of the basis for his vernacular choices.

The theme of the betrayal of civil rights workers by the Democratic Party permeates Brown's counterhistory of SNCC's civil rights history, connecting the Kennedy administration's ambivalent support in the Deep South with the Three-Fifths Compromise, the *Dred Scott* case, the Black Codes, and the segregation of the civil service. Clearly the lack of protection from the FBI concerned and disappointed southern civil rights workers in the early 1960s, but so did the apparent disdain of Attorney General Bobby Kennedy.[111] Brown writes, "In Mississippi, civil rights workers were killed, because Bobby Kennedy said the federal government could not protect them. In Alabama, civil rights workers were killed and the federal government would not move against Wallace. And yet negroes cried over the Kennedys worse than they would've cried for their own mamas."[112] Brown argues that the federal government, despite its insistence on support for civil rights, did little to help the movement and did everything they could to destroy it, including both passive and active support of white supremacists in the South and in the federal government. This political pandering is what creates the exigency for social change; it becomes part of the problem rather than part of the solution. This reaction by liberals is what helps to propel mainstream activists into the Black Power movement where the critique is focused on federal malfeasance, political disingenuousness, and historical inequity propelled by federal inaction or support.

Brown extends his critique of governmental complicity with violence against southern civil rights activists to local police forces in America's cities. Brown connects the make-up of community surveillance with the self-policing of the grassroots organizations. The police would attempt to monitor and patrol poor communities, but their own prejudice, racism, education, and lack of training made them enemies of the same populations that they were sworn to serve just like the soldiers in Vietnam and the South Vietnamese people. Brown's solidarity with Third World peoples in Vietnam is important here because they were fighting the same white authority structure: Black Power advocates were fighting the police and the Vietnamese were fighting the US military.[113]

Rap Brown's regeneration of Black Power reflects the masculine revolutionary ethos of many of his contemporaries, but particularly Malcolm X. Brown's willingness to write frankly about structures of whiteness propels him forward as a "black leader," following in the footsteps of the martyred Malcolm X. He writes, "A lot of people say that it's regrettable that Malcolm got killed. But Malcolm was not an individual. His life didn't belong to him. No revolutionary can claim his life for himself. The life of the revolutionary belongs to the struggle.... Death is the price of revolution."[114] Brown's rhetoric situates Malcolm X as a martyr of Black Power because he was self-sacrificing and always fighting for black liberation. Just as a Malcolm was a revolutionary, so is Brown, and by highlighting Malcolm's service to black people, we can see the kind of leadership model that Brown is emulating in his regeneration of

Black Power and the way that he sees himself as a self-sacrificing revolutionary martyr.

This discussion of the broken promises of white liberals and the law-enforcement community's surveillance and repression of black people provides a transition to a discussion of weapons that illustrates the centrality of self-defense for the regeneration of Black Power. Brown is quite open about the fact that he and his brother Ed constantly carried firearms because of their complete confidence in their ability to use the weapons and in their judgment about when the necessity to use that weapon was a life or death issue. He writes, "Give me a gun before you even give me somebody to work with. A gun won't fail you. People will. I found that out early."[115] Brown's comments about civil disobedience direct the reader to understand the absolute necessity of self-defense, given the racist realities of the police force in the United States. His comments recall the brutality of Birmingham and illustrate Brown's ability to survive as a badman despite such violence. In this logic, the gun became indispensable as a symbol of militancy, as a reassurance of protection, and as a substitute for sell-outs. In characterizing the federal government as treacherous, Brown suggests that only a radical political reorientation among blacks will help them learn to read the disappointment of civil rights as a permanent feature of American life.

In Brown's opinion, the militant must be willing to back up their threat of violence in the same way that law enforcement does. Robert Scott and Donald Smith have pointed out the importance of "symbolic destruction" in rhetorics of confrontation: "[h]arassing, embarrassing, and disarming the enemy may suffice, especially if he is finally led to admit his impotence in the face of the superior will of the revolutionary."[116] Brown's gendered critiques of Johnson and Humphrey illustrate the symbolic destruction that he honed as a master of the dozens, but Brown also argues that everyone is able to practice self-defense, just not many people are willing to do so. Instead, they choose alternative strategies to survive in the midst of racial violence: some accommodate, some assimilate, and some choose nonviolent protest as their means of dealing with their inability to protect themselves from the violence of the state.

Brown turns here from the quandary of self-defense and nonviolence to a polemic about violence as a movement tactic as he reframes state violence and the resistance of the underclasses. He writes, "I began to recognize then the value of being violent. I knew I hadn't done anything to make them white muthafuckas shoot their B.B. guns at me, so I knew that the world didn't run on love. The only thing that was gon' keep white muthafuckas off you was you! . . . America has made it clear that she respects only violence."[117] Brown emphasizes the difference between white violence in America (justified) and black violence in America (crime), although this does make the response to racism an individual responsibility. He continues with a commentary on black violence in the context of Johnson's escalation of the Vietnam War, which bears a longer quotation in full:

> It's legitimate for a Black man to go over there and kill 30 Vietcong and get a medal, but you come back here and kill one racist, red-necked, honkey, camel-breathed peckerwood who's been misusing you and your people all your life, and that's murder. That's homicide, because the white man has the power to define and legitimize his actions.[118]

Linking white violence against blacks in the United States to the war in Vietnam implicitly highlights the similarities between the Vietnamese and black Americans in terms of their colonization and domination, demonstrating the flexibility of the Black Power vernacular. Where the Vietnamese people have the right to fight against the US invasion, so, too, does the whole of black America have the right to rise up against the domestic army of the American police.

For Brown, violence is also a tactical constitutive strategy, rather than simply a response to violence, especially in urban rebellions and confrontations. Brown argues that violence builds solidarity between people and says, "One significant thing about Detroit and Newark was that the violence created a peoplehood . . . And afterwards, there was a real sense of community among the people, a real feeling of pride and togetherness. It came from the fact that they had fought together. It also came from the fact that the honkey cop kills Black people because they're Black."[119] Although Brown talks about peoplehood here, he seems to really be discussing black masculinity because of his interest in violence and the gun as symbols of revolution. Brown uses reversal again to portray the government as the outlaw in contrast to activists fighting for equality. He adds, "When the people cannot find a redress of their grievances within a system, they have no choice but to destroy the system which is responsible . . . for their grievances. The government is the lawbreaker. The people must be the law enforcer. We cannot allow the government to be an outlaw, particularly when the crime is against the people."[120] It is clear from these passages that Brown sees violence as an inherent part of the racial politics of the United States. This serves as a warrant for his claims about the importance of self-defense, his demonization of the police, and his exploration of the utility of violence as an avenue for black liberation. Urban rebellion does, however, have the potential to limit Brown's regeneration of Black Power because it increases the likelihood of imprisonment for leaders and members of the Black Power movement.

Nonetheless, the Black Power vernacular here demands that young black men perform as hypermasculine badmen in confrontations with white liberals and police officers. In the case of urban rebellion, the black male body figures prominently into the construction of both black identity and white identity in clashes between urban populations and white police officers. Herman Gray notes that in the popular imaginary, black men are "logical and legitimate object[s] of surveillance and policing, containment and punishment. Discursively this black male body brings together the dominant institutions of (white) masculine power and authority—criminal justice system, the police, and the news media—to protect (white) Americans from harm."[121] This is even more salient as we examine *Die Nigger Die!* as an artifact, since the cover art is a photo of Rap Brown being handcuffed by four white police officers in riot gear holding batons. Brown is wincing as one of the officers is squeezing the back of his neck and another is helping to hustle him along. As one who has survived encounters with the police as well as prison, this photo of Brown stands to authenticate him as a leader and a hero, fighting the police officers. Here he stands as a bad badman and as a figure of black masculine resistance. In understanding the police as a domestic army that constituted an unremitting threat to black life in America, Brown positions them as the enemies of Black Power and the force that must be resisted in order for Black Power to regenerate. The police, then, become a reliable source of exigency in the creation and maintenance of Black Power organizations and ideologies.

The rebellions in cities like Detroit and Newark became spaces that allowed for the emergence of black revolutionaries to voice the dissatisfaction with the pace of dismantling white supremacy, especially because they featured confrontation with the (white) police of those cities. This rhetorical space was also inherently masculine because the leaders that had been elevated in public spaces were male spokesmen. And as Louis C. Goldberg argues, "It is the role of 'spokesman for rebellion' created by the fact that ghetto rebellions are occurring which is significant, and not Brown or Carmichael specifically. Previously that role was singularly filled by Malcolm X; now new men are moving to fill the gap, rushing to keep up with events more than they are guiding them."[122] In the vacuum created by the death of Malcolm X, men had to fill the role of symbolic leader in his stead, carrying his rhetoric and his ideology through the rebellions following the assassination of King. The goal of many young black protestors and revolutionaries at this time "was to disrupt police order, to make police 'lose their cool,' to produce situations in which police worked until they 'dropped in their tracks' . . . *they are interested not in killing policemen but in humiliating them.*"[123]

By this account, Brown is clearly a "spokesman for rebellion," articulating the concerns of urban blacks (men) and articulating an enemy highly visible in their communities: police officers. His performance of violent confrontation and his elevation of Malcolm X illustrate how Brown sees himself filling the void of masculine leadership that Malcolm's assassination left. Through his rhetoric of both self-defense and violence, Brown shifts away from the gun as a symbol of violence and toward the notion that violence is an important tool in the revolution, particularly in bringing a government to heel for its repression.

Brown's Legacy and the Black Power Vernacular

As Craig Werner has noted, the success of black autobiographies, particularly those written from prison or exile, depends upon the autobiographer's ability to negotiate a "hostile discursive environment in a manner that, in effect, creates a sympathetic audience" especially since "the white audience is likely to have internalized, often on an un-or a semi-conscious level, aspects of the discursive formation that denies or questions black humanity."[124] For black and white readers and listeners alike, Brown's vernacular style, showcased in his speeches but especially in *Die Nigger Die!*, highlighted the white hostility of the discursive environment while calling upon black activists to take up more radical rhetorical space in debates about structural oppression and power. Brown's radical vernacular, particularly in his autobiographical manifesto, successfully documented Brown's lifelong activism along with the constant violence that he experienced as a Black Power activist. In many ways, Brown's manifesto is a bridge between Carmichael's notions of Black Power in the mid-1960s and the evolution of Black Power in the 1970s because he advocates a revolution in black America.

In hindsight, SNCC's organizational structure and its youth propelled leaders like Brown (and Carmichael before him) into the limelight. Howard Zinn described this trajectory thusly:

> But the movement, still with a quality of abandon, still spontaneous and unstructured, refused to be put into a bureaucratic box. The twig was bent, and the tree grew that way. For SNCC, even after it had a large staff, its own office, and money for long-distance phone calls, managed to maintain an autonomy in the field, an unpredictability of action, a lack of overall planning which brought exasperation to some of its most ardent supporters, bewilderment to outside observers, and bemusement to the students themselves.[125]

Zinn's comments highlight how SNCC's student roots influenced the leader-ship of the organization and points to the structural reasons why the Black Power vernacular emerged from SNCC instead of more conservative social spaces like the SCLC. Many SNCC members saw armed struggle as both sym-bolic and prudent because of the pervasiveness of both guns and white vio-lence in the American South.

Brown's support of black self-defense and public dissent certainly marked him as a target from the government, as the introduction of laws named after him prohibiting interstate travel of "agitators" attests. Still, the Kerner Com-mission found that "[d]espite extremist rhetoric, there was no attempt to sub-vert the social order of the United States. Instead, most of those who attacked white authority and property seemed to be demanding fuller participation in the social order and material benefits enjoyed by the vast majority of Ameri-can citizens."[126] In addition to demonstrating that black leaders had no inten-tion of actually overthrowing cities like Newark and Detroit, the commission concluded that urban rebellions did not occur as a response to "a single 'trig-gering' or 'precipitating' incident" but rather emerged out of an increasingly strained social climate where underlying racial grievances remained unre-solved for weeks.[127] Recognizing that the civil disorders sweeping the nation were a result of unresolved racial problems surrounding segregation, housing, employment discrimination, and disenfranchisement in American cities, the Kerner Commission acknowledged that the "Black Power" slogan helped to overcome "the Negro's feeling of powerlessness" that has emerged in response to "his alienation from and hostility toward the institutions of law and gov-ernment" that deprived and victimized black youth.[128]

In his landmark 1973 study, Matthew Holden confirmed the conclusions of the Kerner Commission and argued that urban rebellions influenced Black Power's trajectory, suggesting that the climate of urban repression marked SNCC's forthcoming strategies:

> SNCC was soon charged with, or praised for, advocating violence. But this charge or praise seem to have been, at first, overreaction by both whites and blacks . . .
> The wave of near-panic is related less to what SNCC did than to the *imagery* of incipient black revolt . . . Instead, it seems much more likely that SNCC fell acci-dentally into the posture of appearing to advocate aggressive violence . . . Having done so, it found political benefits to never discouraging that this was its policy.[129]

Despite his faltering ability to build organizations as he had in the heyday of SNCC due to state repression, Brown's legacy at the end of the 1960s is most certainly his persistence in articulating the Black Power vernacular even as he became a prominent target of the FBI's emerging counterintelligence programs.

In using the Black Power vernacular to characterize this new phase of resistance to continued racial oppression, Brown was able to assert a counter-history that highlighted the schisms among the White House, FBI, local police, and civil rights activists and agitate for a new phase of activism that recognized the continuity of repression in the United States against black people. In doing so, he was teaching readers to think critically about racial identification, black adolescence, black masculinity, and black leadership. Brown's manifesto, with its extended commentary about race, gender, and class, provides an important primer for critics of the Black Power movement, since its analysis highlights the rhetorical interventions that Brown was making in the public and within SNCC to change the language of civil rights to reflect different priorities and conversations about identity, globalism, and statism. Kermit Ernest Campbell implores critics to be more sensitive to the social costs in performing black vernacular in the public sphere, writing that "[b]ecause most folks don't see the standard dialect as constitutive of white hegemonic values and worldviews . . . as bearing the ideologies of socially and racially privileged groups in America, they fail to take into account the psychological cost for these youth to assimilate voices, nay, selves that are so closely identified with white middle-class culture."[130]

Brown's conversion to Islam in the 1970s has complicated his relationship to the nation even further, particularly because the Muslim movement in prisons has always been a similar threat to the national order. Consequently, the conclusion will deal with the relationship between Jamil Al-Amin and the nation since his conversion to understand the relationship between Black Power, Muslim movements, and the prison system was, in many ways, *more* of a threat to white supremacy than Brown ever was, particularly in the wake of September 11, 2001. While the conclusion will tackle Brown's most recent incarceration and assess the relationship between the Black Power movement and the war on terror, I want to suggest here that the expansion of the prison-industrial complex during the 1970s and 1980s was primarily justified by the state's framing of black men like Brown as agitators and rabble-rousers needing to be caged.

CHAPTER THREE

Competing Masculinities

Police Brutality, Prison Brutality, and Black Heroes

The morning of December 9, 1981, permanently changed Philadelphia journalist Mumia Abu-Jamal's life as well as the American anti–death penalty movement. In the early hours of that morning, police officer Danny Faulkner stopped a Volkswagen driven by Abu-Jamal's brother, Billy Cook. Cook got out of the car and struck Officer Faulkner in the face as Faulkner attempted to handcuff Cook. Faulkner responded by hitting Cook in the face with a police-issued flashlight when a man darted across the street at the two men.[1] Shortly thereafter, Abu-Jamal was taken to Jefferson University Hospital with a gunshot wound produced by Faulkner's police-issued gun and with trauma inflicted, as witnesses testified, by the police who encountered the scene of the shoot-out. Officer Faulkner was pronounced dead on arrival at the hospital while Abu-Jamal was operated on for two and a half hours before being handcuffed to his hospital bed as the primary suspect in the officer's murder.[2] The weapon was never recovered and all of the eyewitnesses described a man who looked nothing like Abu-Jamal. The murder of Officer Faulkner and the trial of Mumia Abu-Jamal made headline news in Philadelphia for the attention it brought to police brutality and judicial corruption in the city.

The outcry was understandable since, by the early 1970s, Philadelphia had a notoriously racist and corrupt police force. David Lindorff writes, "in the late 1970s and early 1980s, the entire chain of command of both Homicide and Vice were being investigated by the FBI. These were the very units that were investigating [Mumia] Abu-Jamal's case."[3] By the time of Abu-Jamal's arrest, "the Philadelphia Police Department was without a doubt one of the most corrupt and out-of-control big city law enforcement operations in the nation."[4] The *Philadelphia Inquirer* referred to the city as a "petri dish of corruption" and described the "conspiracy of silence" that existed among officers.[5] Investigative reporting "revealed sophisticated networks of corruption grafted on to the police command structure itself" that have been traced to the inception of the Philadelphia Police Department.[6] But the Abu-Jamal case intensified the focus on police misconduct in Philadelphia. For example, the US Attorney's Office in the city was directed by the US Justice Department under "the ardently law-and-order Reagan Administration" to initiate a corruption probe "in the Sixth Precinct and the entire Central Division . . . the very jurisdiction where Faulkner's shooting took place."[7]

By 1982, the indictments emerged and over thirty officers in the division ultimately were convicted of misconduct. A full third of those convicted by the Justice Department were involved in Mumia Abu-Jamal's prosecution and helped to cast him as an unrepentant cop killer.[8] Just two years prior to Abu-Jamal's arrest, the Justice Department sued the city of Philadelphia in an extraordinary move, charging Mayor Frank Rizzo (the former police commissioner) and eighteen top-ranking police officials "with condoning systematic police brutality—the first such charge against an entire police department in American history."[9]

Frank Rizzo was a polarizing force in Philadelphia. Terry Bisson writes, "Philadelphia's answer to the complex problems of urban decline was a walking, talking (sort of) nightstick named Frank Rizzo, a high school dropout, boot-in-your-face patrolman whose outlaw style had earned him the nickname, The Cisco Kid."[10] President Richard Nixon personally supported Rizzo's first "law and order" campaign, which mimicked Nixon's own racial politics at the end of the 1960s. Nixon personally encouraged Rizzo's promotions from beat cop to precinct commander to mayor of Philadelphia while Rizzo promised that he would "make Attila the Hun look like a faggot" in the 1972 mayoral election.[11] When Rizzo ran against black mayoral candidate Wilson Goode, in 1980, his campaign slogan was "Vote White."[12] Rizzo thought that the "fear of punishment is part of every man's life" and this philosophy informed his leadership.[13] The lawlessness and racism of Rizzo's police force "was so routine and so pervasive, that the Justice Department was prepared to sue the city's entire police force for civil rights violations in 1972, until the move was quashed by the Nixon White House."[14]

Rizzo first caught Nixon's attention in 1967, when, as the commander of the city's 7,500-man police department, he clashed with some 3,500 black high school and middle school students who were peacefully demonstrating for a program in black studies. Rizzo ordered "riot plan number three" and the officers surrounded the students and beat them in front of television cameras which recorded Rizzo shouting, "Get their black asses!" as Philadelphia's finest clubbed and stomped the students.[15] Following this public repression, the

Black Panther Party created an office in the city to deal with the persistent police brutality against black residents. In response, Rizzo created a special unit called the Civil Defense (CD) Squad that used "eavesdropping, phone tapping, using undercover agents, trumped up arrests and nighttime raids," which became the prototype for the FBI's COINTELPRO campaign to target, harass, disrupt, and destroy radical groups including the Black Panthers.[16] James Kyung-Jin Lee has documented Rizzo's "reign of terror" in Philadelphia, noting that Rizzo's CD Squad used techniques including manufacturing and "planting" evidence of "bombs" and assassination threats against himself and other city officials, "driving out free speech advocates, and encouraging the use of brutal force among the police rank-and-file against Black residents in the city."[17] This campaign against black activism propelled Rizzo to the forefront of national politics, where his campaign of intimidation and harassment found ample support in the Nixon White House.

By 1969, the FBI's Philadelphia COINTELPRO agents had begun monitoring the political activities of sixteen-year-old Wesley Cook, who would soon adopt the name Mumia Abu-Jamal. Abu-Jamal led students at Benjamin Franklin High School in petitioning to change the name of the school to Malcolm X High School and by 1969, sixteen-year-old Abu-Jamal was the lieutenant minister of information for the Philadelphia Black Panther Party and a permanent target of the FBI. Later, in 1981, in the middle of a successful, award-winning career in journalism, Abu-Jamal was involved in one of the most high-profile trials in the nation's history.

However, Abu-Jamal's community credentials in Philadelphia were solid. He was named by *Philadelphia* magazine as one of the city's "people to watch" in 1981 as the president of the Association of Black Journalists in Philadelphia and as the recipient of the Major Armstrong Award for radio journalism. He had become known as "the voice of the voiceless" for covering police brutality in Philadelphia during Rizzo's tenure. But despite these honors, from the age of fifteen to the time of his trial for the alleged murder of police officer Danny Faulkner, the FBI's COITNELPRO agents in Philadelphia had compiled over seven hundred pages of files detailing his political and intellectual activities.[18] On the back of a photo of Abu-Jamal in his extensive FBI file, one handwritten word appears—"Dead."[19]

This chapter provides a rhetorical analysis of *Live From Death Row* (1995), *Death Blossoms* (1997), and *All Things Censored* (2000), three of Mumia Abu-Jamal's essay compilations since July 2, 1982, when he was convicted of the first-degree murder of Officer Danny Faulkner and sentenced to death by Judge Albert Sabo. All three books were published from death row at SCI/Greene Correctional Facility, where Abu-Jamal remained until 2011.[20] I am interested in how Abu-Jamal's use of the Black Power vernacular marshals the testimony of black intellectuals and his skills as a professional journalist to build his ethos as a Black Power leader, despite the use of the term "cop killer" to circumscribe his penetrating observations about mass incarceration. Where Rap Brown's interventions into the Black Power vernacular often center on his aggressive rhetorical style (the bad badman) as noted in chapter 2, Abu-Jamal's use of the vernacular centers much more on journalistic observation (the moral badman) as he finds new ways to express the economic and political disenfranchisement that characterize black life, especially for the imprisoned. In his texts, Abu-Jamal uses anecdotes to discuss the trajectory of police brutality and the tremendous violence and torture endured by men on death row as evidence of the ongoing crisis of the prison-industrial complex. Additionally, he situates himself within a history of black leadership by turning to historical black (male) leaders to inspire new members for the work ahead.

Contested Terrains: "Cop Killing," Police Brutality, and Black Activism

In many ways, the state constrains dissent, shaping citizens' actions by describing reasonable and unreasonable behavior, sanctioning punishment or retribution, and creating heroes and villains. Within what Walter Fisher has called the "narrative paradigm," stories compete for meaning on the basis of strong reasons (argumentation and evidence), believable stories, characterization of the players, and moral messages.[21] James Boyd White argues that the law can be understood as a series of constitutive rhetorical resources, including "rules, statutes, and judicial opinions, of course, but much more as well: maxims, general understandings, conventional wisdom, and all the other resources, technical and nontechnical, that a lawyer might use in defining his or her position and urging another to accept it."[22] It is precisely because the state controls the narrative resources available to the accused that the vernacular becomes an important resource for the oppressed: they must find other ways to mobilize narratives of their own defense outside of the established legal order, where racism, sexism, and classism reign.

Because of this emphasis on the familiar, the legal narratives often follow predictable patterns, particularly in regard to race, gender, class, and other identity markers as courtroom participants "reflect and refashion cultural artifacts (caste and color) and social norms (character and community)."[23] As lawyers frame their narratives, the media provides another layer of meaning by interpreting these narratives through a lens that often favors the prosecution, rife with unfavorable tropes of racial difference. The narrative strategies of the defense and the prosecution in death penalty cases are particularly problematic in deploying these sensationalized tropes of difference. Two characteristics that death penalty lawyers face when presenting their cases have bearing on this analysis. First, defense lawyers of inmates on death row face increasing hostility because they are representing (mostly) men (of color) who have been charged with violent crime.[24]

Second, because death penalty conviction rates are extremely high, proactive lawyers use narratives to preserve their clients' stories of poverty, abuse, and legal neglect. Austin Sarat writes that the importance of narratives increase as their death becomes immanent within the crucible of mass incarceration. He adds, "As Paul Kaplan has eloquently explained, in the death penalty narratives of the courtroom, a prosecutor's timeline generally begins and ends with the moments just before the crime while the defense's narrative 'often began three generations ago in a sharecropper's cabin.'"[25] Where defense lawyers are often historians of the downtrodden and often critique the legal system to spur social change, the prosecution's stories of those "put away" gain cultural currency in a culture that relies on tropes of security or "law and order."

Because the law is a competitive sport, defense prosecution narratives inevitably vie for attention, especially when dominant metaphors like "security," "terrorism," and "law and order" characterize the discourse. If politicians, police officers, and the media create an environment of insecurity, they must also show how they provide security through the capture, detention, and prosecution of social threats. Sadly, defense lawyers get very few opportunities to counter embedded racial narratives even if they can acknowledge the role of racial stereotypes in narratives of deviance.[26] As Kaplan explains, the prosecution's death penalty narrative "invoke[s] and support[s] dominant and repressive ideologies about what it means to be a victim and a killer," making the introduction of new narratives very difficult, particularly when race is factor.[27]

The pervasiveness of what Anthony Alfieri and others have labeled "race-talk" normalizes racialized, classed, and gendered stereotypes in the legal community, making it difficult to challenge these stories. Alfieri writes that narrative constraints make it extremely difficult to undermine narratives of the defiant black male and that of the deviant black male because they are so normalized in legal communication.[28] This process creates "unreflective deliberative judgment" as legal actors, both knowingly and unwittingly, calcify racist assumptions about black masculinity even as members of the legal community assert the law's colorblindness. Racial narratives that depict black defiance or deviance satisfy the public's hunger for celebrity, and the state's need to enact violence on citizens to keep them distracted and docile, and justify the rhetoric of "law and order," because publics have been conditioned through centuries of stereotypes to fear black men. In these ubiquitous narratives, police officers are the hardworking heroes, black people (usually men) are the pathologically deviant criminals, the judge is the benevolent, competent, unbiased master of ceremonies, and the torture that takes place in the courtroom and in the prison is seemingly justified because the accused is already understood as a criminal. Within this matrix of competing narratives, the stories of the deviant black "cop killer" and that of police brutality are battling for the public's fidelity, particularly within the courts.

The myth of the good cop also contributes to antiblack male sentiment within court culture. Robin K. Magee notes that despite prolific reports of "police brutality and extreme misconduct, the Supreme Court has adopted and inscribed into Fourth Amendment jurisprudence a 'good cop paradigm.' The paradigm has given birth to a good cop myth which falsely portrays officers as necessarily law-abiding and chiefly motivated by law enforcement interests."[29] Because of the good cop paradigm, illegal or illegitimate police motives are converted into legitimate ones, racism of police officers is overlooked, jurors are instructed that all police actions are constitutional and legitimate, and disrespect of black communities is perpetuated by the overwhelming pro-police, antiblack sentiment in court.[30]

The role of narrative in the media coverage of the accused and the police officer in the trial is absolutely central in understanding how this script of the "good cop" is played out time and time again in the case of Mumia Abu-Jamal.[31] One way that the state signifies a person is a threat to the community is to brand them a cop killer. Abu-Jamal was branded a cop killer "despite the fact that all eyewitnesses described the assailant as looking radically different from the accused (the killer was uniformly described as being short, over 200 pounds and wearing an Afro-style hairstyle; Mumia is slender, over six feet tall, weighs 170 pounds and wears his hair in dreadlocks)."[32] Additionally, three witnesses wrote in their statements the night of the shooting that the shooter fled the scene before Abu-Jamal approached Officer Faulkner.[33] Nonetheless, both scholarly sources and news accounts of Mumia Abu-Jamal usually refer to him to as a "convicted cop killer."[34] By deploying "race-talk" that characterizes Abu-Jamal as a deviant black male "cop killer," media outlets, politicians, judges, and lawyers constrain the narratives available to Abu-Jamal in his defense while glorifying the police, even in a force as corrupt as the one in Philadelphia.

Given Abu-Jamal's lifelong career as a journalist, his rhetorical strategies function to bolster his credentials as a black intellectual, "capable of translating the disenfranchised experience of subjugation as an oppositional, ideologically recognizable, vernacularized discourse."[35] These writings demystify the legal system, while marshaling character witnesses, historical narratives, and black heroes, which help him demonstrate the continuity of legal repression against black Americans. Abu-Jamal's Black Power vernacular is deployed to provide analysis of the long-term, systemic violence of the legal system, to expose the horrific conditions of prison, and to mobilize those outside of prison for social change as part of the anti–death penalty movement, as activists for black consciousness-raising, and as new Black Power agitators.

Character Witnesses: Testimony for the Convicted

Despite being branded a cop killer, several spaces emerge in Abu-Jamal's writings to contest this rendering. The first space exists in the introductory comments to each text, which underscore Abu-Jamal's innocence, and they elevate him as a leader for his commitment to black liberation efforts. Like slave narratives that came before, Abu-Jamal's texts are prefaced by comments from well-respected and well-known members of the black intelligentsia, which demonstrate how Abu-Jamal functions as an interlocutor for the history of state violence against black communities. The comments teach the reader oppositional strategies to push back against the race-talk calcified in the cop killer trope.

Black novelist John Edgar Wideman is the first to comment on the importance of Abu-Jamal as a black social critic in the Introduction to *Live From Death Row*.[36] Wideman argues that Abu-Jamal is an important interlocutor for black America because he "forces us to confront the burden of our history."[37] Wideman reminds the reader of the continuity of racial oppression, necessitating Abu-Jamal as a black leader. This is apropos since *Live From Death Row* is composed of several essays on black (male) leaders that remind us of the continuity between slavery and police brutality while also implicitly suggesting the need for new black leaders to navigate state contemporary violence.

To this end, Wideman insists that the reader see Abu-Jamal as part of the lineage of black men uncovering America's racial history and as a leader following in the footsteps of men like Malcolm X and Huey Newton who are celebrated in Abu-Jamal's essays. Wideman notes the outlaw nature of Abu-Jamal's writing, describing his vernacular voice as "dangerous and subversive" to draw the reader into the contested terrain of his writing.[38] Instead of rein-scribing the dichotomous black/white distinction or singling out his own narrative as independent from a larger cultural narrative, Wideman argues that Abu-Jamal anticipates liberation for all people.[39] Here Wideman uses his own vernacular to mythologize Abu-Jamal's as a racial leader and prophet whose very life defies white supremacy:

> The first truth that Mumia tells us is that he ain't dead yet. And although his voice is vital and strong, he assures us it ain't because nobody ain't trying to kill him and shut him up. In fact, just the opposite is true. The power of his voice is rooted in his defiance of those determined to silence him. Magically, Mumia's words are clarified and purified by the toxic strata of resistance through which they must penetrate to reach us. Like the blues. Like jazz.[40]

Wideman's comparison of Abu-Jamal's rhetorical voice to the blues and jazz enhances his ability to praise Abu-Jamal as a subversive and resilient race leader. In doing so, he positions Abu-Jamal within an oral tradition of literary resistance (much like Brown and, as we shall see later, Shakur) that has always persisted under a system of brutality and silencing; he is a modern-day slave whose work is as much a part of black folk life as the blues and jazz. The emphasis on vernacular orality, on voice, is one of the characteristics of the writings in this study that contributes to the elevation of these black leaders as "living martyrs," which I will explore in the final pages of this text.

Likewise, Wideman explicitly compares Abu-Jamal's book to slave narratives, which helps Abu-Jamal regenerate Black Power by connecting slavery and imprisonment as intrinsic to black experience in America. He writes, "The best slave narratives and prison narratives have always asked profound questions, implicitly and explicitly, about the meaning of life . . . Because he tells the truth, Mumia Abu-Jamal's voice can help us tear down walls—prison walls, the walls we hide behind to deny and refuse the burden of our history."[41] By using the collective pronouns "we" and "our," Wideman is able to include the reader in the narrative process and ascribe culpability to the reader for their active participation in either the maintenance of prison or in the struggle for racial parity. This strategy helps to remake the subjectivity of the reader, using historical continuity to build an oppositional consciousness that will help tear down the walls of prison. Here, prisons are the new plantations and Abu-Jamal is the new abolitionist that must be located both in a history of black intellectual resistance and also at the forefront of this new phase of struggle as a truth-teller and leader.

For Abu-Jamal's second book, *Death Blossoms*, professor Cornel West and Julia Wright, the spokeswoman for the Support Committee for Political Prisoners in the United States (in France) and the daughter of novelist Richard Wright, frame Abu-Jamal as a courageous public intellectual. Like Wideman, West proclaims Abu-Jamal a new black prophet, capable of exposing interlocking systems of inequality in the United States.[42] West describes the rich-poor gap that capitalism has created, the white supremacy that maintains "geographical segregation," and patriarchy and homophobia, which are "killing our minds, bodies, and souls in the name of the American Dream."[43] West cites Abu-Jamal's courage and explains that as a prophet, Abu-Jamal "reminds us of things most fellow citizens would rather deny, ignore, or evade. And, like the most powerful critics of our society—from Herman Melville, Theodore Dreiser, and Nathaniel West to Ann Petty, Richard Wright, Toni Morrison, and Eugene O'Neill—he forces us to grapple with the most fundamental question facing this country: what does it profit a nation to conquer the whole world and lose its soul?"[44] In placing Abu-Jamal in the intellectual company of some of the most profound social critics in modern American history, West demonstrates Abu-Jamal's mobility as an interlocutor and marks him as an icon. Vernacular intellectuals, like Abu-Jamal, who find popularity outside of traditional politics are "[i]deologically mobile" moving "back and forth between the popular and political realms. These icons can be, simultaneously, cultural producers or political activists, speaking metonymically for themselves or their constituency—that body of subjects deliberately excluded from formal political debate."[45] West points to the significance of Abu-Jamal's political voice, emanating as it does from death row from jail, noting: "After over fifteen years of nightmarish jail conditions, Mumia Abu-Jamal's soul is not only intact but still flourishing—just as the nation's soul withers. Will we ever listen to and learn from our bloodstained prophets?"[46] West himself is often described as a prophet so his move to catapult Abu-Jamal into the upper reaches of the black intelligentsia marks him as a black prophet, leader, and martyr, for his sacrifices on behalf of black people.[47]

Following West's unrestrained praise, Julia Wright's tribute provides a meditation on the relationship between silence and voice on death row as she chronicles Abu-Jamal's 1995 lawsuit against his prison (SCI Greene) and the Pennsylvania Department of Corrections for violating his human rights. She describes the "high-tech noiselessness" as Abu-Jamal entered the courtroom during this trial and remembers that the "[r]ipples of silence froze in his shackled footsteps. As if on 'a move waves could be stilled, this was a silence of total paradox: the volatile, scarcely hidden presence of loaded police weapons targeting the reined-in love of members of the family in the courtroom—men, women and children who have been unable to touch him for fourteen years."[48] Wright's decision to focus on Abu-Jamal's embodiment in the courtroom functions as synecdoche of death row's sensory deprivation and her comments fill the deafening silence with meaning that builds empathy for him. Likewise, connecting Abu-Jamal to his family resituates him as a community member through the reassertion of his roles as father, grandfather, husband, brother, son, and friend. This rhetorical move counters the race-talk branding him as a "cold-hearted cop killer" and instead humanizes him as a beloved community member.

Importantly, Wright describes how Abu-Jamal's writing forms the basis of his resistance to the silence and constant surveillance that characterize his life as a political prisoner on death row. She writes, "Writing behind locked doors gives durable sound to prison silence, spiritual distance from a madding crowd of politicians and elected judges whose careers are built on the blood of others, creative dimension to the sound and fury of a world lost. In writing, there is a renewed bonding: unshackled hands, grasping notebook, fingers touching pencil, pencil touching paper, paper touched by readers who are in turn touched by meaning."[49] She asks the reader to imagine the intimacy of writing prison texts as well as the acts of care and social love that inform their production. Like Wideman and West, Julia Wright sees Abu-Jamal's voice and the stories he tells as absolutely central to his resistance and to his role as a social critic and leader of this new phase of black liberation struggle.

In his third book, *All Things Censored*, Mumia Abu-Jamal prefaces his essays with a statement equating political resistance with profound love. He writes, "These essays deal with the folk resisting the lure of power, and those struggling to survive against monstrous odds. In that sense, this is their book, for their struggles, their lives are at the core of it." He adds, "By reading (or hearing) these very words, you are participating in a conspiracy of resistance. I welcome you. For the spirit of resistance is, in essence, the spirit of love."[50] Thus, readers of his essays are described as active participants in the conspiracy of resistance, as coconspirators, framing reading itself as a radical, political act. As we shall see in the next chapter, this language of conspiracy also pervades Assata Shakur's poems and works to turn the reader into a coconspirator of the imprisoned revolutionary, rather than an ally of the state, demonstrating the utility of understanding the reading of imprisoned texts as oppositional political strategy.

Poet and novelist Alice Walker provides the foreword to *All Things Censored* and explains that she will no longer write about his innocence, how he was framed or the necessity of a new trial because as she states, "the evidence speaks for itself."[51] Like West, Walker highlights Abu-Jamal as a generational leader imprisoned for exposing state corruption. Because he is on death row, she says, "they think of him as something conquered, a magnificent wild animal they have succeeded in capturing. They feel powerful in a way they could not feel if he were free."[52] Walker's comments create solidarity among black readers as she points to his place in the pantheon of black liberation heroes. Losing Abu-Jamal's voice "would be like losing a color of the rainbow," she says, so essential is his perspective.[53]

Walker also comments on Abu-Jamal's international appeal as a liberation hero, likening black America to the Mexican Zapatistas. She writes, "We are like the Zapatistas of Southern Mexico in many ways: vastly outnumbered, many of us poor, humiliated on a daily basis by those in power, feeling ourselves unwanted, unseen, and un-named. Mumia helps us know how deeply and devoutly we are wanted; how sharply and lovingly we are seen; how honorable is our much maligned name."[54] In highlighting Abu-Jamal's dedication to black pride, Walker points to similarities and compares his Black Power leadership to the Zapatistas who led the Chiapas rebellion in 1994 on behalf of the Indian people of the state, drawing important comparisons between state repression and resistance across the hemisphere. Like the Black Power movement, Tom Hayden reminds us that the Zapatistas are also frequently pronounced dead as a movement, though they resurface every few years to protest Mexican policies through civil resistance.[55]

While literary figures like Wideman, West, Wright, and Walker link Abu-Jamal to a history of black literary leadership and position him as a strong black leader in this new generation of liberation activism, Abu-Jamal's editor Noelle Hanrahan, prison activist and member of Prison Radio, begins the introduction to *All Things Censored* by talking about the limitations of his speech by the prison and the state. She writes, "For over eighteen years Mumia has not only been fighting to stay alive; he has been waging a constant battle for the freedom to write and speak," "despite the unmitigated and unceasing torture" of his confinement.[56] She is unrelenting about exposing the "power of writing" in prisons and sketches a very vivid picture of the surveillance regime and torture to which Abu-Jamal is constantly subjected. She describes the conditions within the prison and asks the reader to actively "imagine your hands callused, cramped, and swollen from writing each day for hours with the cartridge of a ballpoint pen—legal briefs, letters, essays, your master's thesis—and writing everything twice because the prison might 'lose' the copies you send out." She continues, "Imagine your possessions: your books, your notes, your intellectual life, having to fit into a five-inch-deep, fourteen-inch wide box, because that is all you are allowed."[57] In describing the constriction of Abu-Jamal's personal and intellectual space, Hanrahan suggests that prison life creates an endless cycle of brutality, which stifles the intellectual work and voice of someone like Abu-Jamal, committed to public service.

Thus, Hanrahan illustrates how prison dehumanizes prisoners. She writes, "Imagine before and after your weekly two-hour, completely noncontact visit having to submit to a demeaning psychosexual full-body cavity search: 'Strip. Open your mouth. Stick out your tongue. Lift your balls. Pull back your foreskin. Turn around. Spread your cheeks.'"[58] Hanrahan speaks to the specifics of prison degradation, demonstrating how prison life debases people and turns them into animals through psycho-sexual surveillance and assault "designed to break down the human connections between the prisoners, their families, and the outside world."[59] The routinization of this regime in prison is aimed at reducing the prisoner to an asocial, ahistorical object. For Abu-Jamal, this means that the carceral regime is constantly trying to undermine his work as a social critic and imprisoned intellectual; it is turning him from a subject into an object. Nonetheless, Hanrahan's description positions Abu-Jamal as a kind of martyr, exiled to a life of solitude and physical torture. In building Abu-Jamal's credibility as a martyr, Hanrahan strengthens his role as an interlocutor for the voiceless by noting that "Greene County was once a busy stop on the Underground Railroad, and today bears witness to pilgrimages to visit Mumia Abu-Jamal."[60] The reader is encouraged to see the prison system as the newest plantation economy and as a site for the regeneration of Black Power through neo-slave liberators like Abu-Jamal.

By describing the physicality of prison life, Hanrahan moves the reader away from some of the mythic language employed by the black intellectuals and toward a more practical conversation about the severe brutality of death row. For the reader who has never encountered prisons or prison literature, this exercise has the transformative power to elicit empathy for Abu-Jamal as a leader of the disappeared. Hanrahan argues that Abu-Jamal "transcends prison" because of his vernacular rhetorical prowess, writing that he has the "ability to give voice to the dispossessed among us. The topics of his evocative radio essays reach far beyond his prison walls to illustrate the perspectives and the intrinsic human worth of those who exist outside the privileged upper-class world reflected in the media."[61] Because he is able to transcend prison as a speaker and writer, the potential for recruiting new allies in the regeneration of Black Power is limitless, though Abu-Jamal is still depicted as a threat because he has "dared to survive" and has "continued his uncompromising reporting," which "threaten[s] the smooth and orderly functioning of both state-sanctioned murder and modern slavery."[62] Here, Abu-Jamal is a victim, though survivor, of state-sanctioned violence, which undermines his image as a "cop killer" given his role as a journalist, a dangerous truth-teller. Hanrahan highlights how his observations provide a unique position from which to comment on the atrocities of American prison life as a black man revolutionary.

Listening, like reading, is an active process and Hanrahan prepares the reader to become a coconspirator in spreading the writings of Abu-Jamal, even as the government continually attempts to "disappear" him "from the nation's consciousness" because he is one prisoner who dares to challenge "the culture of incarceration" in the United States.[63] She reminds the reader of the sacrifices necessary to get Abu-Jamal's commentaries out of prison, highlighting the threat that Abu-Jamal poses to the state while underscoring the plausibility of his claims as a political prisoner. Again, Hanrahan is careful to emphasize his role as a martyr, disappeared from the nation. Like earlier Black Power advocates who were "disappeared" through COINTELPRO, Abu-Jamal has inspired black readers from death row and solitary confinement.

The prefatory comments by John Edgar Wideman, Cornel West, Julia Wright, Alice Walker, and Noelle Hanrahan offer important authorizing discourses that help draw readers into the movement to save Abu-Jamal's life and to mobilize against capital punishment. Their comments undermine the "cop killer" narrative and create space for readers to empathize with Abu-Jamal because of the prison conditions under which he lives. These writers also have a huge readership in the United States and abroad that provide entrée into the larger world of black *belles lettres* for Abu-Jamal, the "voice of the voiceless." Their comments vouch for his authority to analyze capital punishment, police brutality, and prison politics as a journalist and Black Power leader. Although the public may not directly participate in prison culture, they *can* participate in the exoneration of political prisoners. This is the transformative potential of prison memoirs like those of Mumia Abu-Jamal; prison memoirs tell the untold stories of those silenced by the state.

Targeting Radical Black Organizations

Certainly the authorizing discourses preceding Abu-Jamal's essays in each book function as vernacular counternarratives hailing Abu-Jamal as a Black Power prison leader for a new generation of activists and oppositional activist readers. But Abu-Jamal's own writings function as a second space for the creation of counternarratives that challenge the cop killer trope by challenging *who* can speak about crime and punishment. Describing his career as a journalist and his early affiliation with the Black Panther Party and his later association with the MOVE organization, Abu-Jamal's comments provide context for his emergence as an oppositional reporter. For instance, he writes about the police brutality that he and his friends experienced as they agitated for a name change at his high school prior to his entrance into the BPP: "Well, my political life formally began with the Black Panther Party. I've been in a sense thankful to the Philadelphia police department for kicking and beating me into the Black Panther Party."[64] Abu-Jamal also talks about his time in the Ministry of Information before becoming a journalist after the BPP split. In explaining his calling to his craft, he writes that revolutionary journalism is a consciousness-raising tool:

> When one reads the daily press or listens to what is broadcast on the regular "white" radio stations and TV stations, you will perceive a picture, a slanted picture, of Black life that reflects it in the most improper terms. When media journalism and propaganda is used to reflect a positive side of people, the side that resists oppression, the side of people's inherent worth, no matter what their property or economy value, then that in itself is revolutionary, because this system tends to denigrate people who are poor. And most of the people on planet earth are poor.[65]

Abu-Jamal highlights the racial and class-consciousness that motivates his style of reporting, though gender is conspicuously absent. He writes, nevertheless, from the standpoint of a revolutionary, which influences his views about oppression in black communities. As a black (male) reporter in Philadelphia, Abu-Jamal provided a counternarrative that exposed how white stereotypes and fears frame white news to the detriment of poor people. Providing this oppositional standpoint complicates the narratives of "law and order" as they privilege dominant standpoints on race and "crime." Abu-Jamal's journalistic integrity is informed by a larger political context that acknowledges corruption and racism within the political and legal spheres. As a well-respected journalist committed to uncovering and reporting police brutality in Philadelphia, it is no wonder that Abu-Jamal became a target of the Civil Defense squads, COINTELPRO, and Frank Rizzo as he broadcasted pieces critical of the police for oppressing poor communities of color.[66]

Although Abu-Jamal was clearly targeted because of his affiliation with the BPP as a youth, he was also monitored and harassed because he was affiliated with John Africa's cooperative social group MOVE. The police harassment and attempts at eradicating the communal, progressive MOVE organization began as early as 1974, but climaxed in 1978, when Rizzo confronted MOVE at their home in the Powelton Village section of west Philadelphia.[67] Terry Bisson describes the 1978 MOVE siege this way: "On the morning of August 8, the ex-cop/mayor applied the municipal tool he liked best: The nightstick. Naked, brute force. Hundreds of flak-jacketed riot police moved in. Bulldozers knocked down the fences and splintered MOVE's outdoor platform [which they had built as a forum to negotiate with police so that the public could view the police brutality]. Cranes knocked out the windows of the house."[68] By the time that the MOVE members had surrendered after being flushed from the basement by the high-pressured water from firemen's hoses, police officer James Ramp was dead and nine of the MOVE members were convicted in the killing and are still political prisoners. They were convicted even though the crime scene was totally destroyed by police bulldozers, no guns were found, and the judge said that he "hadn't the faintest idea" about who fired the fatal shots.[69] The 1978 siege became political justification for a second massive MOVE siege in 1985.

The second MOVE siege lasted ten months and dominated Philadelphia's attention in 1985 because it catapulted police brutality back into public conversations about race. On May 31, police attempted to serve MOVE members warrants on charges including "terroristic threats, harassment, criminal conspiracy, possession of explosives or incendiary devices and disorderly conduct."[70] The police "dropped a bomb device from a helicopter onto the roof" of the homes, though "[p]olice claim[ed] the bomb was not incendiary and the fire was started from flammable liquids inside the MOVE home."[71] Emory law professor and former communications secretary for the Black Panther Party Kathleen Neal Cleaver describes the "brutal assault":

> The ensuing explosion ignited gasoline stored in a drum on the roof and the flames spread rapidly to the adjacent row houses. Eventually, as firemen stood in abeyance, two streets were engulfed in flames. The conflagration burned out of control, finally killing eleven MOVE members—five of whom were children—and destroying sixty-one homes, as well as damaging over a hundred others and leaving two hundred and fifty people homeless.[72]

Only two members of MOVE lived through the second siege: Ramona Africa (age thirty) and Birdie Africa (age thirteen). The rest were either shot trying to escape or forced back into the burning building where they died in the flames. Fifty-three row homes were destroyed, displacing more than 250 people, and costing the city over $7 million. The culmination of the yearlong siege of the MOVE house by police divided Philadelphia, which erupted in a storm of protest.

By championing MOVE, Abu-Jamal aligned himself with their role as Philadelphia's new Black Power organization. In *All Things Censored*, Abu-Jamal writes about the May 13 bombing, saying, "Now cops patrol neighborhoods across America, armed like storm troopers, with a barely disguised urge to destroy the very area they are sworn to 'serve and protect'. . . . Are they an aid to the people, or a foreign army of occupation?"[73] Following his critique of the police is a command to the reader: "Organize this very day to resist it [police brutality], to oppose it, to go beyond it. Demand that all imprisoned MOVE members be released and all political prisoners be freed."[74] Abu-Jamal builds the exigency for new Black Power agitation because his description of the police as a standing army demonstrates the continued utility of the colonial analogy to mobilize new activists.

Abu-Jamal's coverage of MOVE highlights how new Black Power organizations were contending with state repression even though the values of a group like MOVE were so different from the Black Panther Party, SNCC, or CORE. MOVE's "values were a pastiche of themes exalted during the 1960s social revolution, such as nonviolence, communal living, racial harmony, self-defense, protection of the environment, physical fitness, and nutritional fads."[75] The MOVE collective first named themselves the Christian Movement for Life, which was shortened to the Movement, and later, MOVE. MOVE was composed of men and women from working- and middle-class backgrounds, from the defunct Philadelphia chapter of the Black Panther Party, from local law schools, and from the civil service. Their teachings were based upon the philosophy of a man they named John Africa.[76] MOVE members believed in exercise, eating raw foods, and refusing electricity and running water; they kept their children out of schools, refused to kill any living creatures, and protested vigorously against social injustices.[77] The organization's values and practices were highly criticized, but MOVE was also controversial because its existence provoked such intense police brutality. The 1978 and 1985 MOVE sieges demonstrate the kind of radical black activism in Philadelphia after the COINTELPRO schemes of the 1970s that had all but eradicated black social action in Philadelphia.[78]

Abu-Jamal recalls that his first impressions of MOVE were negative, since his perspective was influenced by the semi-socialist, paramilitary Black Panther Party. Yet, his conversion testimony serves to underscore MOVE's importance as a new Black Power organization because of their resistance to police brutality. Despite his early dismissal of MOVE, he writes, "in the same way that the Philadelphia Police Department beat me into the BPP, the Philadelphia Police Department's repression of MOVE attracted me to MOVE. Because, even though the repression was extraordinarily severe, brutal, and devastating,

MOVE continued to rebel and resist."[79] Abu-Jamal's conversion testimony highlights how the intensity of MOVE's police repression justified their existence and resistance and gave them credibility as social justice activists.

Abu-Jamal's reflections about the role of police brutality in activating a revolutionary consciousness are important interventions into community history. In an interview with Abu-Jamal, journalist Heike Kleffner asks, "Can you say how it happened that you stood trial for allegedly having killed a cop? Do you feel that the Philadelphia police set you up on the night when you got shot and this cop got killed? I remember reading that the then mayor, Frank Rizzo, once said about you that your 'breed of journalism' needed to be stopped by any means."[80] Abu-Jamal answers by saying, "I think it is undeniable that elements of a set-up existed and that my background as a Panther and as what some people called a 'MOVE journalist' or a MOVE supporter were elements in that." He explains that the Philadelphia Police Department knew who he was because he worked at the radio station next door, adding that his investigative reporting "put me down as a target to be neutralized. One must look back at the coverage of MOVE around the time of the police siege of their house in 1978 to see how demonised, how inhumane, how animalistic the portrayal of MOVE was. When interviews were done with them that showed that they were good, decent and committed people, it challenged the public perception of who they were."[81] Abu-Jamal is quick to analyze the racialist and classist aspects of police portrayals of the black commune, which the state demonized as primitive. Abu-Jamal's commitment to the MOVE supporters illustrates his fidelity to those decent and committed black people opposing police brutality. But this framework also provided the rationale for the police to target Abu-Jamal. Abu-Jamal's coverage of the MOVE siege confirmed what he saw as a Black Panther: that the Philadelphia police were out to remove all signs of black activism from the city. His defiant journalism made him into a hero in the black communities of Philadelphia's West End.

Consequently, the prosecution, Judge Sabo, and the news media mobilized imagery of black deviance in an effort to reduce Mumia Abu-Jamal to the negative media stereotypes of the BPP, an organization that he had not been a part of since his teenage years. Abu-Jamal was not allowed to defend himself, and, when he insisted, he was barred from his own trial. Prosecution witnesses (even those who recanted or changed their stories) were never questioned. Consequently, Abu-Jamal's writings work to oppose the state's deployment of racialized depictions of the deviant black man.[82] In order to transcend the label of cop killer, he offers a competing image of himself, as a credible black journalist and intellectual, and his discourse works to counter the stereotypes of black masculinity that pervade the American justice system. These strategies help to regenerate Black Power activism because they connect both Abu-Jamal and the MOVE organization to a history of black resistance to police brutality, highlighting the need for new activism.

Delegitimizing Incarceration

As Abu-Jamal describes the repression of MOVE, his vernacular pairs his journalistic voice with street talk in a series of critiques that undermine the legitimacy of both the courts and the media to demonstrate how racism and classism influence the adjudication of legal justice. At the center is Abu-Jamal's argument that the death penalty is a political tool of the state designed to decimate poor, black populations and to help elect politicians. Abu-Jamal's eyewitness accounts of death row make him a credible source in a way that is far different from Rap Brown, whose actions and writings were blamed for the repression that Abu-Jamal has been chronicling since the 1970s.

In the preface to *Live From Death Row*, Abu-Jamal argues that civil rights are dependent upon class access, which explicitly builds his moral ethos as a Black Power leader. He writes, "Perhaps we can shrug off and shed some of the dangerous myths laid on our minds like a second skin—such as the 'right' to a fair and impartial jury of our peers; the 'right' to represent oneself; the 'right' to a fair trial, even. They're *not* rights—they're privileges of the powerful and rich."[83] Abu-Jamal's class critique of the notion of "rights" highlights the gross inequalities in his case by generalizing them as the norm within the criminal justice system so as to press the exigency created by a corrupted judicial process. However, his comments also illustrate his commitment to true "justice," which helps illustrate his dedication to struggle thus building his credibility as a leader.

In *Death Blossoms*, Abu-Jamal also writes about disparate sentencing, noting that many convicts "who, by virtue of their wealth and their ability to retain a good private lawyer, are not convicted at all. The criminal court system calls itself a justice system, but it measures privilege, wealth, power social status, and—last but not least—race to determine who goes to death row."[84] By condemning the criminal sentencing, especially to death, as a purely political instrument, Abu-Jamal sets up arguments about the racial bias implicit in the "justice" system. Statements like the one above place Abu-Jamal in the role of both journalist and witness to the brutality inherent in a system that favors the wealthy and the white, and they create a new space for Black Power agitation: the death penalty. This strategy helps to raise Abu-Jamal up as both a leader and celebrity of the movement against the death penalty, which strengthens his ability to spur change.

Abu-Jamal's oppositional reporting from death row helps to galvanize support for the movement against police brutality and the death penalty. To build this support, Abu-Jamal draws upon collective memories of his contemporaries as a way to frame current clashes with the state; this rhetorical strategy helps to contextualize and reassert the necessity for common struggle around the issues of capital punishment, highlighting the importance of dignity to this process. At the beginning of *Live From Death Row*, he writes, "Don't tell me about the valley of death. I live there. In south-central Pennsylvania's Huntington County a one-hundred-year-old prison stands, its Gothic towers projecting an air of foreboding, evoking a gloomy mood of the Dark Ages."[85] In just the first three sentences, Abu-Jamal establishes himself as a witness to America's death row, where he "and some seventy-eight other men spend about twenty-two hours a day in six-by-ten-foot cells. The additional two hours a day may be spent outdoors, in a chain-link-fenced box, ringed by concertina razor wire, under the gaze of gun turrets."[86] His language evokes the austerity and the surveillance inherent in living in a maximum-security penitentiary, yet his tone is measured even as he chronicles the degradation of the state. He comments:

> Mix in solitary confinement, around-the-clock lock-in, no-contact visits, no prison jobs, no educational programs by which to grow, psychiatric "treatment" facilities designed only to drug you into a coma; ladle in hostile, overtly racist prison guards and staff; add the weight of the falling away of family ties, and you have all the fixings for a stressful psychic stew designed to deteriorate, to erode one's humanity—designed, that is, by the state, with full knowledge of its effects.[87]

Abu-Jamal's description highlights the irony of calling such programs "corrections" since in prison, nothing is being corrected; the days are filled with drugs, solitary confinement, violence, and separation.

Abu-Jamal continues by suggesting that imprisonment is an extension of slavery, a familiar trope in the Black Power vernacular, but he does so in a tone that is "articulate and confident in its cadences."[88] He writes, "I remember a front page of the *Black Panther* newspaper, bearing the quote, 'A black man has no rights that a white man is bound to respect,' attributed to Roger Taney, of the infamous *Dred Scott* case, where America's highest court held that neither Africans nor their descendants are entitled to the rights of the Constitution. Deep, huh? It's true."[89] Here, Abu-Jamal mobilizes his previous affiliations to connect him to a recent history of Black Power and to the longer history of black resistance to servitude for an audience that might not make a similar connection. The invocation of *Dred Scott* functions as a rhetorical call to arms about the state of black rights as Abu-Jamal connects himself to a long line of black men suffering at the hands of the state, be they lynching victims or part of peonage systems.

As a man on death row, however, Abu-Jamal is also writing to save his own life, and must comment on his own legal position. He opines, "Perhaps I'm naïve, maybe stupid—but I thought the law would be followed in my case, and the conviction reversed. . . . Even in the face of this relentless wave of antiblack state terror, *I thought my appeals would be successful.* I still harbored a belief in U.S. law, and the realization that my appeal had been denied was a shocker."[90] His comments here are directed at an audience that certainly believes in at least some of the tenets of American "justice" and by expressing his former faith in US law, he counters the stereotypes of his activities in the Black Panther Party. His language is that of a convert, someone not quite willing to believe something until he's seen it with his own eyes. His disappointment permeates these vivid criticisms demystifying the antiblack violence of the US legal system.

Thus, Abu-Jamal asserts the importance of independent media, who are the only journalists committed to reporting on the dispossessed. He warns, "For the powerless and the poor, they are a chimera that vanish once one reaches out to claim them as something real or substantial. Don't expect the media networks to tell you, for they can't, because of the incestuousness between the media and the government, and big business, which they both serve."[91] In tapping into the general distrust of government and the news media as the one to "tell it like it is," Abu-Jamal buttresses his credibility as an oppositional journalist and prison intellectual; he is the ultimate insider, exposing the collusion of two entities that can undermine democracy. In doing so, the "voice of the voiceless" must speak metonymically for himself and other inmates.[92]

Remembering Other Prisoners; Re-Masculinizing Black Power

Stories of police brutality or prison brutality form Abu-Jamal's fourth vernacular strategy. As Austin Sarat notes, "The narrative strategy necessary to write a history of the present in the face of the counternarratives produced in the legal process requires a bold willingness to speak the unspeakable, to tell the story that no one now wants to hear in the hope that future audiences will be more receptive."[93] As the prominent voice from death row, Abu-Jamal uses counternarratives to uncover systemic (in)justice and to position himself as a leader of the dispossessed while recentering the prison in the black liberation struggle.

Abu-Jamal focuses on the effects of the prison system on poor black people in these essays. Barbara Harlow writes that for the prisoner, this kind of writing, "serves to sustain his memory and sense of self and purpose." [94] The political prisoner writes to maintain his or her own sanity, to record and witness abuses by the state, and to sustain a community of resistance, inside and outside of the prison. As an act of solidarity, prison writing encourages oppositional thought within prisons and, in the case of the political prisoner, can recruit prisoners for reform efforts. [95] Angela Y. Davis adds, "The offense of the political prisoner is his political boldness, his persistent challenging— legally or extra-legally—of fundamental social wrongs fostered and reinforced by the state. He has opposed unjust laws and exploitative, racist social conditions in general, with the ultimate aim of transforming these laws and this society into an order harmonious with the material and spiritual needs and interests of the vast majority of its members." [96] Abu-Jamal's persistence as a prison journalist is crucial in recording the histories of those lost inside of the prison system.

Like many political prisoners, Mumia Abu-Jamal's fellow death row inmates haunt his texts as he documents prison deprivation, violence, and torture. For example, in one essay, Abu-Jamal describes the control that the State Correctional Institute at Huntington has over the lives of its inmates. They are routinely "denied family phone calls," "shackled for refusing to violate [their] beliefs," and are on the road to extinction, not to parole. [97] He comments, "As in any quasi-military organization, reality on the row is regimented by rule and regulation. As against any regime imposed on human personality, there is resistance, but far less than one would expect." [98] This is in part because of the twenty-two hours a day that they spend in their "cages," as Abu-Jamal frequently calls them and partly because of the lack of access to the outside world. [99]

In addition to charting the surveillance and intense confinement of death row, Abu-Jamal also describes the intense psychological violence of prison, particularly during visitation when the prisoner is violently strip-searched before being handcuffed and seated in front of the visitor. [100] As Mumia notes in *Live From Death Row*, "The ultimate effect of noncontact visits is to weaken, and ultimately to sever, family ties. Through this policy and practice, the state skillfully and intentionally denies those it condemns a fundamental element and expression of humanity—that of touch and physical contact." [101] This dehumanization of the death row inmates rouses empathy, concern, and certainly shock because Abu-Jamal discusses the effects that these brutal regimes of power exercise over the family. Abu-Jamal's description also serves to underscore the real victims of the justice system: the families of those incarcerated. Parents are separated from children, and families are stressed and strained by even traveling to see an incarcerated loved one. Here, Abu-Jamal connects the pain inflicted on the inmate's body to the black family, skillfully placing the black family at the center of prison resistance. This move reinforces the necessity of black families in new expressions of Black Power and, since the same forms of prison brutality touch millions of families, his potential converts are numerous.

In "Descent Into Hell," Mumia's descriptions of prison violence are even more disturbing, illustrating the need for mental health care, rather than incarceration. He describes a prisoner cuffed to a steel grille in the psychiatric unit whose tremors indicated massive psychotropic drug use. He says, "The spark? Powerful mind-bending drugs, prescribed to prisoners liberally, especially in light of a recent U.S. Supreme Court ruling that allows prison officials free rein to drug prisoners insensate."[102] Abu-Jamal's exposé of the overuse of drugs in prisons includes the story of fifty-seven-year-old Robert Barnes, who threatened suicide if placed in the strip cell they call "the hole." Though he had a history of psychiatric problems and had issued a suicide threat, the row was overcome during midday meal by the smell of burning hair. Robert Barnes had set himself on fire because he had been placed in the hole for twenty-four hours. When he was pronounced dead, over 70 percent of his body was burned.[103] These stories illustrate the psychological trauma of imprisonment that lead to intense desperation and, often, self-harm.

But numerous accounts of violence directed at death row inmates by guards wielding batons, dogs, water hoses, lashes, and mace follow Barnes's story. Abu-Jamal describes solitary confinement, dementia, and horrifying racism perpetuated by an entire brigade of white men with weapons, including the violence directed at a man named Timmy that erupted into a huge brawl in Huntington prison one night. He says, "Armed, armored squads went from cell to cell, pulling, cuffing, punching, bludgeoning, kicking, brutalizing naked prisoners. Men were handcuffed, seized, dragged outside. And thrown into cages, naked, beaten and bloodied."[104] Dozens of stories like this one serve to reinforce Abu-Jamal's outrage at the conditions of death row and yet, his story is told in a matter-of-fact vernacular, without the bravado in a memoir like Rap Brown's or the hostility that might characterize the narrative of a man waiting to be executed. Abu-Jamal's mild, professional tone provides a compelling strategy of identification for a death row inmate, working against the stereotypes of the deviant black male "cop killer."

The key to creating this strategy of identification is intimacy. Because Abu-Jamal is an eyewitness to both victims and perpetrators of prison violence, he has greater credibility as a competing narrative voice. Paul Gready remarks, "The foundation of autobiography's privilege as a source lies in the insider's intimacy with events portrayed, the manner in which experience is claimed as one's own."[105] In autobiographical prison memoirs, the writer is compelled to witness the daily degradation of prisons because prison writing is deemed authoritative and authentic through conceptions of truth that demand eyewitness accounts.[106] Therefore, as a prison journalist, Abu-Jamal builds the case against imprisonment through a multitude of stories that humanize inmates in the face of state violence.

Regenerating Black Male Leadership

In an effort to continue the lineage of black male leadership in the wake of Black Power's decline, Abu-Jamal includes a selection of essays that link the everyday lives of the men on death row to the men of the Black Power movement. While this vernacular strategy continues to demonstrate continuity in black (male) resistance to police brutality and statesanctioned violence, it also masculinizes black liberation history and normalizes the role of black men as the sole leaders of Black Power activism.

In both *Live From Death Row* and in *All Things Censored*, Abu-Jamal eulogizes Malcolm X and Huey Newton as Black Power heroes whose style of black leadership he appreciates and emulates. As discussed in chapter 2, black literary history is full of badman figures for communities to emulate in their resistance to the daily indignities and microaggressions of white supremacy. In the words of Charles P. Henry, "the badman who transgressed totally all of the moral and legal bounds of society, and the strong, self-contained hero who violated not the laws or the moral code but rather the stereotyped roles set aside for blacks."[107] The first kind of hero is what Henry calls a *bad badman* and the second is a *moral badman*. While Abu-Jamal himself adopts the persona of the moral madman, he glorifies the bad badmen, appropriating their popularity, celebrity, and credibility as men who protected their people and their neighborhoods. Malcolm X converted to Islam in prison and was a favorite among prisoners, particularly after his *Autobiography* was published, and as chairman of the Black Panther Party in Oakland, Huey Newton condemned police brutality and did prison time for the alleged slaying of a white police officer. Both heroes survived prison and both became advocates against white violence and police brutality while agitating for prison reform.

As I noted in chapter 2, Malcolm X is often cited as beginning the modern literary renaissance of the *bad badman* figure for his articulate analyses of white supremacy, particularly in his *Autobiography*, which became a template for Black Power agitation.[108] Abu-Jamal reflects on Malcolm's influence in a section entitled "Musings, Memories and Prophecies" that links Abu-Jamal's early association with the BPP to his contemporary work for social justice and highlights the importance of prison writings in the struggle for black liberation.

Here, like Rap Brown, Abu-Jamal positions himself as an heir to Malcolm X, the intellectual progenitor of Black Power. Abu-Jamal writes, "The Black Panther Party considered itself the Sons of Malcolm" and borrowed the notion of black self-defense from his teachings.[109] This would, of course, make Mumia a son of Malcolm as it suggests that the origins of Abu-Jamal's ideology of self-defense are with the BPP.[110] It also precludes the possibility of a *daughter* of Malcolm (even though Malcolm actually had four daughters and Elaine Brown was the chairman of the BPP from 1974 to 1977) emerging to take up the mantle of Black Power and underscores the absence of female heroes in Abu-Jamal's memories of black liberation struggle, potentially limiting the potential of Black Power regeneration. However, Abu-Jamal's embrace of Malcolm X clearly establishes his commitment to self-defense, writing that Malcolm "stood for—and died for—human rights of self-defense and a people's self-determination, not for 'civil rights,' which, as the Supreme Court has indeed shown, changes from day to day, case to case, administration to administration."[111] In pointing to Malcolm's more militant position on self-determination, Abu-Jamal eschews the legal challenges posed by the NAACP and the SCLC, pointing instead to the corruption of the legal system as a constant impediment to black liberation.

For Malcolm X, Mumia Abu-Jamal, and even Rap Brown, civil rights are created and given by white nationalists; black liberation is asserted and taken by the black masses, who recognize the hypocrisy of Christian Americans regarding black civil rights. Abu-Jamal writes that Malcolm X's "message of black self-defense and African-American self determination struck both Muslim and non-Muslim alike as logical and reasonable, given the decidedly un-Christian behavior displayed by America to the black, brown, red and yellow world."[112]

By embracing the black nationalism that Malcolm was known for, Abu-Jamal is using his historical presence as an advocate of self-defense to reinspire a new generation to the politics of Black Power by appealing to them with Malcolm's moral compass, grounded in black experience, and his exposure of Christian hypocrisy. Michael Eric Dyson argues that this kind of invocation transfers Malcolm's moral authority to contemporary readers:

"Malcolm's moral authority was fueled by a moral magnetism so great that it continues to attract people who were not yet born when he met his gruesome death."[113] As a model for black leadership, Malcolm provides a template for how to harness moral outrage and direct it at structural oppression, which is useful as Abu-Jamal marshals nostalgia for him to reimagine black solidarity mass incarceration.

Abu-Jamal continues nostalgia for earlier imprisoned Black Power leaders by emphasizing black love as he remembers Huey Newton's 1989 murder in Oakland. He writes, "I loved him. Huey—self-taught, brilliant, taciturn, strong-willed—molded the righteous indignation and rage of an oppressed people into a national, militant, revolutionary nationalist organization. His courageous spirit touched the downtrodden, black America's so-called *lumpenproletariat* classes and energized them into a balled fist of angry resistance, prompting FBI director J. Edgar Hoover's observation that the party posted 'the most serious threat' to American's internal security."[114] Interestingly, the positive characteristics that he associates with Newton all appear to be ideals that Abu-Jamal is attempting to live up to. Abu-Jamal even instructs us to use Newton's "memory to spark a renewal in revolutionary consciousness."[115] In this way, his eulogy serves a pedagogical function as Abu-Jamal details the affective connections that are sustained by radical collective action.

In eulogizing Malcolm X and Huey Newton, Abu-Jamal taps into collective memories about the "badness" of these formerly imprisoned leaders and their status as martyrs of Black Power. This nostalgia for black liberation heroes from the first phase of the Black Power movement allows Abu-Jamal to mobilize familiar stories, heroes, and histories that make new social movement organizing intelligible to a new generation of activists. In one essay, Abu-Jamal talks about how the hip-hop generation is often lamented as "lost" in the media, largely as a result of their creation of a new vernacular popular culture. But Abu-Jamal argues that they have been "locked out of the legal means of material survival" while being shown the excesses of capitalism as politicians "spit on their very existence." Abu-Jamal adds:

They are not the lost generation. They are the children of the L.A. rebellion, the children of the MOVE bombing, the children of the Black Panthers, and the grandchildren of Malcolm; far from lost, they are probably the most aware generation since Nat Turner's; they are not so much lost as they are mislaid, discarded by this increasibly racist system that undermines their inherent worth. They are *all* potential revolutionaries, with the historic power to transform our dull realities.

If they are lost, then *find* them.[116]

Abu-Jamal sees the hip-hop generation as a group that can be mobilized with the images of Black Power martyrs, and by invoking such figures, he tries to tap into the alienation and rage that characterize the contemporary attitudes of black youth. By seeing this generation as the heirs of Malcolm, the Panthers, and MOVE, he is recruiting them to regenerate Black Power around issues of incarceration, poverty, and police brutality in America's cities through nostalgia for its former leaders.

By marshaling nostalgia for the inspiration of black revolutionary martyrs like Malcolm X and Huey Newton, Abu-Jamal is able to seize the celebrity and heroism of these men as badmen. Abu-Jamal positions himself as the next heir to Black Power by appropriating their leadership styles and ideals. In the case of Malcolm X, Huey Newton, and even in his remarks later about Martin Luther King Jr., nostalgia is seemingly disguised as "a forward-looking restorative impulse" that seeks to reestablish the past in the future.[117]

Although it is often helpful to read the past into the present, activists must resist the urge to prefer "*things as they are perceived to have been*" and instead focus on what can be done now, in the present, with the resources available.[118] To simply indulge in nostalgia reifies the past in the present and acts as tacit consent for the status quo. Although Abu-Jamal's unique insider status provides credibility for his claims about prisons and prison activism, his nostalgia for the brand of black male leadership embodied by Malcolm X and Huey Newton risks both erasing the contributions of women of color in Black Power movement agitation and a kind of atrophy that merely remembers the past.

Still, in using nostalgia for the martyrs of Black Power's previous phase of agitation, Abu-Jamal has positioned himself as historian and social critic, as leader and as black prophet, though potentially at the expense of finding new strategies for social movement organizing and recruiting. This induces his readers to long for a leader like himself who more closely resembles the black (male) leaders of the past. Although Abu-Jamal praises Malcolm X and Huey Newton for tapping into the voice of rage that spoke to many urban blacks, this underscores the neglect of black women and queer black folk in his musing, reminiscing, and eulogizing of black liberation heroes. Black feminist critic bell hooks, in particular, has been an outspoken voice of black rage, but even she notes that, "our efforts to create a renewed black liberation struggle are seriously impeded by the fact that in diverse settings the assumption prevails that we need only to listen to patriarchal men, that our very capacity to move forward as a people depends on strong black male leadership."[119] In hooks's estimation, this regenerative strategy leads to a complete dismissal of black female feminist praxis and promotes and encourages the uncritical acceptance of black male leadership and patriarchy.[120] It is important to note that in these three texts, Abu-Jamal does not comment upon the rich history of black female resistance at all; that history has been eclipsed by the masculinity of black men who were elevated to positions of power within black organizations and to the men who languish on death row. Abu-Jamal is nostalgic for a gendered and decidedly masculine history, and by pledging himself to this partial past, he is regenerating a movement for black liberation that ignores the sacrifices and leadership of black women.

Mumia Abu-Jamal: Movement Leader

In addition to the black intellectuals who speak on Abu-Jamal's behalf in each text, many black activists also place him at the head of this masculinized history of black liberation. In Chinosole's collection of essays, *Schooling the Generations in the Politics of Prison*, Mumia Abu-Jamal and Assata Shakur are the subject of the first two sections of essays designed to discuss this next generation of prison activism. In the section on Mumia Abu-Jamal, Black Liberation Army member Assata Shakur provides the first essay titled, "Message to Mumia." She writes, "His language, his strength, and his intelligence remind me of one man: El Hajj Malik Shabazz, otherwise known as Malcolm X."[121]

In pursuing this kind of rhetorical identification, Shakur praises Abu-Jamal's clear rhetorical voice, and the *absence* of the Black Power vernacular that was so prominent from the Panthers and SNCC leaders, particularly Rap Brown. "Mumia, the only Afrikan political prisoner on death row, didn't use any inflammatory rhetoric. What he said was so clear, so true, that I had to stop everything and concentrate on his message, Mumia Abu-Jamal, journalist, husband, father; he is brilliant. He has the ability to say what needs to be said in the clearest, most vivid way," explains Shakur.[122] One link between Malcolm and Mumia, at least for Shakur, seems to be their clear, uncompromising arguments bearing resolute messages, historical explanations, and new metaphors. She explains that Abu-Jamal has "carried on Malcolm's tradition, and the tradition of so many of our freedom fighters who have risked their lives for the freedom of our people. . . . We can feel Malcolm's energy working through Mumia; we can feel Mumia's energy carrying on Malcolm's legacy."[123] As the heir to Malcolm, Shakur implies a (re)birth of Malcolm's energy through Abu-Jamal, which positions him explicitly as a son of Malcolm. She adds, "If Malcolm X were alive today, I know he would be fighting to save Mumia's life. . . . In the name of Malcolm X, I make a special appeal to you, Sisters and Brothers, to fight tooth and nail to save Mumia's life and to free him from the grips of his oppressors."[124] Shakur asks the reader to be like Malcolm in their actions, agitating against mass incarceration and the death penalty.

Shakur also characterizes Abu-Jamal as a "living hero" in the company of other black revolutionary martyrs and victims of COINTELPRO. She writes:

> When you honor the names of Nat Turner, Harriet Tubman, and Malcolm X, I urge you to honor the names of Geronimo ji Jaga, Sundiata Acoli, Mutulu Shakur, and Mumia Abu-Jamal. I urge you not to forget, and not to betray our living heroes. If we ignore their struggle, we are ignoring our own. If we betray our living history, then we are betraying ourselves. We could not save Malcolm X, but we can save Mumia. We can save him, because we love our Brother, and we need our Brother to help us fight for our freedom.[125]

Shakur encourages new generations of activists to channel Malcolm X through Abu-Jamal because the two leaders are inextricably linked. But this passage also emphasizes the importance of active memory work as Shakur advises readers to remember the slave insurrectionists in the same breath as the Black Power martyrs. Calling it "living history" also invokes this active listening and recollecting alongside calls for saving Mumia. And, although Shakur includes Harriet Tubman in this list of black activists, she also falls into the trap of masculinizing history to help elevate Mumia Abu-Jamal to the status of black liberation hero, even over herself as a leader.

Abu-Jamal emerges as a celebrity and a Black Power leader, but he also transforms into a father figure for the prison population. In this way, he centers the prison-industrial complex in the regeneration of Black Power. But even as his leadership is focused on his similarities with older Black Power martyrs, Abu-Jamal transcends his role as the son of Malcolm, Huey, and the BPP to become a father figure, as a living martyr-prophet who can generate both new sons and new fathers in this new generation of Black Power activism. In an essay titled "Father Hunger," he writes intimately of father-lack and the importance of Black Power as a black family structure: "Without a father, I sought and found father-figures like Black Panther Captain Reggie Schell, Party Defense Minister Huey Newton, and indeed, the Party itself, which, in a period of utter void taught me, fed me, and made me part of a vast and militant family of revolutionaries."[126] He adds, "Many good men and women became my teachers, my mentors, and my examples of a revolutionary ideal—Zayd Malik Shakur, murdered police when Assata was wounded and taken, and Geronimo ji jaga (a.k.a. Pratt) who commanded the party's L.A. chapter."[127] Missing from such configurations are the women in his family or his female comrades. Only Assata is mentioned in passing as he memorializes

Zayd Shakur. Still, this discussion of the father-yearning of his youth illustrates Abu-Jamal's vulnerability while reinforcing this paternity of Black Power as Abu-Jamal sets up himself as a new "father" of Black Power to the men in his all-male prison. This implicitly excludes black women prisoners certainly as leaders but also as followers, which reifies the kind of black male leadership of the past.

This notion of fatherhood sets up Abu-Jamal to be the father and savior of the men on death row and in prisons across America, thereby completing his ascension as a prophet and leader. He writes, "Here in death row, in the confined sub-stratum of a society where every father is childless, and every man fatherless, those of us who have known the bond of father-son love may at least re-live it in our minds, perhaps even draw strength from it. Those who have not—the unloved—find it virtually impossible to love."[128] As a result of this denial of father-love, the men of death row started calling Abu-Jamal "Papa," because of their father-hunger, making the case that collective action is familial. Abu-Jamal notes that while he had his own father, the party, and men like "Geronimo, Delbert, Chuck, Mike, Ed, and Phil; Sundiata, Mutulu, and other oldheads," the other men on death row have had no one.[129] For Abu-Jamal, the absence of the father creates a masculinity crisis that cannot be overcome without substitute or other-fathers who help to instill codes of masculinity within each succeeding generation. Being embraced as "Papa" by other inmates elevates him to the position of the "Father" of the black male masses, thereby completing his transformation. He adds, "I was in denial. For who was the oldhead they were calling? Certainly not me? It took a trip, a trek to the shiny, burnished steel mirror on the wall, where I found my father's face staring back at me, to recognize reality. I am he . . . and they are me."[130]

In this consubstantial Cincinnatus moment, Abu-Jamal emerges as the reluctant prophet, transcending his role as father to his own children and becoming the father to "the people." He becomes a black father to mostly men who are fatherless, much like Malcolm X and John Africa. In such transformations, his transition from death row prisoner to moral badman is made complete by domesticating Abu-Jamal despite imprisonment. The prison, then, is the place of the regeneration of black masculinity, passed along through imprisoned men who become substitute fathers.

Mumia Abu-Jamal: Death Row Celebrity, Intellectual, Leader, and Father

Imprisoned writers, particularly those on death row, provide a very important function for those outside of America's prisons. The significance of

Abu-Jamal's manifestos is that for those incarcerated or, as Dylan Rodriguez has phrased it, those "juridically dead," writing from prison is an act of assertion in the face of misinformation, stereotype, and misconduct. Political prisoners, then, are struggling against the erasure promoted by the state and the media, which attempt to remove them from discussion of the political. Felons are politically disenfranchised in most states and are further removed from public debate by the restrictions on their speech and writing. Mumia Abu-Jamal's case highlights the corruption and brutality that permeate police departments, courtrooms, and prison in America and illustrates the tenacity of his own struggle to overcome this repression and emerge as a leader of a new generation of Black Power activists, committed to a struggle where the prison is central. In this way, we see Abu-Jamal as the heir to the movement toward black liberation, as a celebrity, an intellectual, a Black Power leader, and as a prophetic father figure.

Abu-Jamal's transfer to the general prison population and the decision of the Pennsylvania state attorney general in December 2011 to end the state's quest for the death penalty have only increased the amount of attention that Abu-Jamal has garnered in his thirty years on death row. As his appeals have continued, scholarly attention needs to focus on the decades-long public struggle over his political activism and his incarceration. As black intellectuals testify to Abu-Jamal's innocence and his Black Power leadership, we see in his own writings a political and spiritual calling to expose the police, the courts, and the prisons as broken appendages of justice that must be reformed. As Dale Bauer reminds us, "Personal testimonies and autobiographical criticism in general too often stop at the identification, rather than spell out the persuasion or commitment that is always the next stop in identificatory rhetoric."[131] But Abu-Jamal's books build identification among himself, other prisoners, and the urban black poor as part of the political project of exposing the corruption of the state and the rhetorical project of teaching oppositional reading. This move helps him to build exigency for anti–death penalty activism, judicial activism, and solidarity for his appeals while also countering the "cop killer" race-talk that sought to undermine his credibility. In his essays, Abu-Jamal sketches the exigencies that must mobilize people to act around the issues of police misconduct, injustice in court, the misappropriation of the term *cop killer*, and around the prison violence. As a journalist, Abu-Jamal is committed to a revolutionary oppositional consciousness that infuses his writings with intersectional analyses of the justice system, rendering invisible his own gender politics. In these ways, Abu-Jamal's writings serve to reestablish his loyalty to justice through his expression of oppositional consciousness where black and brown urban communities have been targeted and imprisoned, particularly when they expose corruption.

In elevating himself as a leader, Abu-Jamal's stories of other prisoners help to raise him up as a man of the people, as a spiritual father figure to the men on death row, and as a witness to the atrocities that they endure. Malcolm X and Huey Newton provide templates for Abu-Jamal's brand of black masculine leadership; they provide a cultural resource for nostalgic longing that allows Abu-Jamal to appropriate the ethos of these leaders. Mumia Abu-Jamal regenerates Black Power through black male leadership, possibly at the expense of black women who have been an integral part of the radical black liberation struggle. A critical assessment of this strategy highlights the drawbacks of relying upon nostalgia for black leaders because it occludes the activism of black women of even prominent prison abolitionists like Angela Davis.

In short, Abu-Jamal's writings help to position him as a celebrity and new leader of Black Power agitation because they harness clear, informative, intimate prose that ask the reader to become involved in activism around the prison-industrial complex. Using family metaphors and stories of community action alongside vivid descriptions of prison abuse, Abu-Jamal's text becomes a mandate for social change.

CHAPTER FOUR

Recovering Black Identity and History, Feminizing and Regenerating Black Power

I n 1965, the Johnson administration created the Office of Law Enforce-
ment Assistance as part of the federal government's effort to curb crime.
Consequently, Congress authorized the Omnibus Crime Control and
Safe Streets Act in 1968, thereby establishing the Law Enforcement Assistance
Administration (LEAA). The federal expenditures for the LEAA swelled from
63 million dollars in 1968 to an impressive 895 million dollars in 1975.[1] The
Nixon administration augmented the LEAA in 1969 with riot-control expenditures and new domestic intelligence-gathering operations that would be
useful in "civil disorders" like the rebellions in Newark and Detroit.[2] In equipping the police with so much firepower, the result was that the urban rebellions of the 1960s were almost all ignited by police brutality.[3] Many police
departments acquired weapons that, in Joseph C. Goulden's words, helped
them "tool up for repression."[4]

The LEAA expansion outfitted police with anti-riot gear that became a
symbol of white racism for black communities as police began using them on
black citizens.[5] For example, in their review of the "law and order" policies of
the Nixon regime, the Civil Rights Commission found that police brutality
in the 1960s was so common because the (mostly white) police have found it
relatively easy to avoid positive social interactions with the populations they
are entrusted to protect. Such conditions lead to stereotyping where some
officers conclude that black Americans are "lawless, prone to resist the police,
and likely to require rough handling."[6]

The New Jersey state police have a particularly auspicious record of racialized brutality. In 1967, out of a police force of nearly 1,400 only 150 members of the Newark police force were black, mostly in subordinate positions.[7]

Consequently, black Americans have seen the New Jersey police force, especially in Newark, as an occupying force. Since Newark's black residents lived in neighborhoods that had been white only two decades earlier, nearly all of their apartments and stores were white owned as well, which added to the racial tension in Newark.[8]

In the mid-1960s, a small but significant group of militantly antiblack police officers in cities like Newark and New York organized specifically to crush the Black Panthers and other black nationalist groups in what William C. Kronholm has called "Blue Power."[9] Rather than recognizing the 1960s protests "as an expression of anger by deceived people, [police] saw them as an impudent demand for the good life on the part of people who would not work to earn it."[10] These officers saw protestors as violent agitators demanding special privileges, so police in Newark, New Jersey, for example, spent $331,000 in 1967 to acquire AR-15 rifles and armored cars for riot control.[11]

It is at this intersection of Black Power and Blue Power that the Black Liberation Army (BLA), "a military organization, whose primary objective is to fight for the independence and self-determination of Afrikan people in the United States," grew as the decimation of the Black Panther Party began under COINTELPRO.[12] The prison and exilic writings of Assata Shakur must be located here, during and after the destruction of the Panthers, and in the midst of the fortification of America's police forces. Born JoAnne Freeman in Jamaica, New York, on July 16, 1947, Assata Shakur grew up in a multigenerational, close-knit family. Her life changed forever on May 2, 1973, when Shakur lay near death in a hospital bed after a deadly shoot-out following a "routine" police stop on the New Jersey Turnpike. Shakur was traveling with two friends and members of the BLA, Sundiata Acoli (formerly Clark Squire), and her best friend Zayd Shakur, when two state troopers stopped them for "a faulty taillight."[13] The shoot-out on the turnpike left two men, Zayd and New Jersey state trooper James Harper, dead and both Assata Shakur and New Jersey state trooper Werner Foerster injured.[14] Shakur was a political prisoner of the state for four years before the trial in 1977 where an all-white jury convicted her of killing state trooper James Harper and injuring Werner Foerster with the intent to kill. She was sentenced to life plus thirty-three years in prison. She escaped from the Clinton Correctional Facility in New York on November 2, 1979, and fled to Cuba (after five years underground) where much of her autobiography was written and where she currently lives in exile.

This chapter analyzes the poetry and prose of *Assata: An Autobiography* and contextualizes the memoir within the revolutionary aesthetics of the Black Power vernacular and the political realities of northern Blue Power in the late 1960s and early 1970s. It examines the feminized rhetorical strategies, like the use of poetry, in *Assata* that help to fortify Black Power activism. Like Mumia Abu-Jamal, Shakur situates herself as a leader and as a martyr using nostalgia for Black Power leaders as inspiration for the activism ahead. She uses black history as a rhetorical resource for new political action and highlights the importance of cultural nationalism. In addition, she commits herself to self-defense and Third World solidarity through a gendered articulation of the Black Power vernacular. The black vernacular, as Farred explains, "is ideologically mobile, responsive to crises, adaptable to its situation, able to translate and situate itself in nonnative locales; because of the workings of history and the reduction of geographical distance through cultural proximity, the vernacular has global purchase."[15] Shakur's vernacular is mobile, flexible, and global as she uses the history of slavery in the United States and colonialism abroad to explain the BLA's resistance to "law and order" culture. Finally, she explains the historical and contemporary exigencies that prompt continued action, including police brutality, the expansion of the prison-industrial complex, judicial corruption, and false accusations of cop killing. Still in print, *Assata* demands a place for Shakur's narrative among the prison manifestos of the Black Power movement.

Testimony for the Accused: The Foreword in Shakur's Autobiographical Manifesto

Assata was published in 1987 by Lawrence Hill Books and reprinted in 2001. Shakur chose Lawrence Hill because "they published [Black Panther field marshal and political prisoner] George Jackson's letters" and she felt that she "could trust them with her story" since they had a history of publishing black liberation activists' narratives.[16] Her decision to publish with Lawrence Hill and her solidarity with George Jackson linked Shakur to the prison leadership of the Black Power movement. As the most famous political prisoner of the 1970s (until Angela Davis), Jackson's own prison writings were popular among inmates and those on the outside, who followed the leadership of George Jackson, Angela Davis, and others who fought the "savage repression" of the state.[17]

Like earlier slave narratives and the prison texts of Rap Brown and Mumia Abu-Jamal (mentioned in chapters 2 and 3), Shakur's text begins with two black leaders, Angela Davis and Lennox Hinds, who assert her legitimacy as a revolutionary voice. Former Black Panther Party member Angela Davis pens the first foreword in the 2001 release of the book. As the author of a wildly popular prison autobiography herself and as an internationally renowned academic expert on political prisoners, Davis is a useful commentator on Shakur's situation since Davis's story shares many similarities to Shakur's. Davis was wanted in connection to Jonathan Jackson's attempt at liberating George Jackson from the Marin County Courthouse in 1970. She went underground and was consequently listed on the FBI's Top 10 Most Wanted Criminals list (much like Shakur), sparking one of the most intensive manhunts in US history for a woman who was acquitted of all charges.[18]

Davis begins by discussing how "Blue Power" fueled Shakur's trial and conviction. She notes that Shakur's "image was deployed on official FBI wanted posters and in the popular media as visual evidence of the terrorist motivations of the black liberation movement. Black militants were assumed to be enemies of the state and were associated with communist challenges to capitalist democracy. The protracted search for and public demonization of Assata Shakur served further to justify the imprisonment of vast numbers of political activists, many of whom remain locked up today."[19] Davis describes how dominant media used "law and order" rhetoric to depict Shakur as a terrorist legitimizing the imprisonment of other black female activists. In this way, Shakur's entire text stands not only as a reconstruction of her "personal image, which has been distorted and even destroyed by official documents," but also as an act of solidarity with so many other civilians and activists targeted by the state.[20] Davis resists the state's characterization of Black Power, and, by extension, Shakur, as hostile, describing Shakur as "a compassionate human being with an unswerving commitment to justice that travels easily across racial and ethnic lines, in and out of prisons and across oceans of time."[21] Davis's description highlights the vernacular mobility of Shakur's text while emphasizing her commitment to social justice.

Davis also comments on Shakur's trial and innocence. She explains that under New Jersey state law, "if a person's presence at the scene of a crime can be construed as 'aiding and abetting' the crime, that person can be convicted of the substantive crime itself."[22] Shakur's conviction was won despite three neurologists who all testified that "her median nerve had been severed by gunshot wounds, rendering her unable to pull the trigger, and that her clavicle had been shattered by a shot that could only have been made while she was seated in the car with her hands raised. Other experts testified that the neutron activation analysis administered by the police right after the shootout showed no gun residue on her fingers, meaning she had not shot a weapon."[23] Although she didn't handle any of the weapons, Shakur was also convicted of weapons possession in the attempted murder of state trooper Harper, who sustained a minor injury.[24] Davis's testimony disrupts the official history of Shakur's arrest, acquits her, and positions Shakur as a victim of the state. In this case, Davis's description creates a rhetorical space for Shakur to be silent in the narrative about the details of the trial.

One of Shakur's lawyers, Lennox Hinds (former president of the National Conference of Black Lawyers and law professor at Rutgers University), provides the second foreword in the 2001 edition of the text where he describes Shakur's childhood, humanizing her for the reader. As a defense attorney, Hinds moves back in time to describe the structural circumstances constraining blackness in America and, by extension, Shakur. He writes that "it was the racism riddling every aspect of the early life of this sensitive, intellectually gifted, and life-passionate child, as she struggled to establish her own identity, that led her to seek solutions to the catastrophic impact of racism and economic oppression on all people of color in the United States. It is racist America that provides the context for the making of this Black revolutionary."[25] Hinds's analysis locates the warrant for the black liberation struggle in US racism, describing Shakur as a bright child trying to find solutions to racial and economic oppression.

Following his judgment of Shakur's character, Hinds evaluates her trial. Invoking his authority as a legal professional, he argues that Shakur did not receive a fair trial because of the intense mediation of her story and image.[26] Thus, even before the reader has even encountered Shakur's version of events, two character witnesses of great stature in the black community have exonerated her while documenting the racism inherent in the criminal justice system. He directly addresses the reader, arguing, "we in this society must remind ourselves again how we threaten our own interests and rights when we condone by our silence the government's use of surveillance, attacks on the legitimacy of political activists, and the use of criminal law to suppress and punish political dissent."[27] He warns the reader that because of community negligence, the government silenced Shakur's voice. This rhetorical strategy holds the reader accountable for the consequences of community silence in the face of governmental oppression, demonstrating that Shakur is part of a larger history of antiblack violence. By positioning Shakur as a victim of violence rather than a perpetrator, Hinds connects her persecution to the daily struggles of black Americans, cementing her cause to theirs.

Angela Davis and Lennox Hinds reinforce the illegitimacy of Assata Shakur's trial, provide humanized accounts of her personality, and bolster Shakur's testimony with their own credibility as revolutionary intellectuals. They also discuss the reader's responsibility to civic life in supporting public activism against the government when it seeks out members of subaltern communities to demonize and imprison. This helps to propel readers into activism because it makes them complicit in state violence if they do not act on the behalf of Shakur and those like her. Both forewords orient the reader and frame Shakur's narrative and poetry as the writing of a revolutionary innocent of violence, but committed to the liberation of her people, as a moral bad(wo)man. They also elevate her as a leader by addressing her as a sister, a comrade, and a freedom fighter who has been unjustly imprisoned. In this way, both Davis and Hinds presage the critiques that Shakur provides about her detention, her treatment by the police, her trials, and her unswerving commitment to black liberation through writing.

Writing Revolutionary Power and the Poetry of Liberation

In discussing the means of disciplining prison detainees, Michel Foucault describes "the power of writing," which is essential to surveillance regimes in prison. The "power of writing" allows the prison administration to accumulate massive documentation about detainees, which permits comparisons and the "organization of comparative fields making it possible to classify, to form categories, to determine averages, to fix norms."[28] The result is that the individual detainee is reduced to a statistic that can be compared to others. The prison official, then, is at the center of power in examining and describing the detainee, through systems of surveillance, classification, and description, which reify the pseudo-science of the prison. The ban on writing in prison, "itself provoked by the particular aptitudes of political prisoners, serves to condition in an important way, one of the crucial modes of political prisoner resistance: writing."[29] Writing, then, poses a continued and threatening challenge to the control of prison officials, and poetry, with its ability to be written in bursts and hidden in smaller portions, is a vernacular tradition of resistance that subverts the "power of writing," particularly since the prison denies access to writing materials.

Like many women, Shakur records her experiences in prisons when she can, describing the terrible consequences of solitary confinement. For example, when Shakur arrived at Rikers Island where she awaited her federal trial, she was excited to be out of solitary confinement and around other black women, though the effects of solitary confinement were profound and she could only sit and stare. She writes, "I could barely talk, though . . . My voice was so low everyone constantly asked me to repeat myself. That was one of the things that always happened to me after long periods of solitary confinement: i would forget how to talk."[30] Not only is Shakur's writing limited, but her ability to speak is also damaged by what Foucault calls the "calculated

economy of punishments" meant to shape and discipline the body by forcing obedience to the prison warden, so that the prisoner may be constantly
surveilled.[31] Historically, solitary confinement "was once enforced for 'correc-
tive' purposes by allowing the prisoner to look into himself, to introspect and
meditate on the nature of his crime and eventually be guided to the right
ways, it is also employed to destroy the psychological integrity of the isolated
prisoner."[32] For Shakur, extended solitary confinement was used to strip her of
her voice, personhood, and her dignity; consequently, her writing exists as a
rebuke to the prison system's degradation, and it serves to correct the "official"
accounts of her activities in the BLA.

As the first memoirist of the Black Liberation Army, Shakur's vernacular
resistance justifies the militancy of the BLA with historical and ideological
arguments that explain revolutionary organizing in the wake of COINTEL-
PRO's decimation of Black Power. In this manner, Shakur's text transcends
the Assata Shakur (and certainly the JoAnne Chesimard) of the late 1960s
and negotiates a self that is far more complex because the writer is no longer
coherent as the object of the FBI's ire. Like other autobiographical manifestos,
writings like *Assata* are "texts recording the negotiation of the female self-
in-process between the historical fact of displacement and the possibility of
textual self-presence."[33] Sidonie Smith calls this the "politics of fragmentation"
because the writer has devised a "contestatory autobiographical practice" as
a "means to counter the centrifugal power of the old 'self.'"[34] And, as Caren
Kaplan explains, the refusal "to read testimonial writing by poor and imprisoned women *only* as autobiography links resistance literature with resistance
criticism" as a textual intervention that allies the reader with the writer.[35]

Thus, *Assata* can read as a layered intervention into official history and
memory that allows the text to become a moment of revitalized interest in
black liberations. The text holds out the possibility of significant emancipa-
tory power, both through its prose and, particularly, its poetry. Autobiography
and poetry are interwoven throughout *Assata*, helping to articulate Shakur's
criticisms of the state, her innermost feelings about incarceration, her friends
and family, and her life story, particularly because these are parts of her life
that have been left out of official history and memory. As such, Shakur's text
also works to reconstitute a movement that had receded. To do this, Shakur's
text moves from poetry to prose, from her prison experience to her childhood, and from chapter to chapter, disrupting the linear pattern of storytelling common to traditional autobiography, but encouraging the reader to be
sympathetic to the writer and her political ideologies, rebuilding collective
identification with Black Power.

The Emergent Leader in the Poetry of *Assata*: Lessons of Hope

Shakur's manifesto begins with a poem titled "Affirmation," which provides a mantra of hope.[36] This also provides a positive framework for black liberation, which is a crucial component in recruiting new allies to the receding Black Power movement. To establish herself as a leader of this new phase of the movement, Shakur testifies about her belief system, her personal truth. As a result, most of the lines of this first poem begin with "I believe" or "I have," which firmly position Assata as the legitimate authority over her own life and which demonstrate Shakur's personal, particular truths. These truths include an emphasis on the sanctity of nature and both the "magic" and "wisdom" of the female body. Though she believes in life, she also has seen "destruction" and the "death parade" praying and saluting to the "bloodthirsty maggots" of the state. Still she acknowledges that walls can be broken down, even when they are built and maintained by lawless lawmen.[37]

The presence of the "I" in this particular passage provides documentation of the treatment Shakur received after her arrest. She is able to describe her tormentors but also resist their "truths" about who she "is," what she has "done," and what she should do to repent. Ultimately, in both the poem and in the outside world, it is Assata who triumphs over the state as she reminds us that she literally broke down the wall and escaped her captors; she is the strong leader that can withstand the violence of the state and still be hopeful about the future. This poem, then, provides a foundation of hope for those participating in black resistance projects, in addition to providing a common enemy and a strong ethical component that emphasizes self-determination.

Shakur echoes other black writers using redefinition as a black liberation strategy. For example, in his 1845 *Narrative*, Frederick Douglass certainly expressed it thusly: "I could regard them in no other light than a band of successful robbers, who had left their homes, and gone to Africa, and stolen us from our homes, and in a strange land reduced us to slavery."[38] Former Black Panther Eldridge Cleaver made a similar claim about Robert F. Kennedy when he wrote, "Robert Kennedy has been in some prison of his character for a long time. He's a convict, possibly a lifer, and I got the impression that he lives, like convicts, by one law and one law alone: I shall do only that which is expedient for survival so that I will have one more chance outside of these chains."[39] Shakur indicts "lawless" state officials for their participation in criminal acts against her functions, like those of Douglass and Cleaver, as a way of inverting her relationship to the culture's oppressors.

Just as Shakur highlights the criminality of the American nation-state, she also utilizes birth metaphors, which are repeated throughout the entire autobiography.[40] Here, Shakur introduces the birth metaphor as a vernacular device that is charged with hope for the future, for new generations who struggle, for sailors lost at sea that should not yet be abandoned. Is she talking about people in black communities that are unaware of or participate in their own oppression? Is she reminding us that white people within the hegemonic structure can change? The ambiguity here is useful because in the context of the larger narrative, it can be read as a sense of hope for the nation as well as hope for black liberation. In Shakur's futurist language, hope is expressed through narratives of Shakur's childhood, her family, and the values important to them: black dignity, self-determination, and community.

Constructing a Collective Identity: Dignity, Self-Determination, and Repression in *Assata*

Assata Shakur's text frames and is framed by a dialogue about cultural knowledge production, hope, and love, placing the black family at the forefront of resistance. Shakur's anecdotes about childhood, which center on her adolescence, provide context for her evolution into a liberation hero. A focus on the strength of her family helps Shakur to pay homage to a collective heritage of resistance that fuels her own activism and frames contemporary struggles with the knowledge of the past. This personalization of history also serves to ground her observations in the kind of experiences that a reader, particularly a black reader, might recognize. For example, Shakur writes, "The FBI cannot find any evidence that i was born. On my FBI Wanted poster, they list my birth date as July 16, 1947, and, in parentheses, 'not substantiated by birth records.'" She continues, "Anyway, I was born."[41] The FBI's inability to locate evidence of her birth is indeed a striking commentary on racial being and nothingness much like that of Booker T. Washington, who at the beginning of his autobiography writes, "I suspect I must have been born somewhere and at sometime."[42] Using a convention that recalls the shoddy record keeping of former slaves, Shakur links herself to a history of racial being undermined by white power as she introduces us to her family and early childhood in North Carolina.

This rhetorical strategy highlights the indignity of not knowing the circumstances of one's birth, and it sets up a much larger discussion within Shakur's manifesto about the importance of reclaiming dignity. Shakur's grandparents figure into her early education about black dignity. She writes, "My grandparents strictly forbade me . . . to make subservient gestures when talking to white people. . . . I was told to speak in a loud, clear voice and to hold my head up high, or risk having my grandparents knock it off my shoulders."[43] Shakur's grandparents insisted on respect and taught her how to deal with life in the segregated South, skills that have clearly helped to shape the leader that she has become. Her grandfather would tell her, "Don't you respect nobody that don't respect you, you hear me?" And, her grandmother would say, "Don't you let anybody mistreat you, you hear?"[44] As Shakur remembers the familial support and the values of her grandparents, she notes that respectability and class mobility were connected. She says, "pride and dignity were hooked up to things like position and money. For them, being 'just as good' as white people meant having what white people had."[45]

These anecdotes help to explain the origin of Shakur's oppositional consciousness in the segregated South where surveillance, harassment, imprisonment, and violence have characterized black activist life in the twentieth century. Even her infancy is tainted by the far-reaching arms of the FBI, a conspirator in the creation and maintenance of the prison-industrial complex, and the organization charged with destroying community activism and preserving the integrity of the "nation." In this way, Shakur's text reinvents her individual identity but does so while crafting a group subjectivity that is premised upon dignity, empowerment, and community support. For example, Shakur and her family would go to Bop City, a popular beach in South Carolina, which her grandparents insisted on calling Freeman's Beach. Shakur writes that as an adult she recognized the importance of the name "Freeman" to black communities who changed their surnames after being freed. She notes that after Reconstruction, "many Black people refused to use the last names of their masters. They called themselves 'Freeman' instead. The name was also used by Africans who were freed before slavery was 'officially' abolished, but it was mainly after the abolition of chattel slavery that many Black people changed their names to Freeman. After learning this, I saw my ancestors in a new light."[46] In seeing her ancestors in this new light, Shakur implies that her life, her politics, and her book are assertions of her own freedom as a "Freeman."

Shakur's narration provides a lesson on reading the histories of black resistance that are embedded in naming and positions her within a family tradition of resistance that that can be traced back to slavery. Born JoAnne Freeman (she married Louis Chesimard), Shakur explores the importance of naming as an expression of black agency. And, just as her family would insist on calling "Bop City" "Freeman's Beach," Shakur also changes her name from JoAnne Chesimard to one that reflects her new black identity as she becomes reborn in the black liberation struggle. In Yoruba, "Assata" means "she who struggles," Olugbala (her middle name) means "love for the people," and Shakur means "the grateful." These chosen names are fitting for a revolutionary who has given her life for black liberation and who is positioned to lead the new phase of a movement that struggles with a state constantly under threat of violence.

As Shakur charts the importance of black dignity and self-respect, she also tackles issues of self-hatred in black communities. This strategy is common to generational texts of her era and serves to underscore the pervasiveness of racism as young children internalize inferiority in a white supremacist culture. She talks about calling other kids "nappy head," "jungle bunnies," and "bush boogies" and lists many of the taunts that children would sling at one another. She remembers that "Black made any insult worse" and that she and her peers "had never heard the words 'Black is beautiful.'"[47] Shakur continues by describing the social brainwashing of internalized racism, commenting, "We accepted white value systems and white standards of beauty and, at times, we accepted the white man's view of ourselves . . . And, to varying degrees, we each made them true within ourselves because we believed."[48] These anecdotes highlight the extent to which racism permeates even the lives of children and can be read as a justification for cultural revolution and black self-determination. Shakur's early work with the Black Panther Party and her later work with the Black Liberation Army rejected the negativity surrounding blackness and embracing black pride.

Cultural resistance is a central tenet of Black Power and is spread through processes of cultural identification to movement veterans.[49] In her manifesto, Shakur's poetry positions black culture against the dominant culture that oppresses black America to demonstrate her fidelity to black people and to black liberation. In "Culture," she writes of her disdain for waltzes and symphonies and her connection to black music instead, saying she "hummed the Blues too early" and spent too many nights "out wailing in the rain."[50] The tensions between white art forms like the waltz and resistance arts like the blues underlie the larger questions of culture that form the basis of cultural nationalism. Resistance poems like this "actively engage in the historical process of struggle against the cultural oppression of imperialism, and assert thereby their own polemical historicity."[51] In the 1970s, music played a huge role in redefining black aesthetics as writers began to privilege Third World forms of expression over white norms, usually by opposing symphony (and other forms of European musical culture) and embracing jazz or blues (and other forms of native expression), metered verse to free verse. By positing the blues as the antidote to European aesthetic domination, Shakur is able to highlight the "anti-humanism of Western art and the destructive intellectual and social values sustaining it" by elevating black American art.[52]

Shakur's poems move between the global and the local to connect families to a larger culture of struggle and a vibrant history of black resistance beyond the United States. Shakur's poem, "The Tradition" is the last bit of writing in the text, the bookend to "Affirmation." She begins and continues to repeat, "Carry it on now. / Carry it on" before she describes the places across the globe where "Black People since the childhood of time" carried on the tradition of resistance in "Ghana and Mali and Timbuktu." Shakur remembers and describes the tradition of resistance during the slave trade, on slave ships, and on plantations where slaves resisted daily brutality. Shakur writes that the tradition of black resistance continued through literacy and art in newspapers, meetings, chants and cantatas, in poems and blues songs and "saxophone screams." Black resistance continued in classrooms, churches, courtrooms, prisons, on soapboxes, in picket lines, welfare lines and unemployment lines, in sit-ins, pray-ins, march-ins, and die-ins where it confronted lynch mobs, rifles, water hoses, bulldogs, nightsticks, bullets, tanks, tear gas, needles, nooses, bombs, and birth control. Shakur charts black resistance from Selma and San Juan to Mozambique, Mississippi, Brazil, and Boston, pointing to the internationalist perspective on Black Power. She notes that Black Power survived "the lies and the sell-outs," the "mistakes and the madness," the "pain and hunger and frustration." As Shakur describes how black activists "carried it on," she charts a global history of resistance that should be passed "down to the children" to carry on the struggle for black liberation.[53]

As she moves from the local civil rights movement in Mississippi to global anticolonialist movements abroad, Shakur's poem provides a geography of the African diaspora and the resistance of black people to colonialist violence. H. Bruce Franklin suggests that the "most collective autobiography of the American prison is not any single work, but the body of poetry by Black prisoners," which incorporates "the common oral and musical tradition developed in the songs of Black slavery and extended through the songs of Black peonage and imprisonment."[54] Shakur's own poetry accesses these traditions of black expression and traces the global history of black resistance, labeling it with the language of Black Power as a strong, proud, black tradition, laden with dignity and perseverance as a way of remembering the struggles of the men and women who themselves took risks when others would not. It is this collective history and memory that Shakur is asking the reader to participate in as a witness and as an agent of change. In this process, Harlow notes, "The dismemberment of the poetic identity is reconstructed in ties of solidarity with the people themselves. That dismemberment, part of imperialism's strategy, conditions, however, the new literary and cultural agenda of the poets of the resistance movements and national liberation organizations."[55]

Through both her people's history and her family's history, we are seemingly meant to understand Shakur's commitment to revolutionary change and cultural nationalism as she inspires new generations to agitate for change. We see the continuities of black resistance and also how she uses history as a cultural resource to press the case for black self-determination. Thus, Shakur's poetry emphasizes the role of the black female poet "as both activist and leader" in the face of the pervasive sexism, classism, and homophobia in black intellectual circles of the 1960s and 1970s.[56] Sagri Dhairyam adds, "The only women poets included with any frequency in anthologies of [Black Power] poetry were Gwendolyn Brooks, Nikki Giovanni, and Sonia Sanchez."[57] While these women certainly form a critical part of the Black Arts Movement's cultural canon, the exclusion of poetry written by BPP and BLA members is surprising. Despite her exclusion, however, it seems clear that the poetry within Shakur's manifesto functions to feminize the BPP and the BLA.

Revolutionary Education

Shakur's autobiographical manifesto centers on consciousness-raising, reeducation, and remembering, which epitomize the strategies of regeneration through the rewriting of self-history and black history. As the FBI's war on black liberation organizations destroyed so many movement leaders, members like Assata Shakur provided a counterhistory and a countermemory of the social movement for future generations, contextualizing their lives in the broader historical struggle for black freedom. For example, Assata Shakur comments at length about her own political reeducation through her association with black nationalist organizations, offering readers an alternative history that destabilizes white, male normativity.[58] Like Rap Brown and Mumia Abu-Jamal, Shakur uses anecdotes to "correct" the historical inaccuracies and omissions prevalent in white master narratives, which perpetuate race, gender, and class oppression as early as grade school. She comments, "I didn't know what a fool they had made of me until I grew up and started to read real history. Not only was George Washington probably a big liar, but he had once sold a slave for a keg of rum. Here they had this old cracka slavemaster, who didn't give a damn about black people, and they had me, an unwitting little Black child, doing a play in his honor."[59] Here, Shakur uncovers the limitations and inherent racism of the nation's "official" history, which frames racial discourse. Instead of ignoring the role that education plays in the production of racial ideology, Shakur's black resistance writing stands in opposition to the nation's cultural domination. Shakur describes how children are positioned within a particularly racist framework as unwitting participants in the continuation of their own oppression.

By exploring the foundational myths of American society, Shakur interrogates the relationship between historical narratives and institutional racism. Shakur remembers being the only black child in her fourth-grade class and reciting Whitman's poem "O Captain! My Captain!" because she was excited about Abraham Lincoln. She writes, "Little did I know that Lincoln was an arch-racist who had openly expressed his disdain for Black people. He was of the opinion that Black people should be forcibly deported to Africa or anywhere else. We had been taught that the Civil War was fought to free the slaves, and it was not until college that I learned that the Civil War was fought for economic reasons."[60] Shakur demonstrates how these master narratives make it difficult for black Americans to use history as a resource for resistance.

As an adult, Shakur's knowledge of history was even more limited, but she says, "Harriet Tubman had always been my heroine, and she symbolized everything that was Black resistance to me. But it had never occurred to me that hundreds of Black people had got it together to fight for their freedom."[61] Shakur privileges grassroots organizing in addition to highlighting the importance of leaders to the black liberation struggle. She also acknowledges the gaps in her history, which, when filled, led her to understand her relationship to the nation and its history in a fundamentally different way, as she recognized the continued subjugation of black people. Where many other black revolutionaries cite movement men as their heroes, Shakur breaks tradition to elevate the status of a black female revolutionary. Harriet Tubman is such a foundational figure in black revolutionary history because she was the head of the Department of the South for the entire duration of the Civil War; she was the only American woman to lead both black and white troops in battle; she helped John Brown plan the attack on Harper's Ferry; she spoke on the antislavery lecture circuit, she planned antislavery events; and she was, of course, incredibly active in the Underground Railroad.[62] Tubman can certainly be seen as "a life long militant" and "the godmother of all women who would be fighters for their rights and for human rights."[63] In short, Harriet Tubman was a revolutionary heroine in every way. Shakur connects herself to the feminized revolutionary history epitomized by Tubman.

The recognition of an alternative, revolutionary black history affected Assata Shakur physically as well as intellectually as the emerging counterhistory empowered her. She says, "The day I found out about Nat Turner I was affected so strongly it was physical . . . I had grown up believing the slaves hadn't fought back. I remember feeling ashamed when they talked about slavery in school. The teachers made it seem that Black people had nothing to do with the official 'emancipation' from slavery. White people had freed us."[64] By offering this anecdote, Shakur challenges traditional representations of abolitionists, which allows her to dictate a version of history inclusive of black radical women, who have been traditionally erased from nationalist political movements. It also explicitly makes black America responsible for resisting oppression just as it castigates white racists for perpetuating inequality. By reframing the Civil War for her readers, Shakur contests the version of emancipation that ignores the resistance work of slaves, former slaves, and freedmen in gaining their own freedom and, instead, highlights the agency of US blacks, particularly black women, and their role in their own oppression and liberation.

The lesson that Shakur teaches in these accounts is one that critiques historical memory and the American educational system while reasserting the importance of black heroines and heroes. She explains, "In the same way that we don't hear about a fraction of the Black men and women who have struggled hard and tirelessly throughout our history, we don't hear about our heroes of today . . . Nobody is going to give you the education you need to overthrow them. Nobody is going to teach you your true history, teach you your true heroes, if they know that that knowledge is going to set you free . . . As long as we expect amerika's schools to educate us, we will remain ignorant."[65]

Even her strategies for spelling "amerika" embrace a leftist, New Afrikan grammar in examining the historical omissions of black heroism as Shakur teaches that the silences in history are as important to memory as are the stories that do get (re)told.[66] Shakur is struggling against the erasure of her own voice from the movement, and she is working against the erasure of black heroes and resistance from the larger American culture. This strategy connects her struggles and politics to the larger struggle of black liberation in the United States, which helps to elevate her to the company of black resistance heroes that came before her. This move also asks the reader to do additional intellectual work to guard against the ignorance that comes from avoiding the responsibility for one's own education.

In passages like these where she is providing activist reading and interpretive strategies, Shakur is answering the demand of writers like Nancy L. Arnez who argue: "We need the revolutionary call again. The Black arts movement of the 1960s must be revived. Our artists must again become our prophets, our visionaries. They must again go to the people with the many deadly truths of our putrid, nonproductive lives."[67] Arnez adds: "Our stories for Black children must focus on our heroes—past and present . . . We must prepare our people, young and old, for a protracted struggle for power—for control of the resources of the world."[68] This call for memorializing heroes and martyrs of the movement encourages the cultivation of fresh voices to help craft a new history of radical black action.

In using a partially feminized counterhistory as a resource mobilized against the incomplete, inaccurate, and slanderous history of the Black Power movement, Shakur is able to resuscitate a vibrant, continuous narrative of black heroes and black resistance, which serves to educate new activists with the organizational history of black liberation. Positioning Harriet Tubman at the head of this historical reassessment signifies the historical importance of women to black liberation since this rhetorical strategy, at least partially, disrupts the centrality of traditional male heroes. Such rhetorical moves epitomize the strategies of regeneration because she corrects and documents the black liberation history that is elided by the COINTELPRO propaganda. Counter-history works as a glue, binding together former and current activists and reminds the reader that black women have been a vital part of black liberation through the Underground Railroad and its modern counterpart the Black Liberation Army.

Feminizing Black Power: Metaphors of Birth and Regeneration in *Assata*

Black Power organizations like the Black Panther Party and the Black Liberation Army often saw the reproduction of black revolutionaries as a central political commitment as political assassinations became commonplace during the 1960s. Consequently, the vernacular rhetoric of Black Power often became one of regenerating the spirit of the movement by producing children (the "sons and daughters of Malcolm") to carry cultural and political traditions onward. Kenneth McNeil and James D. Thompson argue, "tribes, families, and societies may raise their own future generations from infancy or childhood, but few complex organizations are able to do so."[69] But, the Black Power movement, in many of its phases and organizations from the Nation of Islam to the Black Panther Party, saw reproduction as a way of sustaining the fight for black liberation. In her classic treatise on motherhood, *Of Woman Born: Motherhood as Experience and Institution*, Adrienne Rich writes, "the Black nationalist movement . . . declared that birth control and abortion are 'genocidal' and that Black women should feel guilty if they do *not* provide children to carry on the Black struggle for survival."[70] Consequently, motherhood and childrearing became central parts of the Black Power movement as groups like the Black Panthers took a serious "interest in the well-being of their activist children" as indicators of the health of the black community as a whole.[71]

For women of the movement, however, reproduction became something of a double-bind because they were often excluded from power if they did not have heterosexual sex or children, but having children made it difficult to patrol the neighborhoods at night or go underground, for example. And, though organizations like the Black Panthers tried to mandate that men and women work on the food programs or in the collective daycare, there was often backlash from men.[72] Nonetheless, because of the state's incessant demand to control black women's bodies and their reproduction through birth control or force, having sex and children were often places where black women tried to wrench control over their bodies and sexualities back from the state.

For black women writers of the Black Power movement, writing and reproduction intersected and created the possibility for women to perform essential tasks of the revolution, which pitted them against the black men within their organizations as well as against the white state. Susan Stanford Friedman persuasively argues, "In contrast to the phallic analogy [of the paintbrush, the pen, the gun] that implicitly excludes women from creativity, the childbirth metaphor validates women's artistic effort by unifying their mental and physical labor into (pro)creativity."[73] Metaphors of birth are useful in expressing the kind of control over sexuality and reproduction that have been systematically and violently withheld from women, especially black women, and the assertion of this literary device serves to underscore the rebellion of black women against the reproductive technologies, regimes, and norms of white culture.

Although Shakur spends ample time in the text talking about important female figures in her life, she also preserves a role in black liberation for black men. In this way, she does not disrupt the importance of heterosexuality to the future of Black Power. In "Story," Shakur writes of her dear friend Zayd Shakur, who, as mentioned earlier, was killed on the New Jersey Turnpike that fateful night. Shakur occupies her own autobiographical subjectivity with defiance and determination, while remembering her beautiful friend. She writes: "You died. / I cried. / And kept on getting up. / A little slower. / And a lot more deadly."[74] This poem occurs in the context of Shakur's recovery at the hospital after police shot her and beat her on the Jersey Turnpike. A black nurse had given her three books to read while she was recovering under watchful police eyes. One was an anthology of black poetry, one was called *Black Women in White Amerika*, and the last was Herman Hesse's *Siddhartha*. As she read the book about black women, she writes of feeling "the spirits of those sisters feeding me, making me stronger. Black women have been struggling and helping each other to survive the blows of life since the beginning of time."[75] Finding inspiration in a black female standpoint demonstrates Shakur's awareness of the legacy of resistance enacted by black women and highlights how female solidarity is a valuable resource for black women in a white supremacist culture.

Shakur's interactions with black women in the hospital or in prison are often positive and therapeutic in her manifesto, a stark contrast to her vicious encounters with (white) state troopers or judges. As she read these books in the hospital following the shoot-out, she recounts how her body began to heal from her wounds and also how she started to regain mobility, empowered by black female intellectualism. She says, "I had three bullet holes. There was a bullet in my chest (it's still there); an injured lung with fluid in it, a broken clavicle, and a paralyzed arm with undetermined damage to the nerves."[76] Even with these wounds, Shakur was determined to find strength in the history and literature of black resistance. Shakur's remembrance of Zayd resists his erasure from public memory just as her recovery signals her defiance of the violence that had left her nearly paralyzed in one arm. She "kept on getting up" as she hobbled around her hospital room and began trying to speak, which was difficult given the damage to her lung. Here, Shakur's remorse itself is articulated as resistance to white America as she remembers a strong, beautiful black man who was publicly demonized and then forgotten. Shakur's homage to men like Zayd Shakur naturalizes the role of men in the revolutionary process; however, Shakur's own insistence at "getting back up" also reflects a key strategy in the rhetoric of regeneration in relation to the Black Power movement.

Shakur's poetry and prose provide a sense of hope that stems from a history of black women's resistance to racism, sexism, and classism in America even as they illustrate the sacrifices that are necessary for the revolution. In her poem "Love," Shakur explains that these sacrifices are made, but they are gendered as she alludes to her prison pregnancy as a form of insurrection. She writes of the two-ness of her struggle using hacksaws and shotguns as metaphors for armed struggle. She writes, "We are pregnant with freedom / We are conspiracy."[77] The prison system exists entirely to shape prisoners into what Foucault identifies as "docile bodies" because of the anxiety about the body that pervades larger Western culture. The modern prison becomes a "policy of coercions that act upon the body, a calculated manipulation of its elements, its gestures, its behavior" where the "human body was entering a machinery of power that explores it, breaks it down, and rearranges it."[78] However, Shakur sees her determination to love and to become pregnant as a reassertion of control over her body. Shakur's pregnancy is the ultimate act of resistance to the prison's "policy of coercions," and she likens it to a "hacksaw," which can cut through the prison bars, and like a shotgun, which can coerce as well as liberate. Shakur appropriates the male metaphors of resistance (gun, hacksaw) and forges her own body as a weapon, a means of (re)generating and (re)growing the black liberation movement. Rather than seeing her body in isolation as a docile, solitary object, she sees it as a part of Kamau (a Muslim deeply influenced by the Nation of Islam who was tried with Shakur for bank robbery), her partner and coconspirator, as she sees her conspiratorial pregnancy as a powerful act of struggle.

This poem concludes with Shakur's description of her pregnancy in jail and her feelings about having a baby whose father and mother would both be locked up for many years. Shakur writes that she thought often of Zayd, and she pledged herself to becoming a mother, recounting that she said, "I'm gonna live as hard as i can and as full as i can until i die. And i'm not letting these parasites, these oppressors, these greedy racist swine make me kill my children in my mind, before they are even born. I'm going to live and i'm going to live and i'm going to love Kamau, and, if a child comes from that union, i'm going to rejoice. Because our children are our futures and i believe in the future and in the strength and righteousness of our struggle."[79] For Shakur, bearing a child would be evidence of the truth of the struggle against white supremacy, and it would serve as inspiration to her to continue the fight.

Shakur describes her pregnancy as "joyous," "spiritual," and a "miracle" and remembers that it was a bit of beauty in a place that was so ugly:

> I was filled with emotion. Already, i was deeply in love with this child. Already, I talked to it and worried about it and wondered how it was feeling and what it was thinking.... Sometimes i felt so helplessly protective, wondering when my baby would be called nigger for the first time, wondering when the full horror and degradation of being Black in amerika would descend on my baby. How many wolves hid behind the bushes to eat my child?[80]

Shakur's pregnancy provided her with hope to continue the struggle, and she saw it as part of a spiritual rebirth as well as a physical process. But Shakur also reflects on the vulnerability of her black child to racism and hatred outside and also inside of the prison. Shakur's pregnancy was terrorized as the prison doctor attempted to cajole Shakur to abort the baby and refused to call in a certified gynecologist to examine pains that Shakur was experiencing. The doctor told her, "Don't worry about it. My advice to you is that you should go to your cell and lie down. Just lie down and rest your mind. Just lie down and stay off your feet. And if you go to the bathroom and see a lump in the toilet, don't flush it. It's your baby."[81] Shakur writes, "[a]s far as I could see, they were out to kill my baby. I couldn't lose this baby now, not now. It was meant to be; this baby was our hope. Our hope for the future."[82] Just as Shakur's own origins were clouded by the state's interference, so was her child under constant threat of death. Her experience highlights an area of agitation that has been historically ignored because imprisoned women of color have been historically marginalized by the state.

In this strategy of regeneration, Shakur's daughter becomes a symbol of resistance and provides continuation to the struggle of which her mother became a part. By having a child in prison, Shakur resists the bodily control that the prison system enacts, and her daughter represents a feminized part of the struggle for freedom. At the same time, however, her act of rebellion in having a child also naturalizes the role of men in the birth process, thereby making them an integral, though sometimes marginalized, part of birth and rebirth. In becoming pregnant, "she becomes one in the very long line of outraged black mothers. . . . Here again the legacy of slavery, which separated mothers and children and refused to recognize maternal love, serves as a powerful context to the birth of her daughter. Like the slave mothers, Shakur has to leave her daughter to the care of her mother."[83] Shakur hopes that her baby will carry on the struggle into the next generation and help rebuild and recreate the movement for black liberation. In an interview on Rikers Island in 1974, she talks at length about the decision to get pregnant. She explains, "What we thought about when we talked about getting pregnant was life and the future. All of us related to the fact that we fight from one generation to the next. And I didn't know if I would even have another chance to have a child. . . . And sitting in the courtroom with all this shit happening it seemed to be the only thing that made sense."[84] The generational rhetoric here definitively connects Shakur's history of black resistance to her contemporary fight for black liberation in a way that positions her child as the terrain of struggle over the future of black activism. As a mother, Shakur, like countless slave mothers, was terrorized during her pregnancy. Elizabeth Alexander reminds us that "these corporeal images of terror suggest that 'experience' can be taken up into the body via witnessing and recorded in memory as knowledge" particularly for those who feel that they might be next in a long line of victims of the US racial tableau.[85]

Where Mumia Abu-Jamal uses a journalistic voice to do this kind of political work, Shakur's feminized vernacular uses affect rather than objectivity to make the case for black liberation. And although Shakur's vernacular style is oppositional toward white supremacy (as I suggest Rap Brown's was in chapter 2), her rhetorical resistance is also gendered producing the black *badwoman* as a rhetorical intervention. In articulating the aggressive masculine outlaw vernacular persona, the Black Power vernacular actively cultivated an idiom that often constrained female participation, but as we see with Shakur, black badwomen can be traced back to Harriet Tubman and other abolitionists. As Farred notes, "For women, the vernacular, even as it seeks to create new possibilities for subaltern articulation, serves as a reminder of how female alienation by the patriarchal/racist complex impacts and manifests itself in the vernacular."[86] The vernacular expression of Black Power was dialectical and oppositional toward white supremacy, but it also framed its cultural resistance in gendered terms that erased the possibility of badwomen contributing to radical black political culture. In articulating an aggressive masculine outlaw vernacular persona, the Black Power vernacular actively cultivated an idiom that often constrained female participation.

However, autobiographical manifestos written by women negotiate the possibilities of feminine identity and subjectivity. Some choose to conform to conventional femininity and some choose to investigate more hybrid possibilities for gender performance, particularly when complicated with explorations of class, race, and sexuality. Bella Brodzki and Celeste Schenck argue that these manifestos also "find a way to challenge inscription into conventional feminine identity and autobiographical representative selfhood while exploiting the textual ambiguity of their partnership with significant others."[87] Shakur, in particular, often employs ambiguity and strategic silence around her relationship with members of the Black Liberation Army, but particularly Kamau (Fred Hilton), who helped her to conceive her daughter in prison.[88] This silence helps to feminize the history of black resistance, though her rhetorical choices in describing her pregnancy acknowledge the important role that men play in (re)producing the movement toward freedom. Interestingly, in feminizing her history, or the history of black resistance, she does not discuss her father or her ex-husband, Louis Chesimard. These two figures, the husband and the father, are often prominent characters in female autobiography, but their absence in Shakur's text evidences just how important it is to her to be writing about black women.

Shakur does, however, write a poem to her four-year-old daughter Kakuya about her daughter's visit to the Clinton Correctional Facility for Women in New Jersey. Her daughter won't play and begins to hit Shakur through the bars with her little fists. Shakur writes:

I tell her to hit me until she is tired. . . . She is standing in front of me, her face contorted with anger, looking spent . . . "You're not my mother," she screams, the tears rolling down her face. "You're not my mother and I hate you." I feel like crying too. . . . I try to pick her up. . . . "You can get out of here, if you want to," she screams. "You just don't want to."[89]

Shakur is devastated by the rejection of her daughter, and she spends the night crying on her cot, resolving to leave prison for good. It is after this encounter with Kakuya that Shakur decided to escape, but she knew that she could not take her daughter with her, either back underground or into exile. And so she writes, "To My daughter Kakuya" of the "shabby dreams," "of some vague freedom," that Shakur has never known.[90] Shakur again makes the connection between birth and freedom in this tribute to her daughter's future. In many interviews, Shakur notes that she has never known freedom, never been able to grow strong and happy without the cultural shame and stigma attached to her blackness and without the poverty of her color. Shakur doesn't want her daughter to be "hungry or thirsty / or out in the cold." She writes, "And i don't want the frost / to kill your fruit / before it ripens."[91] Shakur sees the ways in which race, gender, and class intersect to constrain her present, her future, and the future of her daughter in understanding the ways in which her subjectivity as a black woman of color predicts the kind of future her daughter can expect in a culture that does not provide for its own.

Mothers, daughters, and sisters form the quilt of liberation history. As black feminist scholar, historian, and poet Bernice Johnson Reagon notes, "black women "are people builders, carriers of cultural traditions, key to the formation and continuance of our [black] culture."[92] She continues, "If we understand that we are talking about a struggle that is hundreds of years old, the new must acknowledge a continuance: that to be Black women is to move forward the struggle for the kind of space in this society that will make sense for our people."[93] Shakur places her activism in this larger historical context of black women's struggle for liberation in the United States. Shakur's poem documents her own history as part of the black liberation movement, but this move also points to the "centrality of women in the struggle for justice in the United States," particularly when placed in the company of movement memoirs by Anne Moody, Pauli Murray, Elaine Brown, Angela Davis, and Fannie Lou Hamer.[94] Because of the memoirs of women like Davis, Hamer, and Shakur, the intersection of gender, race, and class in the context of the US prison system rise to the forefront of issues surrounding liberation politics and connect black women from a standpoint that highlights the ways in which black women, in particular, experience the violence of the white supremacist state. Shakur's memoir reinforces the importance of black women to the organization, structure, tactics, and ideologies of black liberation, which feminizes the movement in contrast to the depiction of the black male rage that media outlets often used to stand-in for black liberation projects.

Shakur's feminization of Black Power extends into the prose of *Assata* as she describes the torture of being a black woman within America's prison-industrial complex. She describes the molestation of women in prison as they were stripped, searched, and forced to bathe with a toxic substance for lice and crabs when first admitted. In the last stage of the search before re-entering prison, guards insert their fingers inside of each woman, searching for contraband. If a woman refused to consent to the internal search, she would be placed in solitary confinement. Shakur writes,

> The "internal search" was as humiliating and disgusting as it sounded. You sit on the edge of this table and the nurse holds your legs open and sticks a finger in your vagina and moves it around. She has a plastic glove on. Some of them try to put one finger in your vagina and one up your rectum at the same time. Anyway, I had an instant, mile-long attitude. I wanted to punch the nurse clear to oblivion. Afterward, the guards had the nerve to tell me that a mistake had been made and a doctor would have to make a complete examination . . . He was a filthy-looking man who looked more than a Bowery bum than a doctor. He coughed all over me without even covering his mouth, and his fingernails looked like he had spent the last five years in a coal mine.[95]

Shakur's account feminizes the kind of treatment for female prisoners throughout the text and exposes the gynophobia and violence prevalent in prison facilities. The treatment she describes makes the private horror and humiliation both public and palpable for the reader and punctuates the state's dehumanization of inmates. She demonstrates the ways in which the prison system seeks to control the bodies of its inmates and force submission through inhuman, brutalizing bodily practices, much like the plantation culture of the American slave economy. In part, the affirmations and birth metaphors help to confront the patriarchal system of control over their bodies and reassert a "gynocentric aesthetic based on the body."[96] Passages like the one above also expose such horrible violations of the black female body, that the reader has a physical reaction to the violence enacted upon women, granting permanence to the memory of these details, which may spur the reader to action.

Just as Shakur embraces the birth of her daughter as a moment of regeneration, she also sees her autobiographical manifesto as a moment of (re)birth, producing a whole new history of black women's resistance. The childbirth metaphor allows her to defy patriarchal convention and merge the act of creation, in writing the text, with the act of (pro)creation, in having Kakuya. Shakur's counterhistory is squarely grounded in the history of the black women who came before her and whose spirit she continues to remember. By linking her resistance to that of prior generations of black women, inside and outside of America's prisons, Shakur crafts a continuous, complex narrative of black women's activism that in some ways counter the masculinity of the Black Power movement while still privileging heterosexuality and constructions of motherhood. Shakur's accounts of the violence against black people make the relationship between blackness and poverty irrefutable, which is why her writings continue to be anthologized.

The Police, Prison, and Assata Shakur

Shakur begins by discussing the leadership and goals of the Black Panther Party before describing the COINTELPRO violence that precipitated the BPP's collapse. Although she criticizes Chairman Huey Newton for being a poor speaker, a man unable to take criticism, and a dogmatic reactionary, she also sees the beginnings of Afrocentric education as the most important aspect of BPP life, though she charges that the political education program had no broad understanding of the complex historical circumstances that foster oppression. She also sees the lack of self-criticism in the party as problematic and sexist, especially regarding Huey Newton's public image and the excessive paranoia, which often led to clashes with the police, escalating in violence.[97] The oppositional tone she takes toward the internal politics of the BPP provides an important feminist rendering of an organization that has been discussed, critiqued, and valorized mostly by black men and also provides part of the rationale for why she aligned with the BLA after the Newton-Cleaver split in the organizational structure of the BPP.[98]

Given the extraordinarily brutal methods of state agents against black activists in American history, the use of armed resistance was a central debate among black revolutionaries in combating the terrorism of COINTELPRO and the FBI. Although some saw Newton as a zealot about weapons, it is clear that the rationale for self-defense is one that acknowledges the racist extremism that plagued civil rights organizations. Shakur notes that although the debate raged in her head for many years, she finally understood the need for weapons when she was locked down, and she indicts the utility of moral suasion as a movement tactic, saying, "Nobody in the world, nobody in history, has ever gotten their freedom by appealing to the moral sense of the people who were oppressing them."[99] Nonviolence, according to Shakur, provides no real solution to the classed problem of racial injustice and cannot be a legitimate tactic in the struggle for global liberation because it cannot eradicate capitalism.

Because she felt that the BPP was inadequate for pursuing many of the goals that would lead to a true liberation of black America, Shakur joined up with the BLA, which was mostly underground and decentralized.[100] Those who joined the BLA "were committed to revolutionary struggle in general and armed struggle in particular and wanted to help build the armed movement in amerika," though eventually they were forced underground because of COINTELRPO.[101] She notes, "While i was underground i made it a habit never to remember addresses. I used landmarks to remember a place, and i never had trouble locating any place i had been to once, but even if i visited it a hundred times, i never looked at the address."[102] This really serves as the only time Shakur discusses her life underground, and at no point in *Assata* does she detail or explain her black liberation activities. This silence lends a weight to her activism and serves as a reminder that her comrades are still in danger from the state, so they can't be named or described. It also allows the history of black resistance to be read into her activities, which makes her more likely to be seen as a similar liberation hero rather than a radical activist that could be easily read as a terrorist.

However, the FBI was intent upon disrupting BLA activities. Akinyele Omowale Umoja details the extensive anti-BLA campaigns that East Coast police divisions instituted to destroy black liberation efforts including NEWKILL, which was a program to investigate police killings and which signaled the increased repression of East Coast Panther chapters. Umoja writes, "In an FBI memorandum concerning NEWKILL, J. Edgar Hoover stated, 'The Newkill cases and other terrorists acts have demonstrated that in many instances those involved in these acts are individuals who cannot be identified as members of an extremist group . . . They are frequently supporters, community workers, or people who hang around the headquarters of the extremist group or associate with members of the group.'"[103] Hoover's characterization of the movement participants as terrorists, a move that was prominent in Assata Shakur's trials, precipitated an incredible amount of backlash by East Coast police officers and also an outpouring of support from the federal government, through programs like COINTELPRO and NEWKILL, which decimated the above-ground operations of many liberation organizations and ended the lives of many activists. By branding Shakur a "terrorist," Hoover also explicitly linked her to the hostage situations in Tehran and Libya and the bombings of groups like the Irish Republican Army that dominated headlines during the late 1970s.

Shakur's criticisms of the prison-industrial complex are predicated upon her own treatment in the hands of the state, particularly those police forces empowered by Hoover to undermine and destroy black liberation activism. In the memoir, she provides numerous examples of the brutality of the state, particularly as she describes her interactions with the New Jersey police, following her arrest. She writes, "Every day there were three shifts of police. When they changed shifts, the two troopers would salute the sergeant. Some saluted an army salute, but others saluted like the nazis did in Germany. They held their hands in front of them and clicked their heels."[104] Her aunt and lawyer, Evelyn Williams describes the scene at the hospital after the shoot-out, noting that the open hatred of the state troopers shocked her since they lined both sides of the corridor of her hospital room. She writes that Shakur's "primary concern was the removal of the state troopers from her room—she told me they were threatening to kill her."[105] But the threats were just a part of the kind of harassment and abuse that Shakur was subjected to in the hospital. Shakur adds, "One day one of them came in and gave me a speech about how he fought in World War II on the wrong side . . . He said that if Hitler had won, the world wouldn't be the mess it is in today, that niggers like me, no-good, niggers, wouldn't be going around shooting new jersey state troopers."[106] By examining the culture of patriarchal white supremacy that permeates state police forces, Shakur is exposing the system of lies and deceit that perpetuate race, class, and gender inequity. These officers beat her with the butts of their rifles and consistently threatened to kill her for her opposition to their brutality.[107] Such testimony not only helps constitute the collective memories of the violence against African Americans seeking political and economic justice, but it likewise provides the impetus the regenerative efforts underway in the next stage of the Black Power movement, particularly because police brutality and racial profiling have gotten worse, rather than better.

Finally, Shakur provides a critique of imprisonment that acknowledges the complicated racial history of the penitentiary in the United States, particularly its relationship to labor. She describes refusing to work without pay in prison when a guard demands that she snap string beans. She tells the guard, "I don't work for nothing. I a'int gonna be no slave for nobody. Don't you know slavery was outlawed?" To which, the guard responds, "No, you're wrong. . . . Slavery is legal in prisons." Here, Shakur records the text of the Thirteenth Amendment and argues that, "[p]risons are a profitable business. They are a way of legally perpetuating slavery. . . . Prisons are a part of this government's genocidal war against Black and Third World people."[108] Shakur acknowledges the history of peonage and convict leasing that has provided most of the cheap labor in the United States since Reconstruction and is very clear about the consequences of prison labor for jobs outside of prison (for people of color).[109] This history of peonage connects the prison-industrial complex and political prisoners to a much longer history of state repression and centers the prison system as the enemy. Shakur's critiques of history and of the racist, sexist, and classist nature of the prison system and the police also connect the brutality of the state against her to a prolific history of genocide against black America, starting with slavery. The recounting of such racialized brutalities highlights the continued exigencies for Black Power regeneration and as a documentation of the sacrifice made by those trapped in the prison system.

In addition to recording a feminized counterhistory of resistance, Shakur's anti-imperial language and her use of redefinition are vernacular interventions to rebuild black liberation. On July 4, 1973, Shakur recorded "To My People," an open letter broadcast across the United States.[110] This prophetic discourse emphasizes Shakur's commitment to Third World liberation as a tenet of Black Power. She says, "I am a Black revolutionary, and, as such, i am a victim of all the wrath, hatred, and slander that amerika is capable of. Like all other Black revolutionaries, amerika is trying to lynch me."[111] Shakur directs the listener/reader to think critically about misrepresentations in the media, and she asserts political repression is the modern form of lynching, invoking the racialized and gendered dynamics of Shakur's persecution. Shakur goes on to provide a much more detailed indictment of the "real" criminal, redefining murder as empire-building, asserting: "Nixon and his crime partners have murdered hundreds of Third World brothers and sisters in Vietnam, Cambodia, Mozambique, Angola, and South Africa . . . They call us murderers, but we did not murder over two hundred fifty unarmed Black men, women and children, or wounded thousands of others during the riots they provoked during the sixties."[112] Shakur's criticism of Nixon's "law and order" regime and the expansion of the war in Indochina demonstrate how domestic repression and foreign interventionism are both part of building American empire, which provides the Black Power rationale for Third World solidarity.

Next, Shakur links prison revolt and campus demonstrations to the expansion of the American empire as she continues to invert the label of "murderer": "The rulers of this country have always considered their property more important than our lives. They call us murderers, but we were not responsible for the twenty-eight brother inmates and nine hostages murdered at attica. They call us murderers, but we did not murder and wound over thirty unarmed black students at Jackson State—or Southern State, either."[113] She continues with the public assassinations of black leaders (where government complicity was a contributing factor): "They call us murderers, but we did not murder Martin Luther King, Jr., Emmett Till, Medgar Evers, Malcolm X, George Jackson, Nat Turner, James Chaney and countless others . . . They call us murderers, but we do not control or enforce a system of racism and oppression that systematically murders Black and Third World people . . . For every pig that is killed in the so-called line of duty, there are at least fifty Black people murdered by the police."[114] Shakur's reversal of the label of murderer forces the reader to recognize the tremendous violence utilized and exported by the state to enforce white supremacy and neocolonialism. For Shakur, this pattern began with slavery and theft as the nation was built on the backs of stolen peoples. She says, "it was not we who stole millions of Black people from the continent of Africa. We were robbed of our language, of our Gods, of our culture, of our human dignity, of our labor, and of our lives."[115]

Because of the gross abuses of the West, Shakur argues that such revolutionary action is the only way toward freedom and liberation: "There is, and always will be, until every Black man, woman, and child is free, a Black Liberation Army. The main function of the Black Liberation Army at this time is to create good examples, to struggle for Black freedom, and to prepare for the future. We must defend ourselves and let no one disrespect us. We must gain our liberation by any means necessary."[116] This framework invokes Malcolm X, while acknowledging the importance of armed struggle. As the narrative of a political prisoner, Shakur's book is a source of revolutionary inspiration for those inside and outside of prison because of her analysis.

Certainly, the literary antecedents for her text are not limited to the writings of Angela Davis and George Jackson. Rather, her manifesto is also a part of the emerging revolutionary literary aesthetic in the United States influenced by a wave of anti-imperialist, anticolonialist poets and Négritude writers like Aimé Césaire, Leon Damas, Léopold Sédar Senghor, and Franz Fanon. Like these anticolonial vernacular writers, Shakur uses poetry to bridge the local and the global, which helps her to express anticolonial revolutionary sentiments from within the framework of cultural nationalism and Black Power while still situating her activism in an understandable context: her family.[117] In falling into this canon, Shakur makes the rhetoric of Afrikan liberation accessible to a US audience by deploying poetry as a more palatable, and perhaps accessible, version of this vernacular than, say, treatises on guerrilla warfare like George Jackson's.

Prisons and Black Liberation at the Millennium

Assata Shakur's narrative and poems document state power from the perspective of a political prisoner, countering depictions of her and the BLA in the "official" history. Gready notes that "[t]o be a prisoner is to be variously rewritten, to be contested through writing. Through the confession, state witnesses, legislation, the political trial, and prison regulation the political prisoner is violently and relentlessly rewritten . . . Pain is inflicted and made visible and objectified in the written word enabling it to be denied as personal pain and read as state power."[118] Shakur's memoir provides an entire body of oppositional writing that recovers her story and her poetry from within a Black Power movement that is generally discussed in terms of its black male leaders and their prose. Because of the success of *Assata*, Shakur has become a rallying point for black prison activists because even from exile in Cuba, she continues to inspire black liberation agitation.

Like the Nègritude poets, Shakur's poetry deals with the alienation of blackness, the retreat into the solitude of self as an exile from the larger community, and the agonies of muteness and unfulfilled belonging in daily American life. Her poetry becomes personally cathartic even as she attempts to transcend the personal for the benefit of all black Americans, particularly black women. She expresses her anguish and indignation at the horrific conditions and treatment that she and her fellow humans endure at the hands of the American empire. Thus, Shakur reconstructs the black female self and revalorizes the black women, who have resisted the patriarchy of white supremacist culture and whose history of rebellion is erased, forgotten, or eclipsed by the anxiety surrounding black male revolutionaries. The (re)birth metaphor also reifies the integral role of men in the regeneration of Black Power, through her valorization of their role in the conception of black children who will carry the mantle of Black Power.

Her story repositions the prison-industrial complex and political prisoners at the center of black liberation. In an interview in 1997, she says, "I believe that the only way that people like myself and others who are in prison or exiled will ever be 'safe' is for people to build a strong movement around the issue of political repression. We must build a strong movement to free political prisoners. In conjunction, we must build a strong movement for amnesty for all of those people—those political activists—who were victimized by COIN-TELPRO."[119] By writing and granting interviews, Shakur is still participating in the struggle for black liberation from exile, clearly urging others to build a strong movement around political prisoners. As one voice among many other black people in either exile or prison, she explains that writing is her "duty." She adds, "This goes especially to the case of Mumia Abu-Jamal, who is facing death. We must work and do everything possible to ensure Mumia's release and bring him back into the community where he is so desperately needed."[120] By linking political prisoners like Mumia to Black Power activists in exile, Shakur insists upon collective mobilization and activism for black liberation with a sense of both urgency and duty, which helps to elevate her as a leader. She locates COINTELPRO and the prison system at the heart of the regeneration of the black liberation struggle in the millennium and urges her reader to participate in movement activities centered on exonerating these activists, these targets of the FBI, combating the power structure in the process. Her life and work as a revolutionary reflects the new phase of black resistance where people like Mumia Abu-Jamal are likewise central to the movement's regenerative efforts. Despite the FBI's constant efforts to destroy liberation movements like the Black Power movement, Shakur's poetry asks readers to "become heroes in the cause of liberation," seemingly working to regenerate the will to resist even those who have been partially successful in destroying the leaders of these movements.[121]

Conclusion

Assessing the Role of Prison after the Turn to Black Power

In this book I have attempted to trace how the shift to Black Power was a significant rhetorical and political intervention into discourse about civil rights because of the centrality of the prison and political prisoners, "law and order discourse," and conflict over lawlessness versus social protest. Using a black vernacular steeped in street talk, Third World populism, intersectional analyses of power, and gender performance that utilized irony, hyperbole, anecdote, and history, Black Power autobiographies emerged as a significant space expressing disappointment, alienation, and anger about the pace and content of civil rights reform. Black Power intellectuals embraced a mobile urban vernacular at odds with the respectability politics and Christian sermonizing of public icons like Martin Luther King Jr. These intellectuals have become, in Farred's words, "oppositional cultural icons" who have offered vernacular texts that interrogate the assessments of black activism from within the "law and order" culture of the 1960s.[1] Given the persecution generated by the FBI's COINTELPRO initiatives, the continuing police brutality, and the staggering investment of federal and state taxes into both the militarization of the police and expansion of the prison-industrial complex, it would seem that the role of prison in the movement for black freedom was forced to change as the federal government became even more calcified against civil rights throughout the tumult of 1968.

Activists, excluded from policymaking after the death of King, became even more conscious of their status as outsiders and embraced rhetorical practices that acknowledged their geographic location in urban centers as the movement for black liberation shifted from North to South, using class and gender to shape racial politics for new activists. As Edward Said has aptly documented, texts travel.[2] In the case of Black Power, the vernacular prison texts traveled from the inside of prisons to the outside world, from the hands of political prisoners to black communities in exile. The vernacular shift of Black Power prison writers was strategically and successfully deployed for the white eavesdroppers as well as the Black Power in-group, those allied with Black

Power organizations and ideologies. This book demonstrates how the Black Power vernacular has been a flexible response to racial discrimination and its ever-present, though constantly changing relationship to incarceration.

Nowhere was this changing relationship between Black Power and imprisonment more provocative than in the wake of September 11, 2001, when two hijacked planes crashed into the World Trade Center in New York, another crashed into the Pentagon, and a fourth into a field in Pennsylvania. After 9/11, the passage of the Patriot Act, the outpouring of xenophobia and violence against Muslims in the United States, and the war on terror all ignited another phase of conversation about racial profiling, police brutality, incarceration, and, certainly after Abu Ghraib, international torture. In considering how the Black Power vernacular has stayed relevant since the writers featured in this book first encountered imprisonment in the course of their activism, this short conclusion speculates about Black Power in the political context of the war on terror long after the black liberation movement succumbed to internal and external pressures on black activists organizations in the 1970s. I want to suggest that in refusing to die, disappear, or be silent, all of these intellectuals continue to offer a voice of reproach for mass incarceration in the United States and beyond, linking the history of slavery to American military occupation abroad and to a larger policy of imprisonment throughout the world. In examining the Black Power vernacular within the context of the war on terror, scholars might consider other political contexts after 9/11 that continue to shape the relationship between black resistance and the politics of incarceration.

Rereleasing *Die Nigger Die!*: Regenerating Black Power during the War on Terror

We know that Rap Brown's analysis of race relations was salient for his audience at the time of the first publication of *Die Nigger Die!* in 1969 because it went through an astounding seven printings. The rerelease of the book in 2002 included a new foreword by Ekwueme Michael Thelwell, former SNCC activist and W. E. B. Du Bois Chair at the University of Massachusetts. This new foreword contextualized the book and its author (now known as Jamil Al-Amin) in the post–September 11 climate of anti-Muslim, anti-dissent politics. Thelwell begins by detailing the COINTELPRO schemes to disappear Brown in the 1960s because of his radical, provocative critiques of state power. Then, he argues that Rap Brown has become Jamil Al-Amin, a religious cleric who, despite his denunciation of violence as a means of social change, has been persecuted by the same kind of governmental forces that tried to eradicate him in the 1960s and 1970s. As a strategy of the Black Power vernacular, this renaming of Brown to Al-Amin demonstrates the flexibility of Black Power ideology across time.

But Thewell also suggests that because Brown was such an important Black Power leader, the FBI continues to see him as Brown, as the rabble-rousing agitator of the later 1960s. However, a kind of third persona emerges in the rerelease of *Die Nigger Die!* that blends Brown's Black Power ideologies and Al-Amin's commitments to Islam. Finally, Thewell argues that the circumstances surrounding Al-Amin's current incarceration are suspect, implying that Al-Amin was framed with Islamophobic ideas promoted during the war on terror. Thelwell encourages the reader to see Al-Amin as both an endangered Black Power leader and as Muslim martyr who must be exonerated. Arguing that because Al-Amin was a Black Power leader who advocated armed self-defense and is now an activist Muslim, Thelwell suggests that he has been imprisoned as a part of the legacy of COINTELPRO. By rereleasing the text during his trial, *Die Nigger Die!* seems positioned to both capitalize on new support for Al-Amin and to regenerate Black Power by recirculating the text. This helps elevate him to the status of political prisoner (again), and it makes it easier to link his cause to, say, Assata Shakur and Mumia Abu-Jamal. To understand the way that the rerelease of the text works in 2002, we must first examine how the text travels as a flexible example of the Black Power vernacular during the war on terror.

Thelwell begins by arguing that *Die Nigger Die!* is a crucial artifact of the Black Power movement whose messages have traveled from the past to the present. Calling the book "a vital American historical document," Thelwell points to the fact that like other Black Power autobiographies, this one is "historical almost in the sense of a message found in a time capsule, a missive from another age" that continues to be relevant.[3] Thelwell encourages readers to see *Die Nigger Die!* as a living text, whose messages change over time. John Angus Campbell makes a similar argument when he encourages us to provide accounts "of how a specific rhetorical object—the political consciousness of a people as materialized in their language—creates new rhetorical situations as it moves across time."[4] To do this kind of rhetorical investigation, we must look at the instances when the discourse in question is reintroduced into the political lexicon for this is where radical reflection occurs prompted by the interrogation of individual consciousness and through the forging of collective identities. Campbell adds, "radical reflection occurs when in the present moment of danger an individual (or an individual speaking on behalf of a people) reaches into the magazine of cultural memory and brings forward a fragment of the past around which to crystallize resistance to a present danger."⁵ When the reader or the listener encounters this discursive past in a new present, they embark on the journey of radical reflection and in their judgment; they notice the similarities between the past and the present. "In affirming a previous self-interpretation as their present self-definition, a people treat an entire tradition as though it were a text, 'invent' a relevant parallel to the present case, and rally to repel a perceived threat," writes Campbell.⁶ By utilizing this paradigm, we are able to see the ways that *Die Nigger Die!* bridges 1969 and 2002 to perform its criticisms "at a variety of discursive sites over time."⁷ In this case, the rereleased book connects the black liberation struggle to the war on terror to mark the continuities of imprisonment affecting black lives in the United States and abroad.

Thelwell encourages the reader to see *Die Nigger Die!* as a text that tells us as much about Black Power leaders of the 1960s and 1970s as it does about black (Muslim) leaders today. After providing a brief sketch of Brown's participation in SNCC and the BPP, Thelwell maintains that the pervasive frameups, detention, and assassinations of black leaders in the COINTELPRO era never ended and were intended "to silence and immobilize leadership while forcing groups to redirect energy and resources into raising funds, organizing legal defenses, and publicizing their cases."⁸ The legal spectacles of the Chicago Seven and the Panther 21 trials, among many others, made the black militants into heroes but they also atrophied the Black Power movement by removing leaders from the public eye for months or years at a time while, sadly, directing Black Power financial assets into the legal system. Ultimately, Thelwell's comments here illustrate that Brown was so central to Black Power that the state had to "disappear" him, underscoring Brown's role as a Black Power leader in the past and now, in his current phase of incarceration.

Thelwell highlights the fact that *Die Nigger Die!* served a purpose for the Black Power movement in 1969 when it was first released, but that it serves another purpose now since Al-Amin is a Muslim. Therefore, Al-Amin's leadership as an imam and as a scholarly cleric merges with his persona as a Black Power leader to produce a third persona that is *both* a black radical *and* a Muslim.⁹ Thelwell writes, "The fiery young rebel who speaks out of the pages of this book has long since evolved into an austere religious scholar, disciplined by faith and projecting the aura of a spiritually dispossessed ascetic."¹⁰ There is tension here, though, in seeing Al-Amin as someone totally removed from Brown but then understanding that Al-Amin did not amend the rereleased of *Die Nigger Die!* Because the original text is not revised, Al-Amin occupies a dual space as both Brown, the Black Power firebrand, and Al-Amin, the Muslim cleric, allowing Al-Amin to harness his critiques of the state from 1969 to apply to the context of the present without actually having to utter them again. While this may allow us to try to read the text through the lens of 1969, it also reifies the rigid black badman masculinity, allowing the persona of Rap Brown, and all of the strategies of regenerating Black Power in the text, to remain intact.

This third persona illustrates how explosive Brown was as a Black Power leader but also highlights how Al-Amin's sympathizers want him to be seen as a bookish imam who has changed his opinions on the utility of violence. Thelwell posits "two utterly incompatible and mutually exclusive stories" that may explain why the specter of Rap Brown is still alive in public memory. The first "is the narrative of H. Rap Brown, the armed militant, prone to violence, 'revolutionary' or 'criminal' depending on your take. This old narrative is preserved alive and well in the computerized memory banks of law enforcement and in the film clips and sound bytes of media, a convenient ghost to be summoned up at will over the next thirty years."[11]

The second story is of the bookish, scholarly imam, whose conversion to Islam was complete. As Thelwell assures the reader that H. Rap Brown "is no longer among us," since "[d]uring a period of incarceration by the State of New York" Brown converted to Orthodox Islam, and emerged a Sunni Muslim. Thelwell adds, "Brown went in and Al-Amin came out."[12] Thelwell's description of Brown's prison conversion demonstrates the lasting significance of imprisonment in the transformation of Black Power activists while also positing that while the man changed, the context did not. In particular, Thelwell marshals testimony from Al-Amin's brother Ed Brown, also a former SNCC member, to explore how the state continues to see Brown as the militant firebrand of 1969 despite the transformation that Thelwell describes. Ed says:

Something happens. Say the first attempt to bomb the Trade Center, right? They feed their infallible profile into their computer. Muslim . . . radical . . . violent . . . anti-American, whatever, who knows. Anyway, boom, out spits the names, H. Rap Brown prominent among them. Next thing the Feds come storming into the community and haul Jamil in. This actually happened. Of course it's stupid. And every time they have to let him go. But how do you stop it? A goddamn nightmare, they never quit.[13]

Because Rap Brown declared himself to be an enemy of the state in 1969, Ed Brown argues that the state will consider him an enemy until he is in jail for life or dead, since the state recognizes him as both the militant Black Power extremist that they feared in 1969 and also a radical Muslim. From Ed Brown's comments then, the rerelease of *Die Nigger Die!* can be seen as a strategy of regenerating Black Power to address the continued abuses of the state and its agents, but this cuts against the argument that Brown's transformation into Al-Amin was total.

Rather, Thelwell's perspective attempts to recover an identity for Al-Amin shaped by police harassment for being a radical black Muslim, which helps to make his case that Al-Amin has been accused of crimes he did not commit, of which, this most recent arrest might be similar. The denunciation of violence that Thelwell asserts is problematic, however, because, of the texts in this study, *Die Nigger Die!* is the most committed to violent destruction of the white nation state, at least rhetorically. Thelwell's assertion of Al-Amin's non-violence does very little to undermine the strategies of Black Power regeneration that permeate *Die Nigger Die!* Perhaps this characterization of Al-Amin is meant for the Muslim audience of the text's rerelease as a way of assuaging their concerns about the violence advocated in the text? Perhaps we are to read these statements about Al-Amin renouncing violence as a kind of strawperson argument or as a thinly veiled attempt to exonerate Al-Amin for his murder charge?

Regardless, Thelwell's brief assessment of Al-Amin's character does not destabilize the power of Brown's text to recirculate the Black Power vernacular that embraced badman masculinity, self-defense, and violence. Interestingly enough, though, Thelwell explains that the only objection that Al-Amin had to the rerelease pertained to the "vernacular earthiness of some of the street language," particularly the references to women, but ultimately decided against any corrections to the original text.[14] It is surprising that Al-Amin's concern is with the vernacular, when it is precisely this language that authorizes a contextual and historical pushback against the police state and mass incarceration. Given that the book itself is unconcerned with black female agency, Brown's regrets may, perhaps, reflect the shifting context of feminist and womanist politics that emerged from the 1960s. Nonetheless, Brown's original text stands unmodified, harnessing all of the rhetorical and political agency that Brown had marshaled while he was still chairman of SNCC.

Al-Amin as "Cop Killer"

It seems that on March 16, 2000, Fulton County deputy sheriff Ricky Kinchen was shot and later died, and Deputy Aldranon English was wounded after being shot by a man outside of Al-Amin's corner store in the West End of Atlanta while serving a warrant for Al-Amin's arrest.[15] Al-Amin was arrested in Lowndes County, Alabama, on March 20, 2000, following a four-day manhunt and was subsequently flown back to Atlanta where he was indicted for murder in connection with the shooting death of Deputy Kinchen after Deputy English picked him out of a line-up.[16] He was charged despite the fact that in English's statement on the night of March 16, he claimed to have wounded the shooter and the police were following leads from a trail of blood leading away from the scene where the shooter escaped; Al-Amin was not wounded and showed no signs of injury when he was brought back to Atlanta. The following month, the FBI revealed that they monitored Al-Amin between 1992–1997 for everything from domestic terrorism (specifically the World Trade Center bombing in 1993, for which Abu-Jamal was detained) to gunrunning, to at least fourteen homicides in Atlanta, which certainly illustrated the extent to which the state still perceived him to be a threat. At the beginning of May 2000, the state announced that it would pursue the death penalty against Al-Amin for the shooting of Deputy Kinchen. The next month, Otis Jackson (twenty-six years old) confessed to killing Kinchen but later recanted; however, Al-Amin's defense team was not notified of the confession. Al-Amin was arraigned on January 19, 2001, with a trial date to be set later in the year.

The trial of Jamil Al-Amin for the shooting death of Deputy Kinchen was scheduled to begin on September 13, 2001, but due to the massive outpouring of anti-Muslim sentiment in the United States following the terrorist attacks on September 11, his trial was moved to January 7, 2002, with Judge Stephanie Manis presiding. In cases like Al-Amin's, judges hoped that brief continuances would preserve a fair trial after 9/11, but, as Woods reminds us, "the ensuing war in Afghanistan, heightened terror alerts, and continued threats of new domestic attacks have sustained a certain level of animus toward Muslins in the United States."[17] Judge Manis also imposed a gag rule on Al-Amin because he had proclaimed his innocence to his congregation in a prison letter after his arraignment. On March 9, 2002, a jury convicted Al-Amin of murder and on March 13, 2002, he was sentenced to life in prison without parole, making another phase of incarceration for him.[18]

Although Al-Amin's current phase of incarceration is shrouded in uncertainty, as Thelwell alludes to, he stops short of proclaiming Al-Amin's innocence, choosing instead to focus on the political scene. Thelwell implies that the slayings of so many unarmed black men by police in the preceding year provides context for the police who entered Al-Amin's "Muslim community, under the cover of darkness, heavily armed . . . [and] wearing flakjackets to bring in a respected and beloved religious leader, a figure of a fixed address and regular and predictable habits, at night" particularly "in the service of a warrant for charges they describe as relatively minor."[19] Thelwell's comments provide a provocation that demands the reader understand Al-Amin's current incarceration as more of the same kind of COINTELPRO-style harassment and police brutality that apparently continued through the 1990s.

As he pontificates on the significance of the police brutality in Atlanta and in New York, Thelwell directs the reader to speak about Al-Amin. He writes, "It is now time for the state and his fellow citizens to speak. In the national mood following the horrific events of 9/11, it will be instructive to see what they say."[20] By preempting *Die Nigger Die!* with the framework of September 11, Thelwell implies that the manifesto regenerates its ideologies and strategies for confronting the state even during the climate following the terrorist attacks in 2001. As Al-Amin's trial date neared, the Muslim community began to fear the worst—that Al-Amin would be convicted not because of his guilt but because he is Muslim.[21] Several major polls in the aftermath of 9/11 confirmed that the general American public was suspicious of Muslims and felt that the federal government should tightly monitor them.[22] Thus, Al-Amin became a likely candidate for the death penalty because in the climate after 9/11, the anti-Muslim sentiment added to the lingering racial hatred of black militancy and made finding an impartial jury difficult. For many Muslims, Al-Amin's trial was about more than the fate of Al-Amin himself; it "would test whether a Muslim could really get a fair trial in post-9/11 America."[23] Because Deputy English fingered Al-Amin as the shooter despite the fact that the medical report presented in court found him uninjured, the narrative of the "good cop" was unassailable, particularly because the trial followed the terrorist attacks. Attorney James Curry Woods writes that Al-Amin's trial was a perfect example of how anti-Muslim sentiment clouded trials in the year following 9/11, arguing that "[w]hile criminal defendants facing terror-related charges are more likely to bear the brunt of the anti-Muslim sentiments, litigants of all races and claims may find that changes in American attitudes have affected the jury system as a whole and on many different levels."[24] Woods suggests that Al-Amin's trial was in fact a symbolic showdown between the now-calcified law and order culture that targeted Muslims for mass incarceration in the wake of 9/11.

From these statements, we can see that Thelwell's foreword is suggestive of a *new reading* about *Die Nigger Die!* as the American political and racial context shifted following 9/11. Thelwell's reading of *Die Nigger Die!* positions Al-Amin, *the defendant*, as a kind of third persona blending the Black Power leadership of Rap Brown and the asceticism of Al-Amin. By implying that Al-Amin's most recent arrest is a part of the legacy of both Black Power and COINTELPRO disruption, Thelwell's essay encourages a reassessment of Al-Amin both as a Black Power leader and as a black Muslim resisting the same white structures that have always silenced and disappeared black heroes. And by asking the reader to understand Al-Amin's recent charges and his trial through a post–September 11 climate, Thelwell's new foreword locates *Die Nigger Die!* as an identificatory discourse with the potential to recruit new followers of Al-Amin, either for his Black Power ideologies or for his commitment to Islam. This kind of regenerative strategy has the possibility to build a movement around Al-Amin both during his trial and after the verdict, particularly after a conviction because it (re)frames Al-Amin as a Black Power martyr of the past and of the present, with his religious commitments apparently intensifying his repression. Finally, it suggests that the rhetorical strategies of the "law and order" culture of the 1960s have reappeared in the rhetorical discourses after 9/11 that mobilized Islamophobia to justify domestic repression. Thus, the rerelease of *Die Nigger Die!* marks the convergence of anti–Black Power and anti-Muslim sentiment and, I think, provides the opportunity to ask some pointed questions about how the memoirs of imprisoned and exiled Black Power intellectuals continue to travel in ways that demonstrate the continued salience of the Black Power vernacular.

The War on Terror and the Response from Death Row

The slippage between resistance to state violence and charges of terrorism was not just a feature of the rhetoric surrounding Rap Brown, as Thelwell claims. Rather, it was part of conservative framing of the war on terror that placed radical black intellectuals, particularly political prisoners and other members of the American Left, front and center. Calling people who support Mumia Abu-Jamal "Mumidiots," CNN's conservative commentator Michael Smerconish has suggested that Mumia Abu-Jamal (along with most of the American Left) should be "muzzled" for daring to speak out against the war on terror.[25] Responding to a September 19, 2001, ad signed by civil rights icons, academics, world-renowned authors, politicians, and cultural figures in the *New York Times* published under the banner "Not in Our Name" that condemned the "War on Terror" as a limitless expansion of American military power, Smerconish and conservative commentators after 9/11 worked to rhetorically connect the US Left with domestic terrorism in a fit of hyperbole. In probably the most explicit example, Dinesh D'Souza's book *The Enemy at Home: The Cultural Left and Its Responsibility for 9/11* begins with this claim: "The cultural left in this country is responsible for causing 9/11."[26] In blaming the left for creating the conditions responsible for 9/11, D'Souza writes, "the cultural left and its allies in Congress, the media, Hollywood, the nonprofit sector, and the universities are the primary cause of the volcano of anger toward America that is erupting from the Islamic world."[27] In refusing to acknowledge the US military legacy in Afghanistan or the arms deals brokered between the United States and the *mujahidin*, D'Souza's book, like those of other conservative pundits, glosses the history of US occupation in Afghanistan and instead suggests that the US Left is too strident in pointing out inequality. Particularly important is D'Souza's claim that the *tone* of the left's critiques of neoliberalism has inflamed anti-Americanism abroad. He writes, "the left has actively fostered the intense hatred of America that has led to murderous attacks such as 9/11."[28] By characterizing critiques of the state by the left as "intense hatred" (while simultaneously performing shrill critiques of the state from the right), D'Souza erases any space for positive critique from the left echoing the "law and order" culture of earlier decades.

Conservative critics like D'Souza and Smerconish cannot or will not acknowledge that activists like Abu-Jamal are understood by the left as *political prisoners*. Their imprisonment is political primarily because of what they continue to *say* and *expose* about the relationship between white supremacy and the legal system or about mass incarceration and the destruction of equality movements rather than because of what they've been convicted of *doing*. While the narratives about rabble-rousers and cop killers immediately position the public against the alleged perpetrator, it remains that observations about the legal system uttered by these citizens can be valuable tools in understanding the dynamics of oppression and privilege that shape the legal system and the prison-industrial complex.

Abu-Jamal has remained relevant not simply due to his long stint on death row but also because he continues to write and publish about issues at the intersection of social movements and state violence, particularly after 9/11. For example, in his radio essay titled, "In the Shadow of Abu Ghraib," Abu-Jamal situates the torture of prisoners held without due process in Abu Ghraib prison in Iraq with the history of American penal practices. Responding to over 2,000 photos taken by American prison guards during the occupation of Iraq depicting sexual torture and violence undertaken by the guards against Iraqi captives, Abu-Jamal explains, "Many of the people who are now in Iraq, especially those in the reserves are cops and prison guards. The treatment of Iraqis at Abu Ghraib has the dark precedence in the prisons and police stations across America."[29] He added, "Americans may call it liberation but they're bringing torture, humiliation and domination. It is somehow fitting that these depraved events have happened in one of the most dreadful prisons of the Hussein regime."[30] Abu-Jamal's comments on Abu Ghraib suggest that the language of liberation obscures the politics of mass incarceration, torture, dominance, and disappearance that characterize the US occupation of Iraq. Whether at Guantanamo Bay, where so-called terrorists have been held in indefinite detention with extraordinary rendition, or in Iraq where the photographs of service members mounting prisoners have been circulated around the globe, the torture suggests to Abu-Jamal that the US exports its racial domination. In joining his voice to the chorus of journalists, scholars, and intellectuals dedicated to making the abuses and violence at Abu Ghraib public and visible, Abu-Jamal demonstrates how essential the prison is in maintaining the cultural and military dominance of the United States at the expense of human rights.

In point of fact, one of the main torturers at Abu Ghraib prison, Specialist Charles Graner, had been a reservist working as a guard at the State Correctional Institution at Greene in southwestern Pennsylvania where Mumia Abu-Jamal has been jailed for decades, making the connection between mass incarceration and torture in the United States and similar abuse abroad quite clear and cementing Abu-Jamal's expertise on the matter.[31] *Democracy Now* reported that the Abu Ghraib photos "repeatedly show Spec. Charles Graner Jr. in photographs giving the 'thumbs up' over piles of naked Iraqi men" and that "Graner reportedly worked as a prison guard in Virginia and at the Greene County state correctional institution. Prisoners there claim Graner beat and humiliated inmates while he worked there as a prison officer."[32] Abu-Jamal's commentary on the Abu Ghraib prison abuse scandal connects his comments on prison violence in the United States to a more extensive pattern of prison abuse globally, demonstrating to his readers and listeners how US imperialism uses and abuses incarceration in black sites across the globe. Especially since experts and scholars have been unable to document any usable data gleaned from interrogations garnered in detention sites through torture, Abu-Jamal's coverage brings American prison abuse to a larger audience, exposing the endurance of prison as a space for consolidating white supremacy.[33]

In addition to writing resistance against global mass incarceration precipitated by American empire-building, Abu-Jamal's embodied resistance demonstrates how long-term organizational movements can undermine the death penalty. For example, the success of the "Free Mumia!" movement can be measured by the length of Abu-Jamal's stay on death row. Philadelphia prosecutors finally dropped their pursuit of the death penalty against Abu-Jamal in December of 2011, declaring that Abu-Jamal (like Jamil Al-Amin) will serve life in prison without parole instead. After surviving two executions dates in August 1995 and in December 1999, Abu-Jamal represents a challenge to corporal punishment and his life demonstrates the resilience of black life, even in prison. Thirty-three years after the death of Officer Faulkner, Abu-Jamal's sentence continues to be a lightning rod for conservative backlash against black intellectualism and a mobilizing point for political action against police corruption and racism in the judicial system. His writings demonstrate the ways in which prison intellectuals and their ideas continued to circulate during the war on terror as well as the ways in which their vernacular and political interventions never stop influencing civic deliberation, particularly about the role of the prison (and political prisoners) in the expansion of American imperialism.

Cuba, the Black Liberation Army, and the War on Terror

As a framing discourse of the new millennium, the war on terror provided a new series of images and rhetorical inventions that both imprisoned and exiled Black Power intellectuals used to clarify their opposition to mass incarceration and military occupation. Obviously, Jamil al-Amin rereleased his class tome *Die Nigger Die!* and Abu-Jamal released radio essays about the invasion of Iraq. For her part, Assata Shakur became, once again, the quintessential terrorist. In May 2013, commenting on the reemergence of Shakur's visage as the face of modern terrorism, media scholar Sohail Daulatzai wrote an essay for Al Jazeera Online titled, "Are We All Muslim Now? Assata Shakur and the Terrordome." The essay centered on President Barack Obama's decision to place Shakur on the terror watchlist. He writes, "Assata Shakur is now a Muslim. Well, she didn't actually convert to Islam. But in the eyes of the United States government where 'terrorism' and threats to the state have become synonymous with Islam and Muslims, the recent placement of Assata Shakur on the FBI's 'Most Wanted Terrorist List,' has for all intents and purposes, made her one." [34] Like other critics of the war on terror, Daulatzai points to the expansiveness of who can be defined as a terrorist by the federal government, suggesting that reaching forty years back into time to find easily mobilized symbols for the ideological crusade is symptomatic of overreaching state policies. Daulatzai suggests that the war on terror has been asserted as a "logic of control to systematically target, undermine and destroy any challenge to the domestic and global realms of U.S. power," adding, "it's no coincidence that the figure of the 'black criminal' and the 'Muslim terrorist' both emerged in US political culture in the early 1970s due to the neurotic fears of Black Power domestically, and the threats to an expanding US imperial footprint in Muslim countries abroad." [35] Echoing the arguments of Thelwell in the new prefatory material of *Die Nigger Die!*, Daulatzai points to the intentional conflation of black and Muslim as a rhetorical strategy that collapses a multitude of distinctions to facilitate indefinite detention of both groups domestically.

Daulatzai was hardly the only prominent voice objecting to Shakur's addition to the FBI's Most Wanted Terrorist List. Writing for *The Root*, preeminent Black Power scholar Peniel E. Joseph commented on Shakur's addition, suggesting that it "evokes the triumphant and tragic legacy of the black power movement."[36] Joseph explains, "However ill advised their vantage point, Shakur and hundreds of other 'underground' soldiers of this era . . . viewed themselves as participants in a domestic war for liberation that was less about skin color and the fear of a race war and more about institutions (such as law enforcement and the federal government) that they found to be authoritarian, oppressive and therefore illegitimate."[37] Joseph points to the rationale behind the increasingly radical resistance of the Black Liberation Army as a way of understanding how black liberation became so desperate in the face of COINTELPRO assassinations and disruption, arguing that the intent of their resistance was to expose corruption and racial domination. In doing so, he makes an effort to contextualize the BLA in ways that situate Shakur as a knowable activist rather than a mystified terrorist. And, as Suzanne Oboler notes, the decision to suspend the campaign to pardon Assata Shakur after 9/11 demonstrates how the classification of "terrorists" as "enemy combatants" has helped to expand American imperialism to imprison critics of the United States.[38]

Still, as in the conversations about Jamil Al-Amin and Mumia Abu-Jamal, detractors want to focus on the specifics of the crimes for which they were convicted, a strategy that certainly diverts attention from the structural violence of imprisonment to interpersonal "crime." But the political prisoner framework of all three figures in this study helps us move from analysis of each individual's *case* to their *arguments* about institutional violence in the prisons, courts, and police forces of America. And commenting on Shakur's addition to the FBI's Most Wanted Terrorist List, Angela Davis begs scholars to ask, "What does it mean that an African-American woman, residing in the socialist nation of Cuba, is the target of the newly constituted Department of Homeland Security?"[39] As Daulatzai makes plain, "whether she's innocent or not, the labeling of her as a 'terrorist' has more to do with her political beliefs and the liberation struggles that she was a part of. In fact, it's those very beliefs and activities that led to her (and others) being targeted under the FBI's COINTELPRO, persecuted, put on trial, convicted and then forced to ultimately flee the country and live in exile in Cuba. For the US state, when it comes to labeling a 'terrorist,' innocence or guilt are simply irrelevant details."[40] In this way, Daulatzai, like Thelwell, works to recover a rhetorical space for political prisoners to have a voice in spite of their political and social death in prisons or exile. In creating a space for prisoners to participate in public deliberation about the relationship between mass incarceration, slavery, capital, violence, and state power, the activists in this study and those writing about them seek to add to the larger conversation about American empire.

In writing about this classification of Shakur as a "Wanted Terrorist," Daulatzai adds that it is high time that we "recognise it for what it is: not only a political label used to discredit and undermine struggles for self-determination, but also a legal frame that then gives the state the sanction and power to narrow the scope of dissent and violently crackdown and arrest, incarcerate, torture, bomb, drone, invade, and even assassinate those deemed threats to state interests."[41] Since this was the same rationale for COINTEL-PRO and since the means of undermining civil rights activism appear to be the same, imprisoned and exiled black intellectuals have struggled against the state's definitions of them as noncitizens. Writing in *The Nation*, Mychal Denzel Smith adds, "The United States doesn't like to lose and holds a hell of a grudge. This goes beyond J. Edgar Hoover's declaring the Black Panther Party the 'greatest threat to the internal security of the country' and vowing to eradicate them. This is the fate of anyone, particularly those with black and brown skin, who holds views deemed anti-American—which for them only reflect their status as an oppressed people (there's controversy in asserting that all people deserve the right to food, clothing and shelter)."[42] Smith argues that even if you believe that Shakur was guilty of killing Officer Foerster, "that would make her responsible for one death in the early morning hours on a New Jersey highway forty years ago. If that is terrorism, if the definition is such that this purported crime fits, then in the process of labeling Assata Shakur a terrorist, the FBI has rendered the word all but meaningless."[43]

In addition, rendering the word terrorist meaningless, the conflation of Black Power leaders and Muslim terrorists demonstrates the expansiveness of mass incarceration, racial persecution, and political silencing while also highlighting how threatening the Black Power movement still is in the political imaginary forty years after its zenith. It is clear that the state still sees Black Power leaders as symbols capable of generating the kind of fear and loathing that has always motivated law and order culture. The fact that a now sixty-eight-year-old woman is a major component of the visual definition of terrorist in this age points to the way that historical figures continue to mobilize state repression and resistance.

Assessing the Legacy of the Prison, Imprisonment, and Political Prisoners in the Black Power Movement

Rather than dealing with critiques of the state from the left like Jamil al-Amin, Mumia Abu-Jamal, or even Assata Shakur, commentators from the right would prefer them to be muzzled, truncating public deliberation. For example, Michael Smerconish asserts, "if you had told me that in the year 2020 we would still be arguing what to do with Mumia Abu-Jamal, I would never have believed it."[44] But in penning this sentiment, Smerconish fails to understand that it isn't Mumia himself that is the issue, but what he *represents* as a black leader, intellectual, journalist, and agitator connected to both the history of black resistance to state violence and the connection between black liberation and prison politics. While people may debate the details of each case or brandish the term cop killer around with no racial or historical context, the writings and lives of Jamil al-Amin, Mumia Abu-Jamal, and Assata Shakur continue to have cultural salience because their accounts of state violence sadly still resonate in a culture that refuses to give up racist brutality and mass incarceration. "Beyond the military campaigns in Iraq and Afghanistan, the most significant component of the U.S. war on terror is the use of long-term detention centers to hold enemy combatants," a trend that mirrors the use of imprisonment to confine black Americans after Reconstruction's failure.[45] In fact, looking back on the millennium, it would seem that the Bush administration "perfectly embodied the key themes of the Crime Deal" and "the war on terror would seem to have handed the administration a perfect way to continue the war on crime beyond the traditional legal constraints of criminal justice and national sovereignty."[46] Thus did the war on terror *augment* the war on crime and expand state powers of indefinite rendition and torture, making Black Power histories and critiques of imprisonment even more salient.

In demanding a language of civility, state agents and critics sought to undermine both the medium and the message of Black Power beginning with the birth of Black Power and continuing even through the early years of the war on terror. In writing about African American rhetorical traditions, Voris Nunley has suggested, "Civility tends to privilege the politics and the values of those benefiting from the dominant discourse." Nunley lists rhetors like Maria W. Stewart, Fannie Lou Hamer, Martin Delany, Malcolm X, and others that embraced rhetorical postures that eschewed civility for "telling it like it is," particularly in mixed audiences.[47] I would suggest that the Black Power vernacular was intensely preoccupied with moving past civility into discursive forms that would enable a clearer description of structural inequality. Rap Brown, Mumia Abu-Jamal, and Assata Shakur join Stokely Carmichael, Huey Newton, Bobby Seale, Eldridge Cleaver, and others in choosing a rhetorical posture that, in Nunley's words, "is often misunderstood by the general public as angry, hostile, uppity, arrogant, and uncivil rhetoric."[48] The autobiographies of imprisoned Black Power intellectuals highlight how structural inequality built the prison system, warped the police, and targeted social movements while also connecting the black freedom struggle to issues of gender and class.

Where some readers may look to these autobiographies for representations of how "things really were," this book has used the texts within it for a critical evaluation of the past, attempting to understand the multiple pressures on young Black Power activists building momentum in an increasingly hostile state. After the assassinations of President John F. Kennedy, Malcolm X, and Martin Luther King and with the rise of new conservatism, the Black Power vernacular became increasingly oppositional and confrontational, particularly as repression of activists increased. But as their rhetorical postures embraced revolutionary nationalism and Third World ideologies, it became easier for the federal government and local police forces to justify harassment, imprisonment, and even assassination.

But more important, the autobiographies of Rap Brown, Mumia Abu-Jamal, and Assata Shakur demonstrate how activists have responded to their imprisonment and how their critiques of the prison-industrial complex have helped to shape contemporary activism. Scholars would be wise to remember that race and resistance were major forces shaping the prison-industrial complex in the twentieth century, and the southern civil rights and northern Black Power movements provided tension and justification for ramping up imprisonment. The Black Power movement is a significant element in the emergence of the prison-industrial complex as it changed over the century. As Michelle Alexander has demonstrated, "Following the collapse of each system of control, there has been a period of confusion—transition—in which those who are most committed to racial hierarchy search for new means to achieve their goals within the rules of the game as currently defined. It is during this period of uncertainty that the backlash intensifies and a new form of racialized social control begins to take hold."[49] Alexander suggests that the War on Drugs played a significant role in mass incarceration in the United States, and she is certainly correct, though the expansion of the LEAA, the "law and order" rhetoric of the 1960s, and the COINTELPRO repression of black activists suggest that the War on Drugs emerged in a period that was perhaps the most hostile backlash cycle against black freedom in the twentieth century. Likewise, it perpetuated the elision of black activist and black criminal as a frame for understanding structural resistance to white supremacy, making the criminalization of blackness in the 1980s extremely legible for a white public.

There is no doubt that the oppositional politics of Black Power intellectuals continues to be a source of debate, particularly as Islamophobia and antiblack sentiment converge after the invasions of both Iraq and Afghanistan. However, the strength of the "law and order" versus lawlessness dialectic continues to be a permanent feature of the American rhetorical landscape. The FBI had always considered the BPP and the BLA as terrorists. In a memo concerning East Coast black militants that had allegedly killed police officers, Hoover stated, "[these] terrorist acts have demonstrated that in many instances those involved in these acts are often individuals who cannot be identified as members of an extremist group . . . They are frequently supporters, community workers, or people who hang around the headquarters of an extremist group or associate with members of an extremist group."[50] From Hoover's own assessments, activists in the black freedom movement, especially King and his followers but later even after his assassination were domestic terrorist threats to state power. This political and rhetorical orientation of civil rights intellectuals and activists as "terrorists" made a more confrontational posture inevitable as the young activists encountered more and more efforts of the state to undermine and destroy organizing efforts.

Consequently, this book has attempted to trace how the rhetorical confrontation in the Black Power vernacular, in Paul Gilroy's words, "take[s] us beyond the discourses and the semiotics of 'race' into a confrontation with theories and histories of spectatorship and observation, visual apparatuses and optics. They ask us to rethink the development of a racial imagery in ways that are more distant from the reasoned authority of logos and closely attuned to the different power of visual and visualizing technologies."[51] Centering the prison as a primary space necessary in the interrogation of the semiotics and imaginary of the Black Power vernacular, I have endeavored to demonstrate how Black Power and "law and order" have been co-constitutive discourses, constantly shaping and reshaping through rhetorical and political action and reaction. Constant across time is the fact that quite often agents of the state have worked against equality efforts, complicating and sometimes foreclosing deliberative avenues in the republic. The frustrations, anger, and resistance of young black activists were rhetorical resources that changed their vernacular and its symbols, signs, and images to become more and more confrontational as the promise of racial equality receded. The activists in this study have utilized confrontational rhetorical forms as a strategy of unmasking abuses of power and as a tool in building new forms of racial identification through the deployment of and reframing of metaphors that highlight the persistence of both racial oppression and racial resistance.

As they have written from prison and exile, under duress by COINTEL-PRO and persecuted under the war on terror, Black Power intellectuals have understood the *prison* as a vital space for organizing and for theorizing new politics that harnessed race, gender, and class as mobilizing tropes for resisting police brutality, mass incarceration, and state repression of civil rights activism. Even at the turn of the millennium, Black Power intellectuals sought to use the Bush administration's war on terror as a new lens to continue their agitation against mass imprisonment.

These invocations, travels, and rearticulations of the Black Power vernacular, particularly as it pertains to incarceration, raise questions that need to be pursued in the new millennium, for example: how might scholars understand the ambivalence about Black Power vernacular in more contemporary examples of black liberation activism? Does the ambivalence stem from the rhetorical history of these vernacular choices or from the relationship that the vernacular has to imprisonment? Can the Black Power vernacular continue to function as a rallying cry for activism beyond the social movements of the twentieth century, for example in the #BlackLivesMatter movement? If so, how do rhetorical innovations change or continue vernacular patterns that emerged from the black intellectuals in this study? How has confrontational rhetoric about police brutality or mass incarceration shifted the rhetorical choices of black activists? Of white politicians? Of law and order culture? Does "terrorist" continue to function as a persuasive symbol of black or brown excess? How does the mobilization of the term *cop killer* function in the contemporary political milieu alongside the term *killer cop*? Particularly with the visibility of the #BlackLivesMatter movement, police brutality, mass incarceration, and judicial corruption continue to devastate communities of color and new Black Power vernacular strategies are emerging to challenge state power. It is my hope that this study will help ground new examinations into the Black Power vernacular as Rap Brown/Jamil Al-Amin, Mumia Abu-Jamal, and Assata Shakur continue to circulate as cultural and historical resources for new social movement activists.

NOTES

Introduction

1. Martin Luther King Jr., "A Creative Protest," February 16, 1960, in *The Papers of Martin Luther King, Jr., Volume V: Threshold of a New Decade, January 1959–December 1960*, ed. Clayborne Carson et al. (Berkeley: University of California Press, 2005), 360–70.

2. John M. Sloop, *The Cultural Prison: Discourse, Prisoners, and Punishment* (Tuscaloosa: The University of Alabama Press, 1996), 5.

3. Michelle Alexander, *The New Jim Crow: Mass Incarceration in the Age of Colorblindness* (New York: New Press, 2012).

4. The Watts rebellion occurred in the Watts neighborhood of Los Angles from August 11 to August 17, 1965, in response to a black motorist being arrested for drunk driving. Almost 4,000 members of the California National Guard were mobilized in response to the rebellion as black citizens burned mostly white-owned businesses, and the White House's response was to conflate rioters with criminals.

When prisoners took over the Attica prison in Attica, New York, in September of 1971 after the assassination of San Quentin prisoner and prison writer George Jackson to protest prison conditions, Governor Nelson Rockefeller sent in armed state troops to quell the rebellion, killing 39: 29 prisoners and 10 guards.

5. See Robert S. Cathcart, "Movements: Confrontation as Rhetorical Form," *Southern Speech Communication Journal* 43, no. 3 (1978): 233–47; Leland Griffin, "The Rhetoric of Historical Movements," *Quarterly Journal of Speech* 38 (1952): 181–85; Edwin Black, *Rhetorical Criticism* (New York: Macmillan Co., 1965); Herbert Simons, "Requirements, Problems and Strategies: A Theory of Persuasion for Social Movements," *Quarterly Journal of Speech* 56 (1970): 1–11; Dan F. Hahn and Ruth Gonchar, "Studying Social Movements: A Rhetorical Methodology," *The Speech Teacher* 20 (1971): 44–52.

6. Richard B. Gregg, A Jackson McCormack, and Douglas J. Pedersen, "The Rhetoric of Black Power: A Street-Level Interpretation," *Quarterly Journal of Speech* 55, no. 2 (1969): 152.

7. Robert L. Heath, "Dialectical Confrontation: A Strategy of Black Radicalism," *Central States Speech Journal* 24, no. 3 (1973): 169.

8. Cathcart, "Movements," 245–46.

9. Cathcart, "Movements," 235.

10. Lisa M. Corrigan, "Cross-pollinating the Revolution: From Havana to Oakland and Back Again," *Journal of Post-Colonial Writing* 50, no. 4 (2014): 452–65.

11. Grant Farred, *What's My Name? Black Vernacular Intellectuals* (Minneapolis: University of Minnesota Press, 2003), 17.

12. John Louis Lucaites and Celeste Michelle Condit, "Reconstructing 'Equality': Culturetypal and Counter-Cultural Rhetorics in the Martyred Black Vision," *Communication Monographs* 57 (1990): 13.

13. Farred, *What's My Name?*, 7.

14. Farred, *What's My Name?*, 12.

15. Farred, *What's My Name?*, 12.

16. Robert L. Scott and Donald K. Smith, "The Rhetoric of Confrontation," *Quarterly Journal of Speech* 54 (February 1969): 2.

17. Scott and Smith, "The Rhetoric of Confrontation," 5.

18. Scott and Smith, "The Rhetoric of Confrontation," 5.

19. Ben L. Martin, "From Negro to Black to African American: The Power of Names and Naming," *Political Science Quarterly* 106, no. 1 (1991): 92.

20. Kermit Ernest Campbell, *Gettin' Our Groove On: Rhetoric, Language, and Literacy for the Hip-Hop Generation* (Detroit: Wayne State University Press, 2005), 4.

21. Martin, "From Negro to Black to African American," 83.

22. Farred, *What's My Name?*, 24.

23. Bryan Wagner, *Disturbing the Peace: Black Culture and the Police Power after Slavery* (Cambridge, MA: Harvard University Press, 2009), 1.

24. Maegan Parker Brooks, "Ironic Openings: The Interpretive Challenge of the 'Black Manifesto,'" *Quarterly Journal of Speech* 94, no. 3 (2008): 339.

25. Brooks, "Ironic Openings," 338.

26. Farred, *What's My Name?*, 12.

27. Charles E. Jones, *The Black Panther Party Reconsidered* (Baltimore, MD: Black Classic Press), 77. See, for example, Eldridge Cleaver, "Revolution in the White Mother Country & National Liberation in the Black Colony," *North American Review* (July–August 1968): 13–15.

28. Quoted in Harold Cruse, "Revolutionary Nationalism and the Afro-American," in *Rebellion or Revolution?* (New York: Random House, 1968), 76; originally appeared in *Studies on the Left* 2, no. 3 (1962): 12–26.

29. Kwame Ture (Stokely Carmichael), *Black Power: The Politics of Liberation* (New York: Vintage, 1967/1992), 23.

30. French intellectual Régis Debray developed *foco* theory (also known as focalism) as a revolutionary stratagem using Che Guevara's writings from the Cuban Revolution. The organizing principle of *foco* theory is the notion of vanguardism, which suggests that highly mobile vanguards can focus popular resistance to build a successful coup d'état. Guevara focused on the utility of rural vanguards while Debray's theorizing helped expand the Cuban model to urban revolutionary guerrilla warfare. See Régis Debray, *Revolution in the Revolution? Armed Struggle and Political Struggle in Latin America* (New York: Penguin Books, 1967).

31. George Jackson, *Blood in My Eye* (Chicago: Lawrence Hill, 1973), 74–75.

32. See, for example, Corrigan, "Cross-pollinating the Revolution, 452–65.

33. Huey P. Newton, *Revolutionary Suicide* (New York: Penguin, 2009), 116.

34. Thomas Kent, "On the Very Idea of a Discourse Community," *College Composition and Communication* 42, no. 2 (1991): 425–45. Martin Nystrand originally coined the term "discourse community." See Martin Nystrand, *What Writers Know: The Language, Process, and Structure of Written Discourse* (New York: Academic, 1982).

35. Culpepper Clark and Raymie McKerrow, "The Rhetorical Construction of History," *Doing Rhetorical History*, ed. Kathleen Turner (Tuscaloosa: The University of Alabama Press, 1998), 44.

36. Jennifer Mercieca, *Founding Fictions* (Tuscaloosa: The University of Alabama Press, 2010), 4.

37. Mercieca, *Founding Fictions*, 4.

38. Only Donald Tibbs's *From Black Power to Prison Power: The Making of* Jones v. North Carolina Prisoners' Labor Union (New York: Palgrave Macmillan, 2011) and Dan Berger's *Captive Nation: Black Prison Organizing in the Civil Rights Era* (Chapel Hill: University of North Carolina Press, 2014) have connected Black Power and prisoner conditions to understand prison resistance. However, these monographs are not an examination of Black Power ideology as it was informed by prison culture or an explanation of how Black Power influenced the expansion of the prison system. Rather, these volumes look *within* prisons to see how black prisoners collectivized workers.

39. Stephen J. Hartnett, *Executing Democracy: Volume I: Capital Punishment and the Making of America, 1683–1807* (Lansing: Michigan State University Press, 2010); *Executing Democracy: Volume II: Capital Punishment and the Making of America, 1835–1848* (Lansing: Michigan State University Press, 2012); *Working for Justice: A Handbook of Prison Education and Activism*, ed. Stephen John Hartnett, Eleanor Novek, and Jennifer K. Wood (Urbana: University of Illinois Press, 2013).

40. Wini Breines, "'Sixties Stories' Silences: White Feminism, Black Feminism, Black Power," *NWSA Journal* 8, no. 3 (1996): 108.

41. Breines, "Sixties," 109.

42. Bryan McCann, "Therapeutic and Material 'Victim'hood: Ideology and the Struggle for Meaning in the Illinois Death Penalty Controversy," *Communication and Critical/Cultural Studies* 4, no. 4 (2007): 382–401.

43. Jacqueline Jones Royster and Gesa E. Kirsch, *Feminist Rhetorical Practices: New Horizons for Rhetoric, Composition and Literacy Studies* (Carbondale: Southern Illinois University Press, 2012), 67.

44. Andrew Lakritz, "Identification and Difference: Structures of Privilege in Cultural Criticism," *Who Can Speak? Authority and Critical Identity*, ed. Judith Roof and Robyn Wiegman (Urbana and Chicago: University of Illinois Press, 1995), 12.

45. Dale M. Bauer, "Personal Criticism and the Academic Personality," *Who Can Speak? Authority and Critical Identity*, ed. Judith Roof and Robyn Wiegman (Urbana and Chicago: University of Illinois Press, 1995), 56.

46. Throughout the text, I refer to him as Rap Brown when referring to the SNCC leader and author of *Die Nigger Die!* as he constructed his Black Power persona. I use his new name, Jamil Al-Amin, when talking about him since his conversion to Sunni Islam in 1967.

Chapter One

1. M. A. Jones to Rob Wick, Memorandum on June 20, 1966. *Stokely Carmichael—The FBI Files* (Minneapolis, MN: Filiquarian Publishing, 2009), n.p.

2. FBI File, Stokely Carmichael, July 13, 1966. *Stokely Carmichael—The FBI Files* (Minneapolis, MN: Filiquarian Publishing, 2009), n.p.

3. Reprinted in Ward Churchill and Jim Vander Wall, *COINTELPRO PAPERS: Documents from the FBI's Secret Wars Against Dissent in the United States* (Boston: South End Press, 2001), 107.

4. Hortense Spillers, "The Idea of Black Culture," *CR: The New Centennial Review* 6, no. 3 (2006): 25.

5. Mary Stanton, *From Selma to Sorrow: The Life and Death of Viola Liuzzo* (Athens: University of Georgia Press, 1998), 174.

6. Robert C. Smith, "Black Power and the Transformation from Protest to Politics," *Political Science Quarterly* 96, no. 3 (1981): 432.

7. Donald McCormack, "Stokely Carmichael and Pan-Africanism: Back to Black Power," *Journal of Politics* 35, no. 2 (1973): 390.

8. Vanessa Murphree, *The Selling of Civil Rights: The Student Nonviolent Coordinating Committee and the Use of Public Relations* (New York: Routledge 2006), 7.

9. Theodore Hamm, "The Prisoner Speaks," Review of *Prison Writing in 20th Century America* by H. Bruce Franklin, *American Quarterly* 51, no. 3 (1999): 738–39.

10. H. Bruce Franklin, *The Victim as Criminal and Artist: Literature from the American Prison* (New York: Oxford University Press, 1978), xxii.

11. Franklin, *The Victim as Criminal and Artist*, xv.

12. Franklin, *Prison Writing in 20th Century America* (New York: Penguin, 1998), 3.

13. Franklin, *The Victim as Criminal and Artist*, 108.

14. Franklin, *The Victim as Criminal and Artist*, 101.

15. Franklin, *The Victim as Criminal and Artist*, 101.

16. Farred, *What's My Name?*, 17.

17. V. P. Franklin, "Introduction—To Be Heard in Black and White: Historical Perspectives on Black Print Culture," *Journal of African American History* 95, no. 3–4 (2010): 294.

18. Angela Davis, *Eyes on the Prize*. Interview. May 24, 1989. http://digital.wustl.edu/e/eii/eiiweb/dav5427.0115.036marc_record_interviewer_process.html.

19. Joy James, *Imprisoned Intellectuals: American's Political Prisoners Write on Life, Liberation and Rebellion* (New York: Rowman & Littlefield, 2003), 20.

20. Joy James, "American 'Prison Notebooks,'" *Race & Class* 45, no. 3 (2004): 39.

21. Rhoda Lois Blumberg, *Civil Rights: The 1960s Freedom Struggle* (New York: Twayne Publishers, 1991), 76–80.

22. Martin Luther King Jr., *The Autobiography of Martin Luther King, Jr.*, with Clayborne Carson (New York: Warner Books, 1998), 230.

23. Houston A. Baker, "Critical Memory and the Black Public Sphere," *The Black Public Sphere: A Public Culture Book* (Chicago: University of Chicago Press, 1995), 18.

24. Baker, "Critical Memory and the Black Public Sphere," 18–19.

25. Quoted in Aldon Morris, *The Origins of the Civil Rights Movement* (New York: Simon & Schuster, 1986), 241.

26. In Morris, *The Origins of the Civil Rights Movement*, 241.

27. King, *Autobiography*, 153–54.

28. Charles Sherrod, *Voices of Freedom: An Oral History of the Civil Rights Movement*, ed. Henry Hampton and Steve Fayer (New York: Bantam, 1991), 104.

29. David L. Lewis, *King: A Biography* (Urbana and Chicago: University of Illinois Press, 2012), 149.

30. Sherrod, *Voices of Freedom*, 104–5.

31. Sherrod, *Voices of Freedom*, 105.

32. Quoted in Numan Bartley, *The New South, 1945–1980* (Baton Rouge: Louisiana State University Press, 1995), 326.

33. Pritchett recalls thinking "[w]e're going to out-nonviolent them." Laurie Pritchett, *Voices of Freedom: An Oral History of the Civil Rights Movement*, ed. Henry Hampton and Steve Fayer (New York: Bantam, 1991), 106.

34. "The Albany Manifesto," Martin Luther King Jr., July 15, 1962. http://www.thekingcenter.org/archive/document/albany-manifesto (accessed June 22, 2013).

35. Martin Luther King Jr., "Letter From an Albany Jail," in *The Empire State of the South: Georgia History in Documents and Essays*, ed. Christopher C. Meyers (Macon, GA: Mercer University Press, 2008), 307. As was often the case for his news columns that drew on his written speeches, "A Message From Jail" was ghostwritten with help from SCLC advisers.

36. King, "Letter From an Albany Jail," 308.

37. King, *Autobiography*, 155.

38. David Garrow, *Bearing the Cross: Martin Luther King, Jr., and the Southern Christian Leadership Conference* (New York: William Morrow, 2004), 204.

39. Gerard Hauser, *Prisoners of Conscience: Moral Vernaculars of Political Agency* (Columbia: University of South Carolina Press, 2012), 5.

40. Hauser, *Prisoners of Conscience*, 5.

41. Hauser, *Prisoners of Conscience*, 5.

42. Martin Luther King Jr., *Why We Can't Wait* (New York: Mentor/Penguin, 1963), 29.

43. King, *Why We Can't Wait*, 30.

44. Wyatt Tee Walker quoted in *Voices of Freedom: An Oral History of the Civil Rights Movement*, ed. Henry Hampton and Steve Fayer (New York: Bantam, 1991), 132–33.

45. Walker, *Voices of Freedom*, 133.

46. Hauser, *Prisoners of Conscience*, 6.

47. Martin Luther King Jr., "Hammer of Civil Rights," *The Nation*, March 9, 1964. http://www.thenation.com/article/157742/hammer-civil-rights (accessed December 8, 2012).

48. King, "Hammer of Civil Rights."

49. Hauser, *Prisoners of Conscience*, 5–6.

50. Hauser, *Prisoners of Conscience*, 5–6.

51. Harry McPherson quoted in *Voices of Freedom*, ed. Hampton and Fayer, 338.

52. McPherson, quoted in *Voices of Freedom*, 338.

53. Gary S. Selby, *Martin Luther King and the Rhetoric of Freedom* (Waco: Baylor University Press, 2008), 43.

54. Selby, *Martin Luther King*, 43.

55. King, "Hammer of Civil Rights."

56. King, "Hammer of Civil Rights."

57. Carmichael, *Ready for Revolution*, 202.

58. Carmichael, *Ready for Revolution*, 198.

59. Cheryl Lynn Greenberg, *A Circle of Trust: Remembering SNCC* (New Brunswick, NJ: Rutgers University Press, 1998), 9–10.

60. R. Edward Nordhaus, "S.N.C.C. and the Civil Rights Movement in Mississippi, 1963–64: A Time of Change," *The History Teacher* 17, no. 1 (1983): 97.

61. Late in the summer, several law professors at Harvard drafted and circulated the "Howe Memo," which presented the legal precedent for Justice Department protection of civil rights workers in the US Code (evidenced by Sec. 332 of Title 10) along with the precedent set by President Eisenhower in Little Rock in 1957–1958 and by President Kennedy in Mississippi in 1962 and Alabama in 1962.

62. Clayborne Carson, *In Struggle: SNCC and the Black Awakening of the 1960s* (Cambridge: Harvard University Press, 1981), 117.

63. Maegan Parker Brooks and Davis W. Houck, *The Speeches of Fannie Lou Hamer: To Tell It Like It Is* (Jackson: University Press of Mississippi, 2013), 14.

64. Brooks and Houck, *The Speeches of Fannie Lou Hamer*, 52.

65. Chana Kai Lee, *For Freedom's Sake: The Life of Fannie Lou Hamer* (Urbana: University of Illinois Press, 2000), 52–54.

66. Brooks and Houck, *The Speeches of Fannie Lou Hamer*, 52.

67. Maegan Parker Brooks, "Oppositional Ethos: Fannie Lou Hamer and the Vernacular Persona," *Rhetoric & Public Affairs* 14, no. 3 (2011): 514.

68. Brooks, "Oppositional Ethos," 514.

69. Vicki Crawford, "African American Women in the Mississippi Freedom Democratic Party," in *Sisters in the Struggle: African-American Women in the Civil Rights–Black Power Movement*, ed. Bettye Collier-Thomas and V. P. Franklin (New York: New York University Press, 2001), 133.

70. Cleveland Sellers, *The River of No Return: The Autobiography of a Black Militant and the Life and Death of SNCC* (Jackson: University Press of Mississippi, 1990), 111.

71. Lloyd Earl Rohler, *George Wallace: Conservative Populist* (New York: Praeger, 2004), 45.

72. Roy Reed, "The Big Parade: On the Road to Montgomery," *New York Times*, March 22, 1965. http://www.nytimes.com/learning/general/onthisday/big/0307.html (accessed March 3, 2013).

73. Reed, "The Big Parade."

74. Reed, "The Big Parade."

75. Quoted in Sanford Wexler, *An Eyewitness History of the Civil Rights Movement* (New York: Checkmark Books, 1999), 231.

76. In Wexler, *An Eyewitness History*, 231. Emphasis in original.

77. In Wexler, *An Eyewitness History*, 231.

78. David J. Garrow, *Protest at Selma: Martin Luther King, Jr., and the Voting Rights Act of 1965* (New Haven, CT: Yale University Press, 1978), 53.

79. Hauser, *Prisoners of Conscience*, 19.

80. David Howard-Pitney, *The African American Jeremiad* (Philadelphia: Temple University Press, 2005), 201.

81. Howard-Pitney, *African-American Jeremiad*, 201.

82. Polletta, *Freedom Is an Endless Meeting*, 89.

83. Howard-Pitney, *African-American Jeremiad*, 211.

84. Howard-Pitney, *African-American Jeremiad*, 211.

85. Howard-Pitney, *African-American Jeremiad*, 217.

86. Amy Ongiri, *Spectacular Blackness: The Cultural Politics of the Black Power Movement and the Search for a Black Aesthetic* (Charlottesville: University of Virginia Press, 2010), 41.

87. Tibbs, *From Black Power to Prison Power*, 30.

88. Adam Winkler, *Gun Fight: The Battle Over the Right to Bear Arms in America* (New York: W. W. Norton, 2011), 245.

89. Winkler, *Gun Fight*, 244.

90. Winkler, *Gun Fight*, 245.

91. Roz Payne, "WACing Off: Gossip, Sex, Race, and Politics in the World of FBI Special Case Agent William A. Cohendet," in *In Search of the Black Panther Party: New Perspectives on a Revolutionary Movement*, ed. Yohuru Williams and Jama Lazerow (Durham, NC: Duke University Press, 2006), 160. See also Rod Bush, *We Are Not What We Seem: Black Nationalism and Class Struggle in the American Century* (New York: New York University Press, 2000), 215.

92. Berger, *Captive Nation*, 72.

93. Pinkney, *Red, Black and Green*, 104.

94. Akinyele Omowale Umoja, "Set Our Warriors Free: The Legacy of the Black Panther Party and Political Prisoners," *The Black Panther Party Reconsidered*, ed. Charles E. Jones (Baltimore, MD: Black Classic Press, 1998), 418.

95. Davis, *Autobiography*, 168.

96. H. Rap Brown, Speech at the Free Huey Rally, February 17, 1968. http://www.lib.berkeley.edu/MRC/rapbrown.html.

97. Stokely Carmichael, Speech at the Free Huey Rally, February 17, 1968. http://www.lib.berkeley.edu/MRC/carmichael.html.

98. By 1968, the BPP had chapters outside of the Bay area in Baltimore, Boston, Chicago, Cleveland, Dallas, Denver, Detroit, Indianapolis, Kansas City, Los Angeles, Newark, New Orleans, New York City, Omaha, Philadelphia, Pittsburgh, San Diego, San Francisco, Seattle, and Washington, DC. By 1969, peak was near 10,000, and the Black Panther newspaper had a circulation of over 250,000. See Molefi K. Asante, *Encyclopedia of Black Studies* (New York: Sage Publications, 2005), 135–37.

99. Reprinted in Churchill and Vander Wall, *COINTELPRO Papers*, 130.

100. Immediately after the shooting, at the behest of the FBI, approximately 75–100 LAPD SWAT members descended on the home of Erika Huggins, the widow of John Huggins, greatly exacerbating the tensions between the LAPD and the BPP in California.

101. Amiri Baraka, *The Autobiography of Leroi Jones* (Chicago: Lawrence Hill, 1997), 391–92.

102. See the accounts of these trials in Lazerow and Williams, *In Search of the Black Panther*, 2006.

103. Pinkney, *Red, Black, and Green*, 104.

104. Philip S. Foner, "Introduction," *The Black Panthers Speak*, ed. Philip S. Foner (Cambridge, MA: De Capo Press, 2002), xxxii–xxxiii.

105. Tibbs, *From Black Power to Prison Power*, 7.

106. Carmen Kynard, *Vernacular Insurrections: Race, Black Protest, and the New Century in Composition-Literacy Studies* (Albany: SUNY Press, 2013), 90.

107. Tibbs, *From Black Power to Prison Power*, 51.

108. Huey Newton, *The Huey P. Newton Reader* (New York: Seven Stories Press, 2002), 52.

109. Newton, *Revolutionary Suicide*, 115.

110. Newton, *Revolutionary Suicide*, 71.

111. Eldridge Cleaver, *Soul on Ice* (New York: Delta, 2009), 59.

112. Bridgette Baldwin, "In the Shadow of the Gun: The Black Panther Party, the Ninth Amendment, and Discourses of Self-Defense," in *In Search of the Black Panther Party: New Perspectives on a Revolutionary Movement,* ed. Jama Lazarow and Yohoru Williams (Durham, NC: Duke University Press, 2006), 68.

113. Graeme Abernethy, *The Iconography of Malcolm X* (Lawrence: University Press of Kansas, 2013), 97.

114. Qtd. in Tibbs, *From Black Power to Prison Power*, 32.

115. Reprinted in and Vander Wall, *COINTELPRO Papers*, 181.

116. Ward Churchill, "To Disrupt, Discredit and Destroy," in *Liberation, Imagination and the Black Panther Party: A New Look at the Panthers and Their Legacy*, ed. Kathleen Cleaver and George Katsiaficas (New York: Routledge, 2001), 155.

117. James Baldwin and Margaret Mead, *Rap on Race* (London, UK: Michael Joseph, 1971), 10–11.

118. Peniel E. Joseph, *Waiting 'Til the Midnight Hour: A Narrative History of Black Power in America* (New York: Henry Holt and Co., 2006), viii.

Chapter Two

1. Herbert Haines, *Black Radicals and the Civil Rights Mainstream, 1954–1970* (Knoxville: University of Tennessee Press, 1988), 61.

2. Akinyele O. Umoja, "The Ballot and the Bullet: A Comparative Analysis of Armed Resistance in the Civil Rights Movement," *Journal of Black Studies* 29 (March 1999): 569.

3. Carson, *In Struggle*, 231–34.

4. Carson, *In Struggle*, 221.

5. Floyd McKissick, "The Way to a Black Ideology," *The Black Scholar* 1, no. 2 (1969): 14.

6. James Forman, *The Making of Revolutionaries* (New York: Macmillan, 1972), 504.

7. Haines, *Black Radicals*, 61.

8. "Report From the Chairman," May 5, 1967 (SNCC papers reel 2, 11291130). Quoted in Murphree, *The Selling of Civil Rights*, 145.

9. Nancy Whittier, "Political Generations, Micro-Cohorts, and the Transformation of Social Movements," *American Sociological Review* 62 (October 1997): 762.

10. Whittier, "Political Generations, Micro-Cohorts and the Transformation of Social Movements," 762.

11. David S. Meyer and Nancy Whittier, "Social Movement Spillover," *Social Problems* 41 (May 1994): 279.

12. Carson, *In Struggle*, 257.

13. Carson, *In Struggle*, 255. See also Mac Arthur Herman, *Summer of Rage: An Oral History of the 1967 Newark and Detroit Riots* (New York: Peter Lang, 2013), 132–35; Kevin Mumford, *Newark: A History of Race, Rights, and Riots* (New York: New York University Press, 2008).

14. Hugh Pearson, *The Shadow of the Panther: Huey Newton and the Price of Black Power in America* (New York: Addison-Wesley, 1994), 138. Police officers arrested a black cab driver on July 11 on traffic charges and began to harass and beat him as a growing number of residents from the housing project across the street looked on. A rumor spread that the cabbie had been killed and a mob began to advance on the police officers at the precinct house where they had been scuffling with the cabbie. Police officers responded to the group with tear gas and billy clubs and chaos ensued.

15. Pearson, *The Shadow of the Panther*, 139.

16. *The Riot Report: A Shortened Version of the* Report of the Nation Advisory Commission on Civil Disorders, ed. Barbara Ritchie (New York: Viking Press, 1969), 13.

17. The Kerner Commission was appointed in August 1967 and when it issued its 426-page report, it became a bestseller, demonstrating the national interest in urban rebellion and race relations.

18. *Supplemental Studies for the National Advisory Commission on Civil Disorders* (Washington, DC: Government Printing Office, 1968), 48.

19. *Supplemental Studies for the National Advisory Commission on Civil Disorders*, 62–63.

20. *Report of the National Advisory Commission on Civil Disorders* (Washington, DC: Government Printing Office, 1968), 201.

21. Carleen Basler, Thomas Dumm, and Austin Sarat, "How Does Violence Perform?," in *Performances of Violence*, ed. Carleen Basler, Thomas Dumm, and Austin Sarat (Amherst: University of Massachusetts Press, 2011), 7.

22. Bruce D'Arcus, "Protest, Scale and Publicity: The FBI and the H. Rap Brown Act," *Antipode* 35 (September 2002): 727.

23. Gloria Richardson, leader of the Cambridge movement, invited Brown to speak. See Peter B. Levy, "Gloria Richardson and the Civil Rights Movement in Cambridge, Maryland," in *Groundwork: Local Black Freedom Movements in America*, ed. Jeanne Theoharis and Komozi Woodard (New York: New York University Press, 2005), 97–115.

24. Robert L. Scott, "Justifying Violence: The Rhetoric of Militant Black Power," *Central States Speech Journal* 19 (1968), 98.

25. Qtd. in Carson, *In Struggle*, 255.

26. Qtd. in Carson, *In Struggle*, 255.

27. Pearson, *The Shadow of the Panther*, 139. For an in-depth account of the importance of Cambridge, Maryland, to the movement for black liberation and the role that Rap Brown played in the civil rights struggle in that city, see Peter B. Levy, *Civil War on Race Street: The Rights Movement in Cambridge, Maryland* (Gainesville: University of Florida Press, 2003).

28. Louis C. Goldberg, "Ghetto Riots and Others: The Faces of Civil Disorder in 1967," *Journal of Peace Research* 5 (1968): 120.

29. Michael Lipsky and David J. Olson, *Commission Politics: The Processing of Racial Crisis in America* (New Brunswick, NJ: Transcation Books, 1977), 183.

30. Lipsky and Olson, *Commission Politics*, 108.

31. Carson, *In Struggle*, 256.

32. Carson, *In Struggle*, 256.

33. Rap Brown, "Statement in Washington, July 26, 1967," in *SNCC Speaks for Itself* (Boston: New England Free Press, 1967), 7.

34. Brown, "Statement in Washington," 7.

35. Brown, "Statement in Washington," 7.

36. Editorial in the *Chicago Tribune*, Quoted in Brigitte Lebens Nacos, *The Press, Presidents, and Crises* (New York: Columbia University Press, 1990), 102.

37. Thurmond explained that the act would "deal firmly with those harbingers of anarchy who undoubtedly contributed to the tragedies of our cities." Quoted in D'Arcus, "Protest, Scale and Publicity," 726.

38. D'Arcus, "Protest, Scale and Publicity," 727.

39. Ramsey Clark, Oral History Interview IV with Harri Baker (April 16, 1969), 17, available at http://www.lbjlib.utexas.edu/johnson/archives.hom/oralhistory.hom/ClarkR/clark-r4.pdf (accessed June 12, 2013).

40. Carson, *In Struggle*, 257.

41. The Rabble Rouser Index was renamed Agitator Index in 1968 but it indicated an activist's propensity for violence. Those at the top of the index were Martin Luther King, Stokely Carmichael, Rap Brown, Maxwell Stanford (of the Revolutionary Action Movement), and Elijah Muhammad (of the Nation of Islam), and these men were singled out for special surveillance and harassment. See Kenneth O'Reilly, *Racial Matters: The FBI's Secret File on Black America, 1960-1972* (New York: Free Press,1989), 277.

42. D'Arcus, "Protest, Scale and Publicity," 726.

43. Farred, *What's My Name?*, 25.

44. Sundiata Acoli, "The New Afrikan Prison Struggle," *Imprisoned Intellectuals: America's Political Prisoners Write on Life, Liberation, and Rebellion*, ed. Joy James (Lanham, MD: Rowman & Littlefield Publishers, 2003), 145.

45. Carson, *In Struggle*, 66–82.

46. Brown, *Die Nigger Die!*, 1.

47. Hazel Carby, *Race Men* (Cambridge, MA: Harvard University Press, 1998), 127.

48. This differs from the future of his predecessor, Carmichael, who invoking Black Power ambiguously, insisted that he was not antiwhite and held out for the possibility that all oppressed people would be able to band together against oppression. See Carson, *In Struggle*, 215–28.

49. Henry Louis Gates Jr., *The Signifyin(g) Monkey: A Theory of African-American Literary Criticism* (Oxford: Oxford University Press, 1988), 52.

50. James Jasinski, *A Sourcebook on Rhetoric* (New York: Sage Publishing, 2001), 107. See also James Jasinski, "A Constitutive Framework for Rhetorical Historiography: Toward an Understanding of the Discursive (Re)construction of 'Constitution' in the *Federalist Papers*," in *Doing Rhetorical History*, ed. Kathleen J. Turner (Tuscaloosa: The University of Alabama Press, 2003), 72–92.

51. Don L. Lee, "Introduction," *Die Nigger Die!* (Chicago, IL: Lawrence Hill, 1969), xxxix.

52. Lee, "Introduction," xxxix.

53. Lee, "Introduction," xxxx–xxxxi.

54. Robert G. O'Meally, "'Game to the Heart': Sterling Brown and the Badman," *Callaloo* 14/15 (February–May 1982): 43–44. See also John W. Roberts, *From Trickster to Badman: The Black Folk Hero in Slavery and Freedom* (Philadelphia: University of Pennsylvania Press, 1989).

55. O'Meally, "'Game to the Heart,'" 44.

56. O'Meally, "'Game to the Heart,'" 44.

57. O'Meally, "'Game to the Heart,'" 44.

58. O'Meally, "'Game to the Heart,'" 44.

59. O'Meally, "'Game to the Heart,'" 45.

60. O'Meally, "'Game to the Heart,'" 52.

61. C. P. Henry, "The Political Role of the Bad Nigger," *Journal of Black Studies* 11, no. 4 (1981): 478.

62. Pearson, *Panther*, 139.

63. Cornel West, *Race Matters* (Boston, MA: Beacon Press, 1993), 40.

64. Hazel Carby, *Race Men* (Cambridge, MA: Harvard University Press, 1998), 129.

65. Farred, *What's My Name?*, 13.

66. Farred, *What's My Name?*, 49.

67. Brown, *Die Nigger Die!*, 14.

68. Brown, *Die Nigger Die!*, 14.

69. Brown, *Die Nigger Die!*, 18.

70. Brown, *Die Nigger Die!*, 15.

71. Brown, *Die Nigger Die!*, 15.

72. Brown, *Die Nigger Die!*, 15.

73. Brown, *Die Nigger Die!*, 15.

74. Michael Kimmel, *The Gendered Society* (Oxford: Oxford University Press, 2000), 253.

75. Brown, *Die Nigger Die!*, 17.

76. Brown, *Die Nigger Die!*, 18.

77. Brown, *Die Nigger Die!*, 16–17.

78. Gates, *The Signifying Monkey*, 71–74.

79. Brown, *Die Nigger Die!*, 26–27.

80. Brown, *Die Nigger Die!*, 26.

81. Paul Gilroy, *Against Race: Imagining Political Culture beyond the Color Line* (Cambridge, MA: Harvard University Press 2001), 199.

82. Farred, *What's My Name?*, 12.

83. Brown, *Die Nigger Die!*, 47.

84. Gilroy, *Against Race*, 200.

85. Gilroy, *Against Race*, 200.

86. Brown, *Die Nigger Die!*, 51.

87. Farred, *What's My Name?*, 18.

88. Brown, *Die Nigger Die!*, 52.

89. Brown, *Die Nigger Die!*, 53.

90. Brown, *Die Nigger Die!*, 53.

91. bell hooks, *Black Looks: Race and Representation* (Boston: South End Press, 1992).

92. Henry, "The Political Role of the Bad Nigger," 479.

93. Brown, *Die Nigger Die!*, 39.

94. Brown, *Die Nigger Die!*, 10.

95. Henry, "The Political Role of the Bad Nigger," 479.

96. Brown, *Die Nigger Die!*, 21.

97. Brown, *Die Nigger Die!*, 4.

98. Brown, *Die Nigger Die!*, 4.

99. Brown, *Die Nigger Die!*, 10.

100. Brown, *Die Nigger Die!*, 10.

101. Brown, *Die Nigger Die!*, 13.

102. Brown, *Die Nigger Die!*, 11.

103. Brown, *Die Nigger Die!*, 55.

104. Brown, *Die Nigger Die!*, 45.

105. Brown, *Die Nigger Die!*, 56.

106. Farred, *What's My Name?*, 19.

107. Farred, *What's My Name?*, 19.

108. Farred, *What's My Name?*, 19.

109. Farred, *What's My Name?*, 19–20.

110. Farred, *What's My Name?*, 20.

111. Mary L. Dudziak, *Cold War Civil Rights: Race and the Image of American Democracy* (Princeton, NJ: Princeton University Press, 2000), 156.

112. Brown, *Die Nigger Die!*, 61.

113. Brown, *Die Nigger Die!*, 79.

114. Brown, *Die Nigger Die!*, 85.

115. Brown, *Die Nigger Die!*, 81.

116. Robert L. Scott and Donald K. Smith, "The Rhetoric of Confrontation," *Quarterly Journal of Speech* 54 (February 1969): 4.

117. Brown, *Die Nigger Die!*, 38.

118. Brown, *Die Nigger Die!*, 38.

119. Brown, *Die Nigger Die!*, 39.

120. Brown, *Die Nigger Die!*, 63.

121. Herman Gray, "Black Masculinity and Visual Culture," *Callaloo* 8 (1995): 402.

122. Goldberg, "Ghetto Riots and Others," 124.

123. Goldberg, "Ghetto Riots and Others," 128. Emphasis in original.

124. Craig Werner, "On the Ends of Afro-American 'Modernist' Autobiography," *Black American Literature Forum* 24, no. 2 (Summer 1990): 205.

125. Howard Zinn, *SNCC: The New Abolitionists* (Boston: South End Press, 2002), 38.

126. *Riot Report*, 58.

127. *Riot Report*, 58.

128. *Riot Report*, 70.

129. Robert C. Smith, "Black Power and the Transformation from Protest to Policies," *Political Science Quarterly* 96, no. 3 (1981): 439.

130. Campbell, *Gettin' Our Groove On*, 12.

Chapter Three

1. Daniel R. Williams, *Executing Justice: An Inside Account of the Case of Mumia Abu-Jamal* (New York: St. Martin's Press, 2001), 10.

2. Williams, *Executing Justice*, 6–7.

3. Dave Lindorff, *Killing Time: An Investigation into the Death Row Case of Mumia Abu-Jamal* (Monroe, ME: Common Courage Press, 2003), 33.

4. Lindorff, *Killing Time*, 34.

5. John Dombrink, "The Touchables: Vice and Police Corruption in the 1980s," *Law and Contemporary Problems* 51 (Winter 1988): 201.

6. Dombrink, "The Touchables," 209, 211.

7. Lindorff, *Killing Time*, 35.

8. Lindorff, *Killing Time*, 35.

9. The case against the Philadelphia police was dropped in December 1979, though not for lack of evidence. Instead, the case was dropped because it was seen as outside of the jurisdiction of the Department of Justice.

10. Terry Bisson, *On a Move: The Story of Mumia Abu-Jamal* (Sussex, UK: Plough Publishing House, 2000), 20.

11. Bisson, *On a Move*, 20.

12. Rizzo lost his appeal for a charter amendment that would have enabled him to run in 1980 but was defeated by "a coalition of fed-up Philadelphia businessmen, bankers, lawyers, church groups, black organizations and newspapers—including the American Jewish Committee, the Chamber of Commerce, the Americans for Democratic Action, the Women's International League for Peace and Freedom and the Gay Alliance" and 20,000 more votes were cast on the issue of the charter question than in the vote for governor" (in "A Philadelphia Success Story," *Washington Post*, Sunday, Final Ed. [November 12, 1978], B6).

13. Daniel L. Skoler, "There Is More to Crime Control Than the 'Get Tough' Approach," *Annals of the American Academy of Political and Social Sciences* 739 (September 1971): 30.

14. Bisson, *On a Move*, 21.

15. Lindorff, *Killing Time*, 38.

16. Frank Donner, *Protectors of Privilege: Red Squads and Police Repression in Urban America* (Berkeley: University of California Press, 1990), 205.

17. James Kyung-Jin Lee, *Urban Triage: Face and the Fictions of Multiculturalism* (Minneapolis: University of Minnesota Press, 2004), 216.

18. Van Gosse and Kavita Philip, "Mumia Abu-Jamal and the Social Wage of Whiteness," *Radical History Review* (Fall 2001): 7.

19. Kathleen Cleaver, "The Black Power Movement: Self-Determination, Transformation, and Sabotage," Keynote Address at the Race, Roots, and Resistance: Revisiting the Legacies of Black Power Conference (Urbana-Champaign, IL: March 31, 2006). Author's transcription. See also: "Revolutionary on Death Row: The Story of Mumia Abu-Jamal," *Revolutionary Worker #1003*, April 25, 1999. http://www.revcom.us/a/v20/1000–1009/1003/mumia.htm (accessed July 17, 2015).

20. Timothy Williams, "Execution Case Dropped Against Abu-Jamal," *New York Times*, December 11, 2011. http://www.nytimes.com/2011/12/08/us/execution-case-dropped-against-convicted-cop-killer.html (accessed July 13, 2015).

21. Walter Fisher, "Narration as Human Communication Paradigm: The Case of Public Moral Argument," *Communication Monographs* 51 (1984): 2.

22. James Boyd White, "Law as Rhetoric, Rhetoric as Law: The Arts of Cultural and Communal Life," *University of Chicago Law Review* 52 (1985): 689.

23. Anthony V. Alfieri, "Race Prosecutors, Race Defenders," *Georgetown Law Journal* 89 (2001): 2229.

24. Austin Sarat, "Narrative Strategy and Death Penalty Advocacy," *Harvard Civil Rights–Civil Liberties Law Review* 31 (1996): 356–62. This is especially true since the Clinton Administration supported legislation that limited federal court review of constitutional deficiencies in death penalty cases.

25. Paul Kaplan, *Murder Stories: Ideological Narratives in Capital Punishment* (Lanham, MD: Lexington Books, 2012), xviii.

26. Anthony Alfieri, "Defending Racial Violence," *Columbia Law Review* 95 (June 1996): 1305–6.

27. Kaplan, *Murder Stories*, xviii.

28. Alfieri, "Defending Racial Violence," 1309–11.

29. Robin K. Magee, "The Myth of the Good Cop and the Inadequacy of Fourth Amendment: Remedies for Black Men: Contrasting Presumptions of Innocence and Guilt," *Capital University Law Review* 23 (1994): 157.

30. Magee, "The Myth of the Good Cop," 214–16.

31. The local and national media has utilized outraged widow, Maureen Faulkner, to make claims about Mumia Abu-Jamal's guilt. For more on the use of narratives and stories from the families of victims, see Samuel R. Gross and Daniel Matheson, "Victims and the Death Penalty: Inside and Outside the Courtroom: What They Say at the End: Capital Victims' Families and the Press," *Cornell Law Review* 88 (2003): 486–516.

32. Ward Churchill, "The Third World at Home: Political Prisoners in the U.S.," *Z Magazine* (June 1990), 4.

33. See *Mumia Abu-Jamal: A Case for Reasonable Doubt?*, Dir. John Edington, HBO films, 1996.

34. Just a single Google™ search string of "Mumia Abu-Jamal cop killer" returned 23,000 hits.

35. Farred, *What's My Name?*, 11.

36. John Edgar Wideman pens the introduction to *Live From Death Row* (1996). Wideman, a Pittsburgh native, has written extensively about the racial politics of Pennsylvania and the politics of prison; his own son is also incarcerated.

37. Wideman, "Introduction," xxiii.

38. Wideman, "Introduction," xxx–xxxii.

39. Wideman, "Introduction," xxxiv.

40. Wideman, "Introduction," xxxv.

41. Wideman, "Introduction," xxvi–xxvii.

42. Cornel West, "Foreword," *Death Blossoms* (Farmington, PA: Plough Publishing, 1996), xi.

43. West, "Foreword," xi.

44. West, "Foreword," xii.

45. Farred, *What's My Name?*, 23.

46. West, "Foreword," xii.

47. West is understood as a "professor-prophet" because of his work in tracing the lineage of black (male) leadership. See, for example, Henry Louis Gates Jr. and Cornel West, *The African American Century: How Black Americans Have Shaped Our Country* (New York: Free Press, 2000); Henry Louis Gates Jr. and Cornel West, *The Future of the Race* (New York: Vintage, 1997); Cornel West, *Race Matters* (New York: Vintage, 1994); Cornel West, *Keeping Faith: Philosophy and Race in America* (New York: Routledge, 1993).

48. Julia Wright, "Preface," *Death Blossoms*, Mumia Abu-Jamal (Farmington, PA: Plough Publishing, 1996), xiii–xiv.

49. Wright, "Preface," xvi. Emphasis in original.

50. Mumia Abu-Jamal, *All Things Censored*, ed. Noelle Hanrahan (New York: Seven Stories Press, 2000), 5.

51. Alice Walker, "Foreword," *All Things Censored*, ed. Noelle Hanrahan (New York: Seven Stories Press, 2000), 15.

52. Walker, "Foreword," 15–16.

53. Walker, "Foreword," 16.

54. Walker, "Foreword," 16.

55. Tom Hayden, "Introduction," *The Zapatista Reader* (New York: Thunder Mouth Press, 2002), 2.

56. Noelle Hanrahan, "Introduction," *All Things Censored*, ed. Noelle Hanrahan (New York: Seven Stories Press, 2000), 21.

57. She continues, "Imagine your possessions: your books, your notes, your intellectual life, having to fit into a five-inch-deep, fourteen-inch wide box, because that is all you are allowed" [in Hanrahan, "Introduction," 21].

58. Hanrahan, "Introduction," 21–22.

59. Hanrahan, "Introduction," 29.

60. Hanrahan, "Introduction," 28.

61. Hanrahan, "Introduction," 22.

62. Hanrahan, "Introduction," 22.

63. Hanrahan, "Introduction," 30.

64. Mumia Abu-Jamal and Heike Kleffner, "The Black Panthers: Interviews with Geronimo ji-jaga Pratt and Mumia Abu-Jamal," *Race & Class* 35 (1993): 18.

65. Abu-Jamal and Kleffner, "The Black Panthers," 19.

66. Gottlieb, "State Repression," 185.

67. The *Revolutionary Worker* has reported that there were as many as 400 arrests of MOVE members between 1974 and 1976, totaling bail and fines of more than half a million dollars. "Philly Cops: A History of Brutality in Blue," *Revolutionary Worker* 21 (July 4, 1999), http://rwor.org/a/v21/1010–019/1013/philly.htm (accessed July 14, 2006).

68. Bisson, *On a Move*, 162.

69. Bisson, *On a Move*, 164–70.

70. D. Michael Cheers, "Aftermath of the Fiery and Fatal Siege in Philadelphia," *Jet*, June 3, 1985, 8.

71. Cheers, "Aftermath," 9.

72. Kathleen Neal Cleaver, "Philadelphia Fire," *Transition* 51 (1991): 150.

73. Abu-Jamal, *All Things Censored*, 146–47.

74. Abu-Jamal, *All Things Censored*, 147. Abu-Jamal comments at length about the MOVE organization in *All Things Considered* in additional essays titled: "And They Call MOVE 'Terrorists'!" and "Justice Denied."

75. Cleaver, "Philadelphia Fire," 151. See also Sonia Sonchez's moving poem about the MOVE bombing, "Philadelphia: Spring 1985," which appears in *Callaloo* 26 (Winter 1986): 120–21.

76. John Africa was previously Vincent Leaphart, a handyman who had earned the nickname "Dog Man" for the feral dogs that followed him around town.

77. Cleaver, "Philadelphia Fire," 150.

78. See, for example, Tony G. Poveda, "Controversies and Issues," in *The FBI: A Comprehensive Reference Guide*, ed. Athan G. Theoharis (Westport, CT: Greenwood Press, 1993), 101–42.

79. Abu-Jamal, "The Black Panthers," 20.

80. Abu-Jamal, "The Black Panthers," 20.

81. Abu-Jamal, "The Black Panthers," 20.

82. Bisson, *On a Move*, 186.

83. Abu-Jamal, *Live From Death Row*, 20.

84. Abu-Jamal, *Death Blossoms*, 6.

85. Abu-Jamal, *Live From Death Row*, xvii.

86. Abu-Jamal, *Live From Death Row*, 17.

87. Abu-Jamal, *All Things Censored*, 39.

88. Farred, *What's My Name?*, 19.

89. Abu-Jamal, *Live From Death Row*, 17.

90. Abu-Jamal, *Live From Death Row*, 19. Emphasis in original.

91. Abu-Jamal, *Live From Death Row*, 20–21.

92. Farred, *What's My Name?*, 23.

93. Sarat, "Narrative Strategy," 378–79.

94. Harlow, *Resistance Literature*, 131.

95. The most spectacular example of this is probably the uprising at Attica State Prison in New York, which took place from September 9–13, 1971, included 1,300 prisoners who revolted because of inhuman treatment, brutality, and torture. Inmates were led by prison activists and demanded better living conditions, more vocational training, and less censorship of their mail. In the end, dozens of inmates were killed in the standoff by government-issued weapons as 211 police officers assaulted Attica. The writings and uprising at Attica directed attention at the conditions of prisons in the 1970s as prisoners began to mobilize once again, from their confinement.

96. Angela Y. Davis, "Political Prisoners, Prisons, and Black Liberation," *If They Come in the Morning: Voices of Resistance* (New York: Third Press, 1971), 23.

97. Abu-Jamal, *Live From Death Row*, 6. Also published as Mumia Abu-Jamal, "Teetering on the Brink between Life and Death," *Yale Law Journal* 100, no. 4 (1991): 993–1003.

98. Abu-Jamal, *Live From Death Row*, 7.

99. Abu-Jamal, *Live From Death Row*, 7–8.

100. Abu-Jamal, *Live From Death Row*, 9–10.

101. Abu-Jamal, *Live From Death Row*, 12.

102. Abu-Jamal, *Live From Death Row*, 22–23.

103. Abu-Jamal, *Live From Death Row*, 23–24.

104. Abu-Jamal, *Live From Death Row*, 47.

105. Paul Gready, "Autobiography and the 'Power of Writing': Political Prison Writing in the Apartheid Era," *Journal of Southern African Studies* 19, no. 3 (September 1993): 490.

106. Gready, "Political Prison Writing," 490.

107. Henry, "The Political Role of the Bad Nigger," 473.

108. Henry, "The Political Role of the Bad Nigger," 478.

109. Abu-Jamal, *Live From Death Row*, 132.

110. Although he traces his ideology to the BPP and Malcolm, Abu-Jamal is careful to discuss the importance that Reverend Martin Luther King Jr. had in southern churches but notes that his appeals for nonviolence were met with resistance in the North; consequently, the more militant message of the Nation of Islam was embraced by black youth who saw his struggle to crush white racism as noble.

111. Abu-Jamal, *Live From Death Row*, 136.

112. Abu-Jamal, *All Things Censored*, 243.

113. Michael Eric Dyson, *Making Malcolm: The Myth and Meaning of Malcolm X* (Oxford: Oxford University Press, 1995), xiii.

114. Abu-Jamal, *Live From Death Row*, 167–68.

115. Abu-Jamal, *Live From Death Row*, 170.

116. Abu-Jamal, *All Things Considered*, 144–45. Emphasis in original.

117. Arthur Dudden, "Nostalgia and the American," *Journal of the History of Ideas* 22, no. 4 (1961): 517.

118. Dudden, "Nostalgia and the American," 517. Emphasis in original.

119. bell hooks, *Killing Rage: Ending Racism* (New York: H. Holt & Co., 1995), 63.

120. hooks, *Killing Rage*, 63–64.

121. Assata Shakur, "Message to Mumia," *Schooling the Generations in the Politics of Prisons*, ed. Chinosole (Berkeley, CA: New Earth Publications, 1996), 4.

122. Shakur, "Message to Mumia," 4.

123. Shakur, "Message to Mumia," 4.

124. Shakur, "Message to Mumia," 4.

125. Shakur, "Message to Mumia," 4–5.

126. Abu-Jamal, *Death Blossoms*, 87.

127. Abu-Jamal, *Death Blossoms*, 87.

128. Abu-Jamal, *Death Blossoms*, 87.

129. Abu-Jamal, *Death Blossoms*, 88.

130. Abu-Jamal, *Death Blossoms*, 88.

131. Dale M. Bauer, "Personal Criticism and the Academic Personality," in *Who Can Speak? Authority and Critical Identity*, ed. Judith Roof and Robyn Wiegman (Chicago: University of Chicago Press, 1995), 56–69, 66.

Chapter Four

1. Pamela Irving Jackson and Leo Carroll, "Race and the War on Crime: The Sociopolitical Determinants of Municipal Police Expenditures in 90 non-Southern U.S. Cities," *American Sociological Review* 46 (June 1981): 292. See also Paul M. Whisenand, "Equipping Men for Professional Development in the Police Service: The Federal Law Enforcement Assistance Act of 1965," *Journal of Criminal Law, Criminology, and Political Science* 57 (June 1966): 223–27; Robert F. Diegelman, "Federal Financial Assistance for Crime Control: Lessons of the LEAA Experience," *Journal of Law and Criminology* 73 (Autumn 1982): 994–1011.

2. Jackson and Carroll, "Race and the War on Crime," 299.

3. Robert M. Fogelson, "From Resentment to Confrontation: The Police, the Negroes, and the Outbreak of the Nineteen-Sixties Riots," *Political Science Quarterly* 83 (June 1968): 217. See also Harlan Hahn and Joe R. Feagin, "Riot-Precipitating Police Practices: Attitudes in Urban Ghettoes," *Phylon* 31 (1970): 183–93; Harlan Hahn, "Ghetto Assessments of Police Protection and Authority," *Law & Society Review* 6 (November 1971): 183–94; James W. Button, *Black Violence: Political Impact of the 1960s Riots* (Princeton, NJ: Princeton University Press, 1978).

4. Joseph C. Goulden, "Tooling Up for Repression: The Cops Hit the Jackpot," *The Nation* (November 23, 1970): 520–33.

5. Fogelson, "From Resentment to Confrontation," 222.

6. Fogelson, "From Resentment to Confrontation," 226.

7. Black police were an anomaly in the United States during the 1960s when "only 3.5 percent of all law enforcement personnel in the entire nation were non-Caucasian. By 1962, there were only 36 black state policemen throughout the entire United States, and 24 were located in Illinois"; "Socio-Legal Aspects of Racially Motivated Police Misconduct," *Duke Law Journal* (1971): 759.

8. Bernard Headley, "Black Political Empowerment and Urban Crime," *Phylon* 46, no. 3 (1985): 196–97.

9. William C. Kronholm, "Blue Power: The Threat of the Militant Policeman," *Journal of Criminal Law, Criminology, and Political Science* 63 (June 1972): 294.

10. Ruben G. Rumbaut and Egon Bittner, "Changing Conceptions of the Police Role: A Sociological Review," *Crime and Justice* 1 (1979): 247–48.

11. A. C. Germann, "Community Policing: An Assessment," *Journal of Law, Criminology, and Police Science* 60 (March 1969): 89.

12. Jalil Muntaqim, *We Are Our Own Liberators: Selected Prison Writings* (Montreal, Quebec: Abraham Guillen Press, Arm the Spirit, and the Anarchist Black Cross Federation, 2002), 29. Former BLA member Muntaqim notes that the underground BLA began organizing in late 1968 and early 1969, while the BPP was under attack by the FBI's COINTELPRO programs which caused the leadership split between Huey Newton and Eldridge Cleaver. He writes, "From Los Angeles, California, to Texas, Louisiana, Mississippi and Alabama, armed units were formed and trained in rural areas, and caches were established in Oakland, San Francisco, Detroit, Chicago, Philadelphia, Ohio and New York. Black Panther offices were established to formulate a political relationship with the Black masses in these and other communities across the country" [in Muntaqim, *We Are Our Own Liberators*, 29–30].

13. For Shakur's poem to Sundiata Acoli, see Assata Shakur, "Assata's Poem for Sundiata," *The Black Scholar* 29 (Summer 1999): 67.

14. At the scene, Sundiata Acoli was arrested and he was later convicted of the same crimes as Shakur. He is still a political prisoner.

15. Farred, *What's My Name?*, 24.

16. Assata Shakur, "In Her Own Words: An Interview From Havana 1987," Transcription by author, Freedom Archives Number C78.

17. George Jackson, *Soledad Brother: The Prison Letters of George Jackson* (Chicago: Lawrence Hill, 1970/1994), 27.

18. Davis worked to free the Soledad Brothers, black prisoners held in California's Soledad Prison during the late 1960s. She befriended George Jackson, one of the prisoners who published his prison letters: *Soledad Brother* and also an autobiographical text, *Blood in My Eye*. On August 7, 1970, during an abortive escape and kidnap attempt from Marin County's Hall of Justice, the trial judge and three people were killed, including Jackson's brother Jonathan in a shoot-out at the scene. Governor Ronald Reagan publicly vowed that Davis would never teach in California ever again due to her membership in the Communist Party U.S.A. and her affiliation with Black Power organizations. She was captured in New York City in August 1970 but was released eighteen months later and cleared of all charges in 1972 by an all-white jury. During her incarceration, an international movement to Free Angela Davis gained incredible support and provided a model for activism surrounding political prisoners.

19. Angela Davis, "Foreword," *Assata: An Autobiography* (New York: Lawrence Hill Books, 2001), xi.

20. Helene Christol, "Militant Autobiography and the Case of Assata Shakur," *Black Liberation in the Americas*, ed. Fritz Gysin and Christopher Mulvey (Munich, Germany: Lit Verlag, 2001), 134.

21. Davis, "Foreword," x.

22. Davis, "Foreword," xvi.

23. Davis, "Foreword," xvi.

24. Davis, "Foreword," xvi.

25. Hinds, "Foreword," xi.

26. Hinds, "Foreword," xvii.

27. Hinds, "Foreword," xvii.

28. Foucault, *Discipline and Punish*, 190.

29. Barbara Harlow, *Resistance Literature* (New York: Methuen, 1987), 125.

30. Shakur, *Assata*, 83.

31. Foucault, *Discipline and Punish*, 103.

32. Harlow, *Resistance Literature*, 151.

33. Celeste Schenck, "All of a Piece: Women's Poetry and Autobiography," in *Life/Lines: Theorizing Women's Autobiography*, ed. Bella Brodzki and Celeste Schenck (Ithaca, NY: Cornell University Press, 1988), 287.

34. Sidonie Smith, "The Autobiographical Manifesto: Identities, Temporalities, Politics," *Autobiography and Questions of Gender*, ed. Shirley Neuman (London, UK: Frank Cass & Co., 1991), 187.

35. Caren Kaplan, "Resisting Autobiography: Out-law Genres and Transnational Feminist Subjects," *Women, Autobiography, Theory* (Madison: University of Wisconsin Press, 1998), 125.

36. This poem was reprinted in *CovertAction Quarterly* 65 (Fall 1998): 37.

37. Assata Shakur, *Assata: An Autobiography* (Chicago, IL: Lawrence Hill Books, 1999), 1.

38. Frederick Douglass, *Narrative of the Life of Frederick Douglass* (New York: Dover Publications, 1995), 24.

39. Eldridge Cleaver, *Post-Prison Writings and Speeches* (New York: Random House, 1969), 21–22.

40. Shakur, *Assata*, 1.

41. Shakur, *Assata*, 18.

42. Booker T. Washington, *Up From Slavery* (Oxford: Oxford University Press, 1995), 1.

43. Shakur, *Assata*, 19.

44. Shakur, *Assata*, 19.

45. Shakur, *Assata*, 21.

46. Shakur, *Assata*, 23.

47. Shakur, *Assata*, 30.

48. Shakur, *Assata*, 32.

49. See Doug McAdam, "'Initiator' and 'Spin-off' Movements: Diffusion Processes in Protest Cycles," *Repertoires and Cycles of Collective Action*, ed. Mark Traugott (Durham, NC: Duke University Press, 1995), 217–39; David Strang and John W. Meyer, "Institutional Conditions for Diffusion," *Theory and Society* 22 (August 1993): 487–511.

50. Shakur, *Assata*, 159.

51. Harlow, *Resistance Literature*, 33.

52. Sigmund Ro, "'Desecrators' and 'Necromancers': Black American Writers and Critics in the Nineteen-Sixties and the Third World Perspective," *Callaloo* 25 (Autumn 1985): 573.

53. Shakur, *Assata*, 320.

54. John Hope Franklin, *The Victim as Criminal and Artist: Literature from the American Prison* (New York: Oxford University Press, 1989), 251.

55. Harlow, *Resistance Literature*, 45.

56. Dhairyam, "Remapping the Contours," 240.

57. Dhairyam, "Remapping the Contours," 232.

58. Shakur's associations with black nationalist organizations included the Golden Drums, the Black Panther Party, and the Black Liberation Army.

59. Shakur, *Assata*, 33.

60. Shakur, *Assata*, 33.

61. Shakur, *Assata*, 175.

62. Earl Conrad, "I Bring You the Sesquicentennial of Harriet Tubman's Birth," *Black Scholar* 1 (January/February 1970): 4.

63. Conrad, "Harriet Tubman," 7.

64. Shakur, *Assata*, 175.

65. Shakur, *Assata*, 181.

66. She alternately expresses her dissatisfaction by spelling "amerikkka" highlight the role of white supremacy and the Ku Klux Klan in the nation. For a short discussion on New African grammar, see Chokwe Lumumba, "Repression and Black Liberation," *Black Scholar* 5 (October 1973): 36.

67. Arnez, "Black Poetry," 18.

68. Arnez, "Black Poetry," 19.

69. Kenneth McNeil and James D. Thompson, "The Regeneration of Social Organizations," *American Sociological Review* 36 (August 1971): 629.

70. Adrienne Rich, *Of Woman Born: Motherhood as Experience and Institution* (New York: W. W. Norton & Co., 1986), 75.

71. Alonda Nelson, *Body and Soul: The Black Panther Party and the Fight Against Medical Discrimination* (Minneapolis: University of Minnesota Press, 2011), 34.

72. Elaine Brown, *A Taste of Power: A Black Woman's Story* (New York: Anchor Books, 1992), 190–92.

73. Susan Stanford Friedman, "Creativity and the Childbirth Metaphor: Gender Difference in Literary Discourse," *Feminist Studies* 13 (Spring 1987): 49.

74. Shakur, *Assata*, 17. Her poem for Sundiata appeared in the summer 1999 issue of *Black Scholar*.

75. Shakur, *Assata*, 16.

76. Shakur, *Assata*, 17.

77. Shakur, *Assata*, 130.

78. Foucault, *Discipline and Punish*, 138.

79. Shakur, *Assata*, 93.

80. Shakur, *Assata*, 124.

81. Shakur, *Assata*, 126.

82. Shakur, *Assata*, 126–27.

83. Christol, "Militant Autobiography," 141.

84. Assata Shakur, "Partial Interview with Assata Shakur at Rikers Island Women's House of Detention," *Assata Speaks . . . and the People Speak on Assata*, ed. Bibi Angola (Bibi Angola: 1980), 7.

85. Elizabeth Alexander, "Can You Be BLACK and Look at This: Reading the Rodney King Video(s)," *The Black Public Sphere: A Public Culture Book*, ed. Black Public Sphere Collective (Chicago: University of Chicago Press, 1995), 87. This essay first appeared in *Public Culture* 7 (Fall 1994).

86. Farred, *What's My Name?*, 13.

87. Bella Brodzki and Celeste Schenck, "Introduction," *Life/Lines: Theorizing Women's Autobiography*, ed. Bella Brodzki and Celeste Schenck (Ithaca, NY: Cornell University Press, 1988), 11.

88. This strategic silence is actually quite pragmatic. Jalil Muntaqim writes this of the BLA, "It is our policy not to reveal the names of comrades who have acted within our organizational underground formations" (Muntaqim, *We Are Our Own Liberators*, 37).

89. Shakur, *Assata* 257–58.

90. Shakur, *Assata*, 259.

91. Shakur, *Assata*, 259.

92. Bernice Johnson Reagon, "My Black Mother and Sisters, or, On Beginning a Cultural Autobiography," *Feminist Studies* 8 (Spring 1982): 81.

93. Reagon, "My Black Mother and Sisters," 82.

94. Marla F. Frederick, *Between Sundays: Black Women and Everyday Struggles of Faith* (Los Angeles: University of California Press, 2003), 95.

95. Shakur, *Assata*, 84.

96. Friedman, "Creativity and the Childbirth Metaphor," 66.

97. Shakur, *Assata*, 220–27.

98. The Newton-Cleaver split (1970) was borne out of the extensive political repression of the BPP by COINTELPRO and the increasingly paranoid expulsions of party members by Newton. The official split happened while Newton was doing a television interview about the Panthers with Eldridge, who was on the phone from Algiers, where he was in exile. Cleaver expressed his disdain for Newton's leadership since his exile and he demanded the resignation of the chief of staff, David Hilliard. Cleaver also criticized the children's breakfast program, which he saw as reformist, and demanded a more confrontational strategy. Newton expelled Cleaver from the Central Committee and Cleaver joined the Black Liberation Army (which had already been created by Alprentice Carter and was underground).

99. Shakur, *Assata*, 139.

100. Shakur, *Assata*, 241.

101. Shakur, *Assata*, 241.

102. Shakur, *Assata*, 82.

103. Akinyele Omowale Umoja, "Repression Breeds Resistance: The Black Liberation Army and the Radical Legacy of the Black Panther Party," *Liberation, Imagination, and the*

Black Panther Party, ed. Kathleen Cleaver and George Katsiaficas (New York: Routledge, 2001), 13.

104. Shakur, *Assata*, 10.

105. Williams, *Inadmissible Evidence*, 80–81.

106. Shakur, *Assata*, 10.

107. See also Robin D. Barnes, "Blue by Day and White by Knight: Regulating the Political Affiliations of Law Enforcement and Military Personnel," *Iowa Law Review* 81 (1996): 1079–1172.

108. Shakur, *Assata*, 64–65.

109. See also Angela Y. Davis and Gina Dent, "A Conversation on Gender, Globalization, and Punishment," *Signs* (Summer 2001): 1235–41.

110. This letter was reprinted in the October 1973 edition of *The Black Scholar*, pages 16–18 as well as in Shakur's manifesto.

111. Shakur, *Assata*, 50.

112. Shakur, *Assata*, 50

113. Shakur, *Assata*, 51.

114. Shakur, *Assata*, 51.

115. Shakur, *Assata*, 51.

116. Shakur, *Assata*, 52.

117. Négritude is a pan-African literary movement on the part of French-speaking African and Caribbean writers who lived in Paris during the 1930s, 1940s, and 1950s including Césaire, Damas, Senghor, and others, who decried colonialism. The concepts of Négritude were embraced throughout the twentieth century by Afrikan Liberation movements, which utilized the form and style to mobilize the masses against neocolonial and imperialist projects in the Third World.

118. Gready, "Political Prison Writing," 499.

119. Assata Shakur, "Assata Shakur: A Revolutionary Life," *Covert Action Quarterly* 65 (Fall 1998): 42.

120. Shakur, "A Revolutionary Life," 42.

Conclusion

1. Farred, *What's My Name?*, 32.

2. Edwards Said, *The World, the Text, and the Critic* (Cambridge, MA: Harvard University Press, 1983).

3. Ekwueme Michael Thelwell, "Foreword," *Die Nigger Die!* (Chicago, IL: Lawrence Hill, 1969), vii.

4. John Angus Campbell, "Between the Fragment and the Icon: Prospect for a Rhetorical House of the Middle Way," *Western Journal of Communication* 54 (Summer 1990): 351.

5. Campbell, "Between the Fragment and the Icon," 351.

6. Campbell, "Between the Fragment and the Icon," 352.

7. Campbell, "Between the Fragment and the Icon," 352.

8. Thelwell, "Foreword," xxi–xxiii.

9. It is also important to note as well that Brown has penned one other text since the original publication of *Die Nigger Die!* titled *Revolution by the Book: The Rap is Live*. In this book, Al-Amin emphasizes the importance of a spiritual as well as political change in consciousness to accompany the revolution. He tackles such issues as ways to worship, dress, food, family life, etc. He concludes the text by arguing, "Revolution comes when human beings set out to correct decadent institutions. We must understand how this society has fallen away from righteousness and begin to develop, Islamically, the alternative institutions to those that are in a state of decline around us" (in Jamil Al-Amin, *Revolution by the Book: The Rap is Live* [Beltsville, MD: Writer's Inc. International, 1994], 163). In fact, throughout the text, Al-Amin applies Black Power ideologies to Islamic theology to promote a revolution in consciousness that replaces the capitalism of the nation-state. The publication of this treatise on Islam is also significant because its title, too, links Al-Amin to Rap Brown by referencing his former persona and by linking the two in a "Prologue" that highlights Brown's Black Power career. Although the space here does not permit an in-depth study of Al-Amin's 1994 text, suffice to say that despite the references to Brown, the majority of the text does deal with interpretations of passages of the *Quran*. Nonetheless, by referencing his persona as Rap Brown in *Revolution by the Book* and by re-issuing *Die Nigger Die!*, it seems that Al-Amin wants his former and current lives to coexist. He certainly has not distanced himself from the black revolutionary or in any way dampened his commitment to Islam. The continuity of his commitment to ideologies that do not conform to white standards helps Al-Amin to regenerate both Black Power and black Islam.

10. Thelwell, "Foreword," ix.

11. Thelwell, "Foreword," xxvii.

12. Thelwell, "Foreword," viii.

13. Thelwell, "Foreword," xxviii–xxix.

14. Thelwell, "Foreword," ix.

15. They were trying to deliver an arrest warrant to Al-Amin for failure to appear in court in January 2000 on charges of theft by receiving stolen property and impersonating an officer. These charges date back to an incident in May 1999.

16. He was indicted on one count of murder, four counts of felony murder, two counts of aggravated assault, and six other lesser charges.

17. James Curry Woods, "The Third Tower: The Effect of the September 11th Terrorist Attacks on the American Jury System," *Alabama Law Review* 55 (Fall 2003): 212.

18. The jury was composed of nine black people, two white people, and one Hispanic-American.

19. Thelwell, *Die Nigger Die!*, xxxv.

20. Thelwell, *Die Nigger Die!*, xxxviii.

21. Woods, "The Third Tower," 209.

22. Woods compiled the relevant data on the post–September 11 polls: "In the weeks following the attacks of September 11, 2001 . . . the prejudiced eye of suspicion turned against Muslim Americans. A *Los Angeles Times* survey conducted in the days following the

attacks found that 43 percent of Americans were more suspicious of people who appeared to be of Arab descent. Eighty-seven percent of Americans were concerned about another major terrorist attack on the United States. In another survey conducted the week after the attacks, almost half of respondents (44 percent) believed the terrorist attacks represented the feelings of Muslim Americans toward the United States. More than half of Americans (58 percent) felt there should be tighter controls on Muslims traveling on US planes and trains, while 83 percent thought that tighter restrictions should be imposed on immigrants from Muslim or Arab countries. A CNN/USA Today/Gallup poll showed that 35 percent of Americans had less trust in Arabs living in the United States as a result of the September 11 attacks. Also, one-third of Americans, and 55 percent of those between the ages of eighteen and twenty-nine, reported that they had heard negative comments about Arabs in America" (Woods, "The Third Tower," 210).

23. Woods, "The Third Tower," 213.

24. Woods, "The Third Tower," 214.

25. Michael Smerconish, *Muzzled: From T-Ball to Terrorism—True Stories That Should Be Fiction* (Nashville, TN: Thomas Nelson, 2007), 183.

26. Dinesh D'Souza, *The Enemy at Home: The Cultural Left and Its Responsibility for 9/11* (New York: Random House, 2007), 1.

27. D'Souza, *The Enemy at Home*, 1–2.

28. D'Souza, *The Enemy at Home*, 2.

29. Mumia Abu-Jamal, "In the Shadow of Abu Ghraib," *Democracy Now!* http://www.democracynow.org/2004/5/10/in_the_shadow_of_abu_ghraib (accessed September 1, 2014).

30. Abu-Jamal, "In the Shadow of Abu Ghraib."

31. Abu-Jamal, "In the Shadow of Abu Ghraib."

32. Abu-Jamal, "In the Shadow of Abu Ghraib."

33. See, for example, David P. Forsythe, *The Politics of Prisoner Abuse: The United States and Enemy Prisoners after 9/11* (Cambridge: Cambridge University Press, 2011).

34. Sohail Daulatzai, "Are We All Muslim Now? Assata Shakur and the Terrordome," *Al Jazeera*, May 9, 2013. http://www.aljazeera.com/indepth/opinion/2013/05/20135712155495678.html (accessed September 10, 2014).

35. Daulatzai, "Are We All Muslim Now?"

36. Peniel E. Joseph, "Why Is the FBI Going After Assata Shakur Now?" *The Root*, May 3, 2013. http://www.theroot.com/articles/politics/2013/05/assata_shakur_on_fbi_most_wanted_terrorists_list_a_reminder_of_a_complicated_racial_past.html (accessed September 1, 2014).

37. Joseph, "Why Is the FBI Going After Assata Shakur Now?"

38. Suzanne Oboler, *Behind Bars: Latino/as and Prison in the United States* (New York: Palgrave Macmillan, 2009), 271.

39. Angela Davis, "A Vocabulary for Feminist Praxis: On War and Radical Critique," *Feminism and War: Confronting U.S. Imperialism*, ed. Robin L. Riley, Chandra Talpade Mohanty and Minnie Bruce Pratt (London: Zed Books, 2008), 26.

40. Daulatzai, "Are We All Muslim Now?."

41. Daulatzai, "Are We All Muslim Now?."

42. Mychal Denzel Smith, "Assata Shakur Is Not a Terrorist," *Nation*, May 7, 2013. http://www.thenation.com/blog/174209/assata-shakur-not-terrorist# (accessed July 29, 2014).

43. Smith, "Assata Shakur Is Not a Terrorist."

44. Smerconish, *Muzzled*, 249.

45. Jonathan Simon, *Governing through Crime: How the War on Crime Transformed American Democracy and Created a Culture of Fear* (Oxford: Oxford University Press, 2007), 270.

46. Jonathan Simon, "From the New Deal to the Crime Deal," in *After the War on Crime: Race, Democracy and a New Reconstruction*, ed. Mary Louise Frampton, Ian Haney Lopez, and Jonathan Simon (New York: New York University Press, 2008), 56.

47. Vorris L. Nunley, "From the Harbor to Da Academic Hood: Hush Harbors and and African American Rhetorical Tradition," in *African American Rhetoric(s): Interdisciplinary Perspectives*, ed. Elaine Richardson and Ronald L. Jackson II (Carbondale: Southern Illinois University Press, 2004), 231.

48. Nunley, "From the Harbor to Da Academic Hood," 231.

49. Alexander, *The New Jim Crow*, 21–22.

50. J. Edgar Hoover, quoted in O'Reilly, *Racial Matters*, 321.

51. Gilroy, *Against Race*, 43.

INDEX